D0849533

Renegades and Rogues

« TODD B. VICK »

Renegades and Rogues

THE LIFE AND LEGACY OF
ROBERT E. HOWARD

University of Texas Press ⤶ AUSTIN

The "Box of Monkeys" photo of Hester Jane Ervin and her half-siblings is used by permission of Terry Baker. The photo of REH, Lindsey Tyson, and Tevis Clyde Smith is used by permission of Robert L. Tyson and family and the Howard House and Museum. The photos of Truett Vinson and Herbert Klatt are used by permission of Christopher Oldham. All of the remaining photos are used by permission of the Robert E. Howard Foundation.

LIBRARY OF CONGRESS CATALOGING-IN-PUBLICATION DATA

Names: Vick, Todd B., author.
Title: Renegades and rogues : the life and legacy of Robert E. Howard / Todd B. Vick.
Identifiers: LCCN 2020019514
 ISBN 978-1-4773-2195-9 (cloth)
 ISBN 978-1-4773-2196-6 (library ebook)
 ISBN 978-1-4773-2197-3 (nonlibrary ebook)
Subjects: LCSH: Howard, Robert E. (Robert Ervin), 1906–1936. | Authors, American—Texas—Biography. | Fantasy fiction, American—Texas—History—20th century.
Classification: LCC PS3515.0842 Z89 2020 | DDC 813/.52—dc23
LC record available at https://lccn.loc.gov/2020019514

doi:10.7560/321959

For my wife, Kasha

Shine, little light

Contents

Renegades and Rogues

Who Is Robert E. Howard?

On myriad occasions people ask me to name some of my favorite authors. As I call out names—Charles Dickens, Jack London, Victor Hugo, J. R. R. Tolkien—their heads nod in recognition. Invariably, when I say "Robert E. Howard," they furrow their brow and ask, "Who is Robert E. Howard?" Chances are, these same people will recognize his most famous character. So I ask if they've heard of Conan the Barbarian. Often this is followed by a tepid response, a nod or a simple "yes." I then launch into a routine narrative: back in 1932, in Cross Plains, Texas, Robert E. Howard created Conan. They tilt their heads and gently nod as I gradually present my defense for enjoying this somewhat lesser known (to the general reading public) Texas writer and his globally famous barbarian character. On occasion, their faces reveal an uncertainty about why I would like such a thing. It's an interesting look of confusion, surprise, and curiosity. Sometimes I defend my response with a hearty explanation that Howard wrote many different kinds of stories (and characters): western, horror, action adventure, historical fiction, and hundreds of poems. Their heads tilt in surprise, and they say, "Really?" And the conversation ends. I'm left wondering if they walk away better for having heard about Robert E. Howard. I wonder if they will actually attempt to read his work, if for no other reason than that he made the list of my favorite authors.

That's the thing about Robert E. Howard. He's written all these wonderful stories and created fascinating protagonists, but the general public basically knows him for one character. And this character has gradually eclipsed his creator in familiarity via popular culture since his first appearance in print back in 1932. I don't mean this as a pejorative strike against Conan. He was one of the first twentieth-century characters to loom large in the wider field of popular culture. The general public, especially in the United States, has grown accustomed to larger-than-life stories and characters. I'd say they've come to expect it and are disappointed when a story or character falls short of this expectation. Conan was fulfilling this need long before it became a criterion in today's pop culture media, and that's why Conan overshadows his creator: the public's focus has been on the character, not the creator.

When I ask people if they've ever heard of Conan, I wonder if images of Arnold Schwarzenegger in the 1982 film *Conan the Barbarian* come to their minds. Knowing that this is likely the case makes me wish they would read one of Howard's Conan stories. I could certainly name a few that would give them a better idea of both the character and his creator. And then I realize that Robert E. Howard is perhaps the greatest unknown author in the state of Texas, maybe even the world. Practically everyone knows who Conan is, but few know the man behind the character. This is a bittersweet reality. Howard's famous character and those stories have been critically important and trendsetting within the framework of fantasy fiction, as well as popular culture, and their influence has been incalculable. But there is so much more to Robert E. Howard's literary oeuvre than merely his Conan stories.

Considering all of Howard's literary output makes me realize how important that question is: who is Robert E. Howard? Whether we as fans or scholars of the man and his work like it or not, Howard has too often been swept into a literary corner that is dismissed or overlooked because his stories originated in the pulp magazines of the 1920s and 1930s. Current academic pulp studies are gradually addressing this neglect, but to date, Howard's work has not been presented as serious literature to the degree that the works of writers like Ernest Hemingway, William Faulkner, or even H. P. Lovecraft have. These three were popular fiction authors in the 1920s and 1930s who are now studied in literary circles. It's been an uphill climb, but writers like Howard are finally gaining some of the same literary ground. With this in mind, it's important that we understand Robert E. Howard, the man and writer, and what makes his life and work so important to both fans and scholars.

Robert E. Howard was an enigma. At times even his closest friends and regular correspondents were left second-guessing him. Unpacking his life is a complicated task. Aside from what his stories tell us, much of what we know about Howard has been gleaned from his friends, via interviews and letters. Howard's letters reveal much about his personality and provide a deep glimpse into his private life, thoughts, and ideas. In some letters, he is at his most vulnerable, baring his real self, his real personality. Some of these letters, however, must be read with several grains of salt, since Howard was ever the storyteller. Sifting through his exaggerations and tall tales is an arduous task, but a necessary one. Even in those moments when Howard is showboating or spinning tall tales as if they are real, this behavior is a measure of his true nature.

The greatest percentage of Howard's letters were written to the pulp writer H. P. Lovecraft. Recently, through the work of S. T. Joshi and David E. Schultz in editing Lovecraft's personal correspondence, we have obtained a glimpse of what Howard's literary contemporaries said about him. Understanding his prowess as a writer, Lovecraft praised Howard's ability to incorporate his own southwestern history into his stories, even certain Conan stories. He also called Howard a phenomenally gifted poet and had always hoped to see a collection of Howard's poetry in print.[1] Lovecraft told his fellow writer E. Hoffmann Price that Howard "had gifts of an order even higher than the readers of his published work could suspect, and in time would have made his mark in real literature with some folk-epic of his beloved southwest."[2]

Lovecraft declared that no writers could excel at their craft unless they took their work seriously and wholeheartedly. And in terms of being able to communicate smells, fear, impending doom, brooding horror, or stark, living fear, "what other writer is even in the running with REH?"[3] Fans of Howard's works have known this for decades. Not until recently has the literary community finally caught up with the fans. New academic articles, university theses, and dissertations are now being written about Howard and his work.

When Robert E. Howard died, buried with him was his assumption that his work would probably fade into obscurity. I don't think he could have ever imagined his creations having the impact they have had. His life and work have been far-reaching, changing and influencing countless other writers. Almost one hundred years after his death, George R. R. Martin's book series *A Song of Ice and Fire* (*Game of Thrones*) owes its chops in part to Robert E. Howard. Martin has admitted as much on talk shows and his own blog. Among other notable writers, Pulitzer Prize–winning author Michael Chabon, while visiting Dallas, Texas in 2017 to present his own work at the Dallas Museum of Art, made a five-hour round trip to Cross Plains, Texas, to visit the Robert E. Howard House and Museum, a trip Chabon declared he had wanted to make for some years. Interviewed in the *Dallas Morning News*, Chabon explained that he was a huge fan of Robert E. Howard and revisited Howard's works every couple of years.[4] Chabon said that the experience of being in the room where Howard wrote his stories was quite moving.

In the years since his death, a considerable amount has been printed about Howard's life, some of it deprecatory, some of it exaggerated and misleading. And an inestimable amount of misinformation has circulated. I hope that this book will help remedy that. Utilizing newly discovered information about the Howards that has surfaced over the last decade or so—most of it previously revealed only on blogs for a handful of readers who are ardent fans of the writer—I hope this book will reach a wider audience, especially those who have perhaps heard of Conan but don't really know the man behind the character. I've attempted to present this material in such a way that the seasoned fan of Howard, the newly introduced curiosity seeker, and those who have never heard of the man will all benefit from reading the book.

Robert E. Howard is an important writer, in both early twentieth-century literature and popular culture. He is especially important to the state of Texas, and being among the state's earliest writers, he should be recognized as one of the state's own. Howard's works have reached millions around the world, been translated into multiple languages, and have had a great impact on popular culture. This is why, now more than ever, the question, Who is Robert E. Howard? is a critical question for us to ask. This book is my answer to it.

CHAPTER ONE

Pioneering Stories

THE FAMILY OF ROBERT E. HOWARD

I suppose I've done less traveling than any of my family, for hundreds of years back. They were always a race of wanderers, all branches of my various lines, and seldom stayed long in the locality in which they were born.

ROBERT E. HOWARD, IN A LETTER TO AUGUST DERLETH, JANUARY 1934

There are two roads one might travel to encounter Robert E. Howard.[1] There is the shorter and more direct route, filled with tall tales and the typical family struggles, care, and protection. This road winds its way to Robert from his parents. The other, longer route runs through hills and plains, rivers and native people—the landscape of Texas, where Robert was born and raised. The first road is a private path, one that Robert for the most part kept to himself. He rarely lived apart from his parents. Family was an integral part of his life, and each parent contributed part of their own history, passions, and personality to their son. Those who are unable to visit or live in Texas can experience the second road through Robert's stories. Texas was the architect that built Robert E. Howard into the person and writer we know today. Both roads provide a tumultuous, sometimes breathless, and always enthralling ride. And both help define the man and the writer.

Almost from birth, Robert heard tales about his pioneering relatives. He was quick to repeat these stories later in life to friends and correspondents, and sometimes he used elements from them in his fiction. Many of these family stories were exaggerated in his various recitations, to which Robert brought a highly romanticized imagination. For him, the old stories provided a freedom he longed for but had never experienced. They recounted a way of life that seemed to him ideal but too far in the past to be realized outside of a vicarious participation in the hearing and retelling. These stories of Robert's family and many of their Texas and southern settings shaped him and were embodied in the stories that he wrote.

Robert's mother, Hester Jane (Ervin) Howard, was born July 11, 1870, into a large affluent family in Hill County, Texas. She was the eighth child of "Colonel" George W. Ervin[2] and his wife Sara Jane. All but one of her older siblings were born in Mississippi. Robert declared that his maternal grandfather "was a planter [farmer] and not a cattleman."[3] This was likely the case while the Ervins lived in Mississippi, but Mr. Ervin's farming career was short-lived after the family moved from Mississippi to Texas in 1866. It is uncertain why they did so.[4] Perhaps they were drawn there by the rapid expansion in Texas at the time, or simply by new opportunities. Whatever the reason, Mr. Ervin eventually became a businessman, operating stores and hotels, investing in real estate and mineral deposits, and for a time sitting on the board of directors for the Dallas and Wichita Railroad in Dallas.

The tales that Robert told about his grandfather often portrayed a monumental character, and one wonders how much of them was true. In one account, Robert writes:

> My grandfather Colonel George Ervin came into Texas when it was
> wild and raw, and he went into New Mexico, too, long before it was a
> state, and worked a silver mine—and once he rode like a bat out of Hell
> for the Texas line with old Geronimo's turbaned Apaches on his trail.[5]

For sheer action and adventure, this account is enthralling. Ervin did come to Texas with his wife and kids when it was "wild and raw" in 1866. He also owned a portion of a silver mine at Steins Pass near Steins, New Mexico, in 1889, prior to New Mexico becoming a state. The *Lampasas Leader* reported that Ervin took business trips to Hidalgo County, in New Mexico, to invest in a silver mine.[6] This business venture garnered a modicum of fame in parts of West Texas. Even the *El Paso Times* reported the purchase.[7] It is uncertain when Ervin began scouting Hidalgo County for silver mines. It is certain, however, that Geronimo and his Chiricahua Apache tribesmen were raiding, killing, and driving out miners in Hidalgo County and the surrounding areas. As it happened, Geronimo was captured in 1886 just forty-five miles, as the crow flies, southwest of Steins Pass. Whether or not his grandfather was actually chased out of the area by Apaches, Robert was captivated by the story. The circumstances and exhilarating nature of the tale are reminiscent of Howard's action desert adventure stories featuring Francis Xavier Gordon (El Borak). It is likely that Robert heard this account about his grandfather from his mother or his step-grandmother, Alice Wynne.

Robert never met his maternal grandmother, Sarah Jane Ervin. She died on June 2, 1874, possibly because of complications giving birth to her daughter Lizzie, who died shortly after Sarah.[8] This was a terrible misfortune for Mr. Ervin and his family. Suddenly he became a single parent with four children still living under his roof. And on the brink of the tender age of four, Hester (Robert's mother) lost not only a younger sister but also her mother. The burden of providing care for his children and remaining active in his business and community duties may have been softened by the older siblings' willingness to help when they were able. George Ervin's mother, Jane (Tennyson) Ervin, who had remained with the family after her husband died, most likely took over Sarah Jane's role and helped raise Hester and her other grandchildren.

Robert heard stories about his grandmother Sarah Jane from his mother, Hester. But the only maternal grandmother Robert knew and spent time with was Alice Wynne, Hester's stepmother, whom George Ervin married in April 1875, about a year after Sarah Jane died. Robert had fond memories of his step-grandmother, whom he visited as a child. In a December 1932 letter to H. P. Lovecraft, he recalled one such visit:

> I remember the peach-cream I used to eat at my grandmother's home, up in Missouri. She had a big orchard, including many fine trees of El-bertas, which, when allowed to ripe properly, are hard to beat. At night, when everything was still, I'd wake up occasionally and hear, in the quiet, the luscious squishy impact of the ripe peaches falling from the laden branches. These peaches, mushy-ripe, and cut up in rich creamy milk, made a frozen delicacy the like of which is not often equaled.[9]

When Robert's maternal grandfather remarried, he moved his family to Lewisville, Texas, and began investing in land with mineral deposits. It was in Lewisville that Hester began her education. Almost two years after the Ervins moved, "Lewisville opened two schools—one for whites and one for blacks—in 1877."[10] In Texas in the 1870s, children were required to begin public school, with free tuition, between ages eight and fourteen.[11] Because of this law, Hester's education began in 1878, when she was eight. Being female, she was not required, nor expected to for

that matter, to complete a public education through high school graduation. Since she could read and write, it is likely that she attended public
school for at least six years, if not longer.[12]

However long her education, Hester was devoted to the task. She had
a passion for literature, poetry, and especially drama and stage perfor-
mance. Later in life, Dr. Howard recalled that "Robert's mother was a
poet. She also loved the stage. It was her ambition when a young girl to
prepare herself for the stage, but her father opposed it. She often spoke of
it as a great disappointment. I am sure she had the talent."[13] She instilled
this passion in her son, reading and reciting literature and poetry to him
as a child. "Written poetry by sheets and reams, almost books of it, was
stored in her memory so that from Robert's babyhood he had heard its
recital. Day by [day,] he heard poetry from his mother."[14] Her devotion
to poetry instilled a passion for the craft in her son. Robert penned over
seven hundred poems, and many were published in various magazines
and anthologies. In addition to reading poetry and literature to her son,
Hester probably taught Robert to read and write early enough in his life
that he was relatively proficient at both by the time he began his own formal education.

In late 1885, a few months after Hester's fifteenth birthday, the Ervins
moved from Lewisville to Lampasas, Texas. There were any number of
reasons for this move. Most likely, Mr. Ervin heard about the newly discovered Hancock mineral springs, which had made Lampasas a health
resort town. His mother (Robert's great-grandmother) was aging, so it
is possible that the move was made so that she could benefit from the
mineral springs. Shortly after relocating to Lampasas, Ervin, keeping to
his typical business practices, invested in land. The family settled into
a large two-story house where Mrs. Alice (Wynne) Ervin cared for her
young children[15] and her husband's aging mother. Sometime later, at the
age of seventeen, Hester lost her paternal grandmother, Jane (Tennyson)
Ervin. This left the Ervin family with no real reason to remain in Lampasas, other than Ervin's land investments, which were eventually sold.
By 1890, when Hester was twenty years old, her family had moved to Exeter, Missouri. Up to this point, Hester's family had moved four times,
enabling her perhaps to cultivate a unique patience for the transient
lifestyle that she would later experience with Robert's father, Dr. Isaac
Howard.

In Exeter, Hester spent most of her time helping her stepmother settle into their house and caring for her younger stepsiblings. Between 1891
and 1904, she had no prospective suitors. She did, however, have robust

financial support from her father and a substantial amount of freedom. Being a social butterfly, she took advantage of both and traveled to Texas to visit her siblings. Hester's older brother, William V. Ervin, had married Ida Ezzell and, in doing so, inadvertently embarked on a career in journalism. In Robert Lee, Texas, he became the proprietor of the local newspaper, *The Rustler*.[16] Sometime later, William and Ida moved to Ferris, Texas, where William purchased and operated another newspaper, the *Ferris Wheel*.[17] On several occasions, Hester visited Ferris, Texas, and the friends she made there among her older brother William's in-laws, especially Frank Ezzell, would have an indelible impact on her life. Her visits and relationships in Ferris would have a ripple effect later in her life on the Howard family dynamic.

During her visits to Ferris, Hester befriended her brother's sister-in-law Lesta (Ezzell) McCarson and his business partner Frank Ezzell, who was Lesta's brother. Her friendship with Lesta McCarson lasted the rest of her life. It was probably through Lesta that Hester met Frank. Beginning in May 1899,[18] Hester stayed in Ferris for six weeks at Lesta McCarson's home. During her stay, and most likely during her previous visits to Ferris, Hester spent large blocks of time with the Ezzell family. This included time spent with Frank Ezzell. Frank and Hester may have gone on several outings together or spent long hours at Lesta's home conversing over tea or coffee. According to the "1900 census, Frank Ezell is found living at the house of his sister Lesta, in Ferris, in the very house Hester Jane had spent six weeks in the year before."[19]

Frank was about the same age as Hester, and it is possible that a romance developed between them during this time. Years later, it was reported by Annie Newton Davis,[20] a neighbor of the Howards in Cross Cut, Texas, that "Mrs. [Hester] Howard was in love with a friend, had been, a young man. And she expected to marry him." While Annie Newton Davis could not recall the young man's first name, she did declare that his last name was Ezzell, confirming the likelihood that it was none other than Frank whom Hester had expected to marry.[21]

In the summer of 1899, after her six-week visit, Hester left Ferris and traveled to see a sister in Abilene, Texas. She remained in Abilene a little over a year. By 1901, she had moved to Mineral Wells, Texas, to live with another relative. It is reasonable to think that while in Abilene and Mineral Wells, Hester corresponded with her good friend Lesta McCarson and kept up with the goings-on of Frank Ezzell and the *Ferris Wheel*. It is also conceivable that during this period Hester waited for Frank Ezzell to propose marriage. However, since no letters to or from Hester exist for this period, and the only known surviving copies of the *Ferris Wheel* end with the September 9, 1899, issue,[22] whether Frank intended to propose to Hester remains a mystery.

By 1903, Hester was thirty-three and had never married. Socially she may have been feeling some pressure to tie the knot, especially since women in the late 1800s and early 1900s were typically married before their midtwenties. Even so, she enjoyed her freedom, her ability to travel, and her time spent with friends and family. She may have also still been waiting on Frank Ezzell's proposal. Whatever the case, while Hester lived in Mineral Wells, Annie Newton Davis recalled, "this dashing young doctor came along, and she hurriedly married him. Then the rest of her life, she lived in disappointment."[23] To what degree Hester was unhappy in her marriage to Dr. Howard will never be known. Annie Newton Davis also reported that Hester spent time around Goldthwaite, Texas—more specifically, in a town between Goldthwaite and Lampasas called Lometa, where several of the Ezzell family members retired.[24] This information certainly implies that Hester kept in contact with the Ezzell family. Moreover, it's not known if Robert was aware that his mother was in love with another possible suitor before meeting his father. Robert never discussed the situation in any of his letters, not even with his closest friends. He may have simply never been told.

Frank Ezzell remained single the rest of his life and did well for himself financially. He died in 1947. Is it possible that he intended to propose to Hester only to discover that she had married Dr. Howard? Did Hester simply tire of waiting for Frank to propose? Unfortunately, answers to questions regarding Frank and Hester were lost with their deaths. Hester did, however, maintain contact with the Ezzell family the rest of her life, and she and Lesta remained close friends. Through Lesta, Hester may have maintained contact with Frank or received updates about his life and whereabouts.[25] Possibly testifying to Hester's frustration was the report from neighbors that on certain occasions Dr. Howard declared that Hester had kicked him out of their home.[26] If this is true, Robert must have known that something was amiss between his parents. And yet he remained silently stoic.

Robert's father, Dr. Isaac Mordecai Howard, was a persuasive and charming man who had a confident manner, good listening skills, and an acutely honed ability as a master storyteller. He easily adapted to almost any situation and was highly ambitious. All things considered, it is understandable that Hester fell so easily and quickly in love with him. However, unlike Hester's father George Ervin, Isaac Howard was not an astute and savvy businessman. He remained poor his entire life, and Hester seems to have struggled with the lack of money in the household.

Isaac Mordecai Howard was born on April 1, 1872,[27] to poor struggling farmers in Ouachita County, Arkansas. Poverty and the struggle to overcome it would occupy the larger part of his entire life. Isaac's parents, William Benjamin and Louisa "Eliza" (short for Elizabeth) Henry Howard, had nine children. Isaac was their eighth child and fifth son. All their children were born in Arkansas except their eldest, Mary Elizabeth, who was born in Mississippi. Writing about the paternal side of his family, Robert declared:

> My branch of the Howards came to America with Oglethorpe [in] 1733 and lived in various parts of Georgia for over a hundred years. In [18]49 three brothers started for California. On the Arkansaw River they split up, one went on to California where he lived the rest of his life, one went back to Georgia and one, William Benjamin Howard, went to Mississippi where he became an overseer on the plantations of Squire James Harrison Henry, whose daughter he married.[28]

Robert's paternal grandfather, William B. Howard, about whom Robert heard many a tale from his own father, began his farming career on his future in-laws' plantation in Mississippi. It was there that he met and married Eliza Henry, while working for her father, James W. Henry.[29] A few years after William and Eliza married, both the Henry and Howard families moved to Arkansas. The Howards stayed in Arkansas until Eliza's father, James W. Henry, died in July 1884, leaving his family a small fortune, $30,000, to be split eleven ways, between his wife and ten children. With their portion of the inheritance, William and Eliza Howard moved to Hill County, Texas. Having heard, as a youngster, wild-eyed tales about his paternal grandfather working on a plantation, southern plantations would loom large in much of Robert's horror and weird fiction.

Her father's experience and success in Texas was probably one reason Eliza Howard gave her husband the idea of moving to a still relatively feral state. Eliza's father, James W. Henry (Robert's great-grandfather), upon forced retirement from service in the Confederate Army during the Civil War,[30] moved from Arkansas to Texas while it was still a frontier. "He took his slaves and went to Texas where he raised cotton until the end of the war, hiding bales so cleverly that even the carpet-baggers couldn't find them." Robert claimed that his great-grandfather was quite successful at this cotton venture. It lasted several years, avoiding the Comanches who roamed the Texas countryside and potential revolts by his slaves because of the Civil War. James W. Henry "was the only Southerner I ever heard of who made more money at the close of the Civil War than he had at the beginning."[31] Though Robert was often prone to telling (and hearing) tall tales about his family, considering that James W. Henry moved back to Arkansas and had $30,000 to disperse among his children and wife upon his death, this story is likely for the most part true.

William and Eliza, along with their kids, moved to Hill County, Texas, in 1884, when Isaac was twelve. A short time later, in 1887, Isaac lost his older brother, James H. Howard, and then his father, William B. Howard, died in late 1888.[32] The causes of their deaths are unknown. With both men gone, his brother David Terrell Howard (born in March 1866), who was nearly six years older than Isaac, became the head of the Howard family. Eventually the Howards ended up in Limestone County, Texas, as farmers, and most of the family except Isaac remained there. It is uncertain what the relationship was like between David and Isaac at the time of their father's death. David was "described by his family as 'a very stern man and hard to work for.'"[33]

There was immense difference between David and Isaac Howard. When suddenly made head of the family at an early age, David quickly developed a stern sense of responsibility and a need to be firmly grounded, anchored in one place, in order to rise to the task of providing for his family. Isaac, even as a child, was always fiercely independent, a trait he later handed down to his son Robert. Discontented with the notion of being tied to one place or forced to do something undesirable, Isaac was consumed with wanderlust. According to several of his nieces and nephews, he was "not content on the family farm in Limestone County and decided, instead, to practice medicine."[34]

In March 1885, Isaac struck a deal with his brother to sell his half of a hundred-acre tract of land for $140. David "put a down payment of 'ten dollars cash in hand' and agreed to pay the rest by November 1, 1895."[35] The interesting thing about this situation is that Isaac was thirteen years old in March 1885. At such a young age, he already had other plans besides farming. Isaac's proclivity for adventure and regular change was beginning to germinate. But David did not fulfill his side of the agreement by the agreed-upon date. It took three additional years before the sale was completed and filed, on February 12, 1898, when Isaac was twenty-six. So what happened to Isaac in the years between these two documents?

March 1885 to April 1899 was a critical time for Isaac. After agreeing to sell his portion of the family land to his brother, he probably finished his education and graduated from high school before turning his attention to his chosen profession. Where he studied medicine has garnered much speculation. It is often assumed that he went back to Arkansas to apprentice with his maternal uncle, J. T. Henry, "an 1873 graduate of the Medical Department at the University of Nashville [who] was practicing medicine in Eagle Mills, back in Ouachita County, Arkansas."[36]

In those days, it was common for a young man to apprentice with a seasoned physician who was also a family member. And J. T. Henry had a good reputation and strong credentials. Since Isaac was fresh out of high school, it is possible that his mother helped him get a ticket on a coach or train and sent him to her brother in Arkansas to follow his dream of becoming a medical doctor.[37] If this is what happened, then Isaac apprenticed with J. T. Henry for about eight or nine years, which is a long time to be an apprentice. Perhaps Isaac waited a year or two after high school before starting his apprenticeship.

Isaac did have local apprenticeship options. In late 1893, when Isaac was twenty-two, David Howard married Fannie Elizabeth Wortham, who came from a family with several physicians. Fannie's father was a medical doctor in Prairie Hill, Texas, where the Henrys and Worthams lived. She also had a sister whose husband was a medical doctor in the adjacent county. What this means is that "in the early 1890s we've got a young Isaac Howard, purportedly not interested in the family business of farming. He's got a doctor uncle in far-off Arkansas who seems to be doing pretty well for himself, and his older brother Dave marries into a family with at least two doctors, one of whom is practicing in the very town in which they live, the other in a nearby county."[38] Keep in mind, during this same time Isaac and David were in the middle of their land agreement. And David may have been making incremental payments to Isaac, who could have used that money to pay David's doctor in-laws to train him in the practice. Whether Isaac traveled to Arkansas or stayed in Texas, on "April 19, 1899, [he] was granted a 'Certificate of Qualification to Practice Medicine in all its branches throughout the State of Texas' by the Medical Board of Examiners, Fifth Judicial District, Texarkana, Texas."[39] With his freshly printed certificate and a sudden and vast amount of independence, Dr. Howard found himself free to navigate the map in search of people to help.

Howard never settled down in a large city, such as San Antonio, Dallas, or Houston, to practice medicine. Instead, he moved from one small town to another, never really staying more than two or so years in a single place. He was a skilled doctor with a wonderful bedside manner, excellent people skills, and a healthy compassion for humanity. But these same traits often hurt him financially. Robert confirmed this when he declared, "There is no better physician in the state of Texas, though there are many who have made more of a financial success. The reason he is not a rich man is because he's been more interested in humanity than in dollars." Robert further explained that his father often refused money from his poorer farming clients in these smaller communities. "The charity work he's done would run up into the hundred thousands, and the bills people have beat him out of would about equal that figure."[40] While that figure is probably exaggerated, the circumstances are not. Dr. Howard could have been wealthier had he demanded monetary payment from all his clients. But as Robert revealed, his father's compassion for those in need outweighed his desire for monetary gain.

Once Howard earned his state Board of Medical Examiners certificate, "the first place he appears is Freestone County, [Texas,] where he registers his new credentials on July 20, 1899."[41] Eventually, he worked between Freestone and Limestone Counties for about two years before he moved to Montague County, Texas, in May 1901. He had an uncle, George Walser, who lived in Montague County. Interestingly, Robert used that great-uncle's last name as a nom de plume—Sam Walser—for several stories published in the spicy pulp magazines, like *Spicy Adventure Stories*. George Walser may be the reason Dr. Howard registered to practice medicine in that county. However, in the early twentieth century, the populations of several Texas counties that bordered the Red River were booming owing to railroads and the discovery of oil. His adventurous spirit and what he thought were open doors to opportunity led Dr. Howard to migrate to boomtowns. In addition to Montague County, the 1902 *Polk's Medical Register and Directory of North America* shows Dr. Isaac Howard living and practicing medicine in Petersburg, Oklahoma, "just across the Red River in Indian Territory, and not far from where his sister Willie had moved after marrying Oscar McClung."[42] He very likely may have made this move to help his sister raise her children while her husband Oscar was in prison.

By 1902, Dr. Howard was registered and practicing medicine back in Palo Pinto County, Texas. He practiced there for several years, making trips to Mineral Wells, Texas, the largest town in the county and a flourishing hot spot for tourists and businesses. On one of these visits to Mineral Wells between 1903 and 1904, Isaac Howard met the love of his life, Hester Ervin. The two dated for a short spell and married on January 12, 1904. He was almost two years younger than Hester, as she probably discovered while they dated. At the time, patriarchal social conventions indicated that the male in a married couple ought to be older than the female. It is not known whether Hester revealed her actual age to her husband, but since neither of them was prone to convention, her age probably did not matter.[43]

Around the time Dr. Howard and Miss Ervin were married, the medical industry began to change, with "physicians in larger cities in Texas pushing for stronger regulation of medical education and licensure." To strengthen his credentials and education, Dr. Howard began correspondence courses at Gate City College of Medicine and School of Pharmacy in Texarkana. In 1903, the Arkansas State Medical Association (ASMA) determined that Gate City College was a fraudulent school, merely a "diploma mill." But before the ASMA could shut the school down, Gate City College relocated to Texas. Dr. Howard received a diploma from the school in 1905. The school continued to operate in Texas until "the newly created Board of Medical Examiners in November of 1907 [began] to bar graduates of the school from examination, and thus from licensure, in the state." Fortunately for Dr. Howard, when the new Board of Medical Examiners in Texas was created, "doctors currently practicing were 'grandfathered in,' and he would have been no exception, but now he had a medical degree."[44] Being grandfathered in allowed Dr. Howard to continue his practice and have his medical degree recognized as legitimate. Even so, he would later attend reputable medical schools, such as the Tulane University School of Medicine in New Orleans, to strengthen his education and credentials.

On May 12, 1905, just weeks after receiving his medical degree from Gate City College of Medicine, Dr. Howard registered his new credentials at the Parker County courthouse in Weatherford, Texas. Parker County is adjacent to Palo Pinto County, so he could now work in both counties, which he did until 1908. While the Howards spent most of their early marriage living in Christian and Oran, Texas, by late 1905 they had settled, at least temporarily, in Peaster, Texas (Parker County), where they made plans to begin a family.

CHAPTER TWO

From Birth to Bagwell

*My family has been prone to follow booms, and I have lived in oil
boom towns, land boom towns, railroad boom towns, and have
seen life in its crudest and most elemental forms.*

ROBERT E. HOWARD, *ARGOSY ALL-STAR MAGAZINE*,
JULY 20, 1929

The past few days have been so warm and pleasant that work is
the only thing upon the minds of everybody. The rattle of the
trace chains, the sound of corn dropping in the feed trough
at daybreak, the clicking of the stalk-cutter, the fire and smoke leaping
toward Heavens, the 'clinking' of the blacksmith hammer on the anvil,
and the jolly ha! ha! of the country merchant, presents to one's mind the
sublimity of a country life."[1] So reported the special correspondent from
Peaster, Texas, to the *Weatherford Daily Herald* on January 26, 1906.
In this unseasonal warmth and bustle, Dr. Isaac M. and Hester Howard gave birth to an unexpected boy. And though Dr. and Mrs. Howard
could have never known the fate of their child, each would play a pivotal
role in who this boy became.

In the first few years of their marriage, the Howards had trouble con-
ceiving. Given Mrs. Howard's age, there was probably some urgency on
her part to have children right away. When the trouble ensued, the couple approached Dr. Howard's brother, David Terrell Howard, who was
still "farming in Limestone County at the time, some 125 miles southeast of Christian, and had quite a large family (six children in 1904, and
twelve before he was finished having children in 1919)."[2] The Howards
asked David about adopting his youngest child, Wallace. As an adult,

Wallace Howard confirmed that this happened when he declared, "They come to mama and papa and wanted to take me and raise me as their— their foster-son."[3] By 1905, while the Howard brothers were discussing the possible adoption, Mrs. Howard discovered that she was pregnant. And on January 22, 1906, in Peaster, Texas, the Howards received the pleasant surprise of the birth of Robert Ervin Howard, named after his great-grandfather, Robert Ervin.[4]

Mrs. Howard was approaching thirty-six years of age when she gave birth to her son. Besides being old enough to be at risk of medical complications, Mrs. Howard, in 1906, faced the even greater risk of being at the mercy of the archaic state of medicine and its practice in those days. Despite the risks, Robert was born without complications.

There are various discrepancies regarding the actual date of Robert E. Howard's birth on official state documents and landmarks.[5] The attending physician in Peaster, J. A. Williams, recorded January 24, 1906, as the date of Robert's birth on the birth certificate filed at the Parker County courthouse—the same date that is recorded on the Parker County birth registry. However, the Howard family Bible[6] has Robert's birth date as January 22, 1906. Robert himself indicated that his date of birth was January 22,[7] and that same birth date appears on his death certificate. More than likely, J. A. Williams made a simple clerical error.

Shortly before Robert was born, *Polk's Medical Register and Directory* for 1904 listed the Howards' place of residency in Christian, Texas, which no longer exists.[8] A year later, the *Weatherford Weekly Herald* declared, "Drs. Blackwell and Howard will soon have under construction a nice office which will add to their convenience and that of the patient very much."[9] The implication is that, around September 1905, the Howards moved from Christian to Peaster so that Dr. Howard could partner with Dr. Blackwell. Around this same time, Dr. Howard began making land purchases in Oran, Texas. Hester probably planted this idea in her husband's mind, inspired by her father's tremendous success at land investments. In addition, the Texas and Pacific Railway had announced its intent to lay tracks from Mineral Wells to Salesville, Oran, and on to Graford in 1907. Anticipating that Oran would become a railroad boomtown, Dr. Howard had a potent incentive to buy land plots in those areas while he and Hester resided in Peaster.

Peaster, Texas, was established as a single-family settlement in the 1870s when a pioneer from Georgia—H. H. Peaster—purchased 160 acres of land nine miles northwest of Weatherford. A small community rose up next to his land and called itself Freemont. Later, in 1885, the community changed the name to Peasterville, in homage to its first settler. During the decade prior to the twentieth century, the town shortened its name to Peaster and established US postal service. The population of Peaster at the time was around 100 people.[10] When Robert was born, Peaster had been a town for only thirty-six years but had grown to a population of 260. The town had a dozen businesses, a gristmill, several churches, and even a small school. It was an agricultural community producing mainly grain, wheat, and cotton. A month after Robert was born, the *Weatherford Weekly Herald* declared, "Dr. Howard is boasting of the only boy baby of Peaster in 1906."[11] It had appeared that Dr. Howard might keep his family in Peaster, but they moved thirty-five miles west to the Dark Valley region shortly after Robert's birth. The move from Peaster to Dark Valley was unusual, especially since Dr. Howard had already established a partnering medical practice in Peaster. This move is a prime example of Dr. Howard's restlessness. For the better part of Robert's formative years, Dr. Howard's wandering spirit would keep his family assiduously roaming. Even so, the proximity of Dark Valley to Peaster was such that Dr. Howard could travel between the two when necessary.

Though Robert was just an infant when the Howards lived in Dark Valley, he claimed to have had ominous memories of the area, and he attributed the gloominess of his own nature to having lived there. Dark Valley was "a long, narrow valley, lonesome and isolated, up in the Palo Pinto hill country."[12] This description, from a letter to his friend H. P. Lovecraft, is accurate even today. Robert's account became even gloomier. "So high were the ridges, so thick and tall the oak trees that it was shadowy, even in the daytime, and at night it was as dark as a pine forest— and nothing is darker in this world." Trying to impress Lovecraft, Robert shifted his narrative of Dark Valley to one more akin to his horror fiction, exaggerating its dismal effect. "The creatures of the night whispered and called to one another, faint night winds murmured through the leaves and now and then among the slightly waving branches could be glimpsed the gleam of a distant star. Surely the silence, the brooding loneliness, the shadowy mysticism of that lonesome valley entered in some part into my vague-forming nature."[13] However embellished this account, it seems that Dark Valley did play a germane role in Robert's life, since similar settings eventually appeared in his stories.

While in Dark Valley, the Howards lived with W. H. Green and his wife Nora. Their house was nestled next to Dark Valley Creek, just northwest of the Brazos River.[14] The Howards stayed with the Greens temporarily while their own house was being built in nearby Oran. A birth certificate is on file in the Palo Pinto County courthouse for the Greens' daughter, who was born July 26, 1906, probably while the Howards were staying with the Greens. Dr. Howard's signature confirms that he was the attending physician.

Within eighteen months of Robert's birth, he became restless, sickly, and cried relentlessly. Whatever Robert suffered from is not known since Mrs. Howard never revealed or even suggested what the issue might have been. Nonetheless, in the last few months of her life Mrs. Howard confessed to her caregiver, Kate Merryman, that the situation with Robert may have caused her to miscarry a second pregnancy. She explained that Robert would cry for hours and hours, and so she would "jiggle the bedsprings" and bounce him on the bed to soothe him.[15] When she grew tired of bouncing him on top of the bed, she would place Robert on the bed, lie on her back, and use her legs and feet to bounce the bed. Mrs. Howard assumed that this caused her miscarriage. Of course, Dr. and Mrs. Howard probably never said as much to their son, not wanting him to blame himself. The experience certainly reinforced Mrs. Howard's protective instincts for her only child. From then on, she vigilantly guarded her son, as any mother would have done under the circumstances.

The Howards lived in Dark Valley for at least a year before moving to Oran, Texas, in late May of 1907. Having made multiple land purchases, they seemed to be preparing to settle down in Oran. And they did for a brief seven months—from May until early December—while Dr. Howard practiced medicine in and around the Oran area. His land purchases appeared to be sound investments. By this time, the T&P Railroad had laid tracks and the train was traveling from Weatherford to Oran. As people began to migrate into the area, the town grew. The area around Oran was conducive to cotton farming, and Oran soon gained a cotton gin, a livery stable, and even a weekly paper. But the growth would not last. The boll weevil destroyed the cotton crops, causing a small exodus of farmers from Oran to other more productive areas and leaving Oran with around forty people. If the land purchases had been closer to Mineral Wells or Weatherford, they would have been better investments. But since they were in Oran, a place whose agricultural fortunes had withered, they failed.

On December 20, 1907, Dr. Howard reregistered his medical license at the Palo Pinto County courthouse to record his change of address to Oran, Texas. A few days later, and with payments still due on their land purchases, the Howards moved west to Seminole, Texas. At this time,

Robert was approaching the age of two. On their way to Seminole, they took a slight southward detour to visit Hester's older brother, William Vinson Ervin, in Big Spring, Texas.[16] William Ervin was the editor of the Big Spring newspaper, the *Enterprise*. As folks were prone to do back then, Ervin announced Dr. Howard's stay in Big Spring in the January 3, 1908, issue of the paper. He reported that Dr. Howard left for Seminole on the previous Monday, December 30, to determine if his family might settle there. In this same report, Ervin gave his readers a short description of Dr. Howard: "He is a polished gentleman, a fine physician and the people of that town will be fortunate if he decides to locate there."[17]

A follow-up report published on January 24, 1908, explained that one or more of the Howards had become ill while Dr. Howard was in Seminole and that this was the reason for the three-week delay in their move. The Howards had finally left at the first of that week to relocate to Seminole.[18] This would put the Howards in Seminole by the end of January 1908, the same month Robert turned two.

From 1905 to 1906, a few years prior to the Howards' arrival in Seminole, Gaines County was established and a group of New York investors purchased land in the area and donated it to the county, which divided it and sold it in small lots. There was no real reason to move to Seminole in the early 1900s other than western expansion in Texas and the availability of inexpensive land, but apparently this was enough for the hundreds of people who settled in the area.

The news about inexpensive land in Gaines County spread far and wide. Over six hundred miles away, the *Brownsville Daily Herald* in Brownsville, Texas, announced on June 21, 1907, that state land was for sale in Gaines County. The article declared, "Because of the new land law, J. T. Robinson, chief clerk of the General Land Office, has had circulars printed, showing the procedure one must go through to acquire this land. There are now 1,000 sections which will go on the market."[19] The article reported that Gaines County had three sections of land that would be available in August and October of that same year. This was one of the final waves of western expansion in Texas and was set in motion primarily by the control and removal a few decades earlier of the Native Americans who once roamed and hunted over Texas and its neighboring states. Robert was raised listening to many accounts of Texas expansion and Native American stories. The Howards' participation in that period of historical Texas expansion, with their move to Seminole, ultimately played a pivotal role in Robert's life as a writer.

The first wave of settlers, which included the Howards, suffered severe hardship. Because water was scarce in the area, lumber had to be freighted in from nearby Big Spring and Midland, and there was little farming. Food, clothing, and most all other supplies had to be hauled to Seminole by freight wagons.[20] The earliest industry in Seminole was cattle, which began almost simultaneously with the selling of land lots in the area. Several decades after the Howards had already left Seminole, irrigation was established, making the area safer and easier for farming and leading to a more substantial population boom than in the early 1900s.

On February 3, 1908, a few weeks after their arrival, Dr. Howard registered his medical license with Gaines County.[21] Almost immediately he was busy. The lack of water in the area was detrimental to early settlers, and the hot West Texas temperatures took a steep toll on some of the people. Several settlers became severely dehydrated. While growth in the area was steady, the poor conditions made Seminole's future look bleak. The Howards stayed less than a year, probably owing to the harsh conditions and the delayed construction of a railway connection into town. The last known date for the Howards in Seminole is July 24, 1908, the day Dr. Howard filed a register of death for an infant at the Gaines County courthouse. Shortly thereafter, it is likely that the Howards traveled back to Big Spring to regroup and rest, but not for long. If they did in fact rest in Big Spring for a brief spell, it would certainly explain why they soon found themselves in Bronte, Texas. On September 14, 1908, Dr. Howard filed his medical license at the Coke County courthouse.[22] This was followed by an indication in the *Texas State Journal of Medicine* of an address change for the Howards between February 15 and March 18, 1909.[23] Dr. Howard moved his family from Seminole to Bronte in Coke County, north of San Angelo, shortly after Robert turned three.

The likeliest reason the Howards chose to move to Bronte was news regarding completion of the Kansas City, Mexico, and Orient Railway in 1907, making Bronte a railroad boomtown. Hester's brother in Big Spring, William V. Ervin, had once lived in the town of Robert Lee, just twelve miles west of Bronte. William may have informed the Howards about the potential boom in the area due to the upcoming railway service. The primary agriculture in the county—cotton—also brought a continuous flow of new people migrating to the area. To accommodate the railway, Bronte relocated a mile closer to where the tracks would be laid so that when the first train arrived the community would be prepared to use the railway for its cotton commerce.[24]

After Dr. Howard filed his medical license in Coke County, he wasted little time getting involved in the community. He was the attending physician for several births[25] and provided other medical services when needed. By 1910, Bronte's population was over six hundred, and the town had a bank, two cotton gins, and a newspaper. Even so, in predictable fashion, the Howards would stay there only about a year before uprooting and moving again. Robert mentioned the town only once in passing when he gave accounts of the various places where his family had lived in his early years. Apparently, the town left little to no impression on him. But as we will see, the incessant travel did.

The Howards left Bronte in early September 1909.[26] Their whereabouts up to November 20, 1909, remain, for the most part, a mystery.[27] However, recent research seems to indicate that during this three-month hiatus the Howards were braving the length of the Nueces River in a covered wagon, traveling to Crystal City, Texas.[28] This excursion—one of Robert's earliest memories—instilled in him a romantic passion for pioneer life. The experience of the covered wagon, the river, the wildlife, and outdoor cooking and living carved a deep notch into the psyche of the young lad. In a nostalgic attempt to revive the romance of this early experience, Robert revisited the area as an adult, but was sorely disappointed. He briefly described both trips to his friend Lovecraft:

> And one of my earliest memories is being lulled to sleep in a covered wagon camped on the Nueces River, by the howling of wolves.
>
> When they built Crystal City twenty years ago in Zavalla county, some forty miles from the Mexican Border, the wolves came howling to the edge of the clearings. The woods were full of wildcats, panthers and javelinas, the lakes were full of fish and alligators. I was back there a couple of years ago and was slightly depressed at the signs of civilization which disfigured the whole country.[29]

The letter is dated October 1930, and Robert declared that the covered wagon trip occurred "twenty-years ago." As people are often prone to do, Robert probably rounded his time frame to the nearest whole number, give or take a few years. This would make him three to four years of age at the time, and the year around 1909 to 1910. He thought it important to mention Crystal City by name, which is next to the Nueces River in the lower Rio Grande Valley. Another reason for the family to visit Crystal City was that Dr. Howard had a sister—Willie Price Howard McClung—who lived there. Her daughter, Fanny McClung Adamson, confirmed the Howards' visit to Crystal City when she declared, "We must have moved there [Crystal City] in 1908 and it was either 1909 or 1910 when he [Dr. Howard and family] was there."[30]

The experience in the lower Rio Grande Valley in the covered wagon is also found in a letter that Robert wrote to the editor of *Dime Sports Magazine*, published in June 1936:

> About the first half of my life was spent in various parts of West, East and South Texas and western Oklahoma, mostly following land booms and railroad booms. As a child I crossed the South Plains, not in a covered wagon indeed, but in a buggy, in what was about the last big colonization movement in Texas—the settlement of the Great Plains. (I did go down the Nueces in a covered wagon.) I also saw the beginning of the development of the Lower Rio Grande Valley. The last half of my life has been lived in the oil-belt towns of Central West Texas.[31]

Crystal City was established in 1905 with the purchase of ten thousand acres of land by Carl F. Groos and E. J. Buckingham. The land was sold to buyers as farmland and the settlement was fully established by 1908 when the area received its US post office. Around 1909 or 1910—about the time the Howards arrived—people were coming from various locales to settle in and around the area. The town was incorporated in 1910, the same year that the Uvalde Railway established service to the area and the first school was being built. So Robert did in fact witness the beginning of the development of the Lower Rio Grande Valley.

From November 20, 1909, to around the beginning of January 1910, the Howards stayed in San Antonio. On January 8, shortly before Robert's fourth birthday, Dr. Howard registered his medical credentials in Atascosa County to practice medicine in the area. That registration indicated a mailing address in Poteet, just south of San Antonio. Additionally, according to the *Texas State Journal of Medicine*, a "J. M. Howard" changed addresses from Bronte to Poteet between January 20 and February 20, 1910.[32] Following the paper trail, the family's next appearance is in the May 16, 1910, census, which lists them as living back in Palo Pinto County (Oran, Graford, Dark Valley, and so on).[33] *Polk's Medical Register* for that same year has Dr. Howard listed as residing in Graford, Texas. So their stay in Poteet was a meager four months.[34]

In several of his letters, Robert mentions that as a child he lived on a ranch in south Texas.[35] The location of this ranch has never been determined, but it is likely to have been close to Poteet in Atascosa County. By this time in the Howards' nomadic lives, Robert was four years old

and his family had moved six times, in addition to visits to several locales for brief spans. Robert was gaining a strong sense of freedom during this period of his life, and the nomadic lives of several of his most
popular fictional protagonists would clearly reflect this part of his early
life. These frequent changes of address and travels around Texas at such
an early age inculcated in Robert a deep sense of adventure and a peripa-
tetic spirit that would characterize his later stories.

The likeliest reason for the Howards' move back to Palo Pinto County
in the late spring of 1910, aside from Dr. Howard's incessant wanderlust,
was its familiarity: they had lived there before. In addition, Dr. Howard
still owned land in Palo Pinto County, and it was finally paid off in May
1908. In late December 1910, Dr. Howard's name begins to appear on several birth certificates in Palo Pinto, listing his address in Oran. In January 1911, Robert would be five. Based on birth and death certificates and
the "Purely Personal" section of Weatherford's *Daily Herald*, the Howards stayed in Oran for nearly two years.[36] The Howards had never lived
this long in any one area since Robert's birth. Being five to nearly seven
years old at the time, Robert was old enough to recall details about Palo
Pinto County and Oran. He had also heard fascinating stories and some
tall tales about the pioneers and Native Americans in the region.

Palo Pinto County was first settled by cattlemen who braved the
frontier when it was largely populated by the Comanche and Kiowa. In
1857, a twenty-one-year-old open-range cattleman named Charles Goodnight settled in Black Springs (present-day Oran) in the Keechi Valley.
Goodnight was "destined to become one of the most famous cattlemen
in Texas, and one of the originators of the great cattle drives." Soon after he settled in Black Springs, 1860 would go on record as one of the
"bloodiest years on the frontier."[37] In the winter of that year, Goodnight
would lead a posse of eight men in search of a band of Comanche raiders led by Peta Nocona. Nocona and his raiders had not only killed several settlers in the area but earlier that year may have killed another cattle rancher named John Brown. Brown had been the husband of Mary
(Brown) Crawford,[38] whom the Howards knew in Oran.

In a letter to Lovecraft, Robert retold a story that Mary Crawford related to him when he was an impressionable six-year-old. "I remember
the story she used to tell of the fate of her first husband, a Mr. Brown, in
the year 1872."[39] He continued: "One evening some of the stock failed to
come up and Mr. Brown decided to go look for them. The Browns lived
in a big two-storied ranch-house, several miles from the nearest settle-

ment—Black Springs." Robert explained that Brown heard the sound of a horse-bell fastened to one of his horses. Knowing his horses must be close by, Brown walked in the direction of the sound:

> Mrs. Brown stood on the porch of the ranch-house and watched her husband striding off among the mesquites, while beyond him the bell tinkled incessantly. She was a strange woman who saw visions, and claimed the gift of second sight. Smitten with premonition, but held by the fatalism of the pioneers, she saw Brown disappear among the mesquites. The tinkling bell seemed slowly to recede until the tiny sound died out entirely. Brown did not reappear, and the clouds hung like a grey shroud, a cold wind shook the bare limbs and shuddered among the dead grasses, and she knew he would never return.

John Brown, attacked by a raiding band of Comanches, was scalped and killed. The Comanches stole his horses and headed straight for the ranch house at full speed. In a panic, Mary Brown ran into the house, called for her servants—an African American woman and boy. She then "put buckets of water where they would be handy in case of fire, [and] she armed the terrified blacks, and led them into the second story of the ranch-house, there to make their last stand."[40]

The Comanches approached the ranch house and shot arrows into the windows, all the while whooping at the top of their lungs. In the commotion, with a rifle steadily aimed at the Comanches, Mary Brown noticed that several of the Comanches' horses were her own. She also heard the horse-bell that had lured her husband to his death. The Comanches circled the ranch house a few times and then rode away, disappearing over the horizon. As a child, Robert would hear this and other firsthand accounts from pioneers who settled the area as early as the 1850s. And while Robert sympathized with the Native Americans' plight, the infringement upon their hunting lands and their way of life, he also had a passion for the pioneers, albeit a romanticized view of their bravery, struggles, and freedom. This sympathy for the Native Americans and romanticism about pioneer freedom would be sustained by Robert for the rest of his life, finding expression in stories such as "Beyond the Black River."

After two years in Oran, Dr. Howard decided that it was time to move. On October 18, 1912, he filed the last birth certificate for a birth he attended in Palo Pinto County. Two months later, his medical credentials were filed in Clay County with a post office address in Byers, Texas. Chances are that the family moved to Byers because of an oil boom in Clay County and several surrounding counties.

Byers, Texas, is almost within walking distance of the Texas and Oklahoma state line. It sits next to the Wichita River, which flows into the Red River separating Texas and Oklahoma. When Dr. Howard filed his medical credentials on December 19, 1912, in Clay County, Robert was nearing his seventh birthday. Several booms had occurred in and around the Clay County area. Almost ten years prior to the Howards' arrival in the area, the Wichita Falls and Oklahoma Railway connecting the city of Wichita Falls with Byers was completed. The area was also well known for cattle breeding, grazing, and marketing. Cotton crops were abundant, and Byers touted several cotton gins. With the aid of the railway, cotton dealers could easily sell and transport their cotton out of the area.

There were almost six hundred people in Byers when the Howards arrived. The town had one bank, a weekly newspaper, a variety of shops, and even several furniture dealers. Additionally, Byers was "near the old North Texas oil-fields."[41] These oil fields lay beneath a small network of Texas towns in Wichita County (adjacent to Clay County) that included Electra, Old Burkburnett, Burkburnett Townsite, and Northwest Extension. In 1912, when the Howards lived in Clay County, these towns had recently struck oil and tens of thousands of people were moving to Wichita Falls and the surrounding area. Even though no record of medical registry for Dr. Howard exists in Wichita County, Byers was close enough that he could have practiced medicine in both Clay and Wichita Counties. And yet, despite the railroad, cattle, cotton, and oil booms in this area, after four months the Howards moved again.

There was nothing remarkable about Bagwell, Texas, when the Howards arrived there in April 1913. The town was just under twenty miles from the Oklahoma border, and slightly less than one hundred miles from the Arkansas border. Originally settled by a blacksmith named Milas Bagwell, Bagwell was a crossroads for several small nearby towns. Not only did Bagwell use his blacksmith skills to help others in the area, but he also established a tannery for the local hunters. When the T&P Railroad built tracks through the county around 1876, farmers began to colonize the area to grow cotton and grain crops, and now the town needed a cotton gin and a gristmill. By 1914, the town population had surged to around three hundred. It had a district school, a church, and a sawmill.

With the T&P Railway transporting lumber and cotton out of the area, Bagwell had a steady stream of income and soon established two banks.

It is believed that Dr. Howard moved his family to Bagwell at the request of a Dr. Stephens, a friend from Gate City Medical College in Texarkana, though which friend is unclear:

> There were two doctors named "Stephens" in Bagwell, Dr. Willis Commodore Stephens and his son, Willis Walter Stephens. And it turns out both had attended the Gate City Medical College in Texarkana during the years that Isaac Howard was studying there—the younger Stephens graduated in 1904, Howard in 1905, and the elder Stephens in 1906.[42]

It is not known which Stephens invited Dr. Howard to the area. Even so, he registered his medical license at the Red River County courthouse on April 30, 1913, and the Howards established residency in Bagwell. Even though the Howards' time in Bagwell was relatively short—a little over a year and a half—it would have a profound impact on seven-year-old Robert, who began his formal education there. The town's population included a number of former slaves whose history, culture, and stories provided lively material for Robert in his writing career.

This part of Texas has a rich pioneer history that begins in the early 1800s, when "the first Anglo-Saxon settlement in Texas was begun in 1814 in Red River County on what is now the western border of Bowie and the east border of Red River County."[43] Shortly thereafter, in 1833, James Clark settled the area and created a township. Through an act of the Texas Congress in 1837, Clarksville was incorporated and quickly became an agricultural and, eventually, educational center for the surrounding areas. Bagwell was later established eight miles northeast of Clarksville in the middle of what is known as the piney woods in Red River County. With agriculture being the primary source of trade and income in those pioneer days, slaves migrated with their owners to the area. When slavery ended, the African American population typically remained where they were living and continued to work on the farms and plantations. As a result, during the time the Howards lived there, Red River County had a diverse population.

In Robert's formative years, Bagwell was the first place where he experienced African Americans and their culture. The seven-year-old was entertained with an assortment of stories about ghosts, voodoo, and black magic by a former slave named "Aunt" Mary Bohannon. As an adult, Robert detailed these experiences in his correspondence with Lovecraft. "As regards African-legend sources, I well remember the tales I listened to and shivered at, when a child in the 'piney woods' of East Texas, where Red River marks the Arkansaw and Texas boundaries."[44]

Born into slavery in Kentucky,[45] Mary Bohannon was "brought to Texas sometime between 1850 and 1860, along with nine other slaves, by Henry C. Bohannon,[46] who left his farm in Breathett [sic] County, Kentucky and relocated to a farm east of Clarksville." Not too long after settling in Red River County, on March 31, 1861, Bohannon's wife, Pauline Bohannon, died. She was forty-one. Just a few short years later, Henry C. Bohannon died as well, on July 14, 1863. This left their two children, daughter Mary F. and son Logan, with the slaves and land. "Upon his father's death, Logan, then aged 18, accepted $1700.00 as his part of the estate and returned to Breathett [sic] County, Kentucky: he apparently never returned to Texas."[47]

While the Civil War escalated and would soon be the central event in America's consciousness, Mary F. Bohannon married William J. Swain, on December 24, 1861. William Swain thus became the executor of the Bohannon estate, retaining the land and the slaves. When the Civil War ended on May 9, 1865, and slavery in the United States was abolished in December of that same year, "Aunt" Mary Bohannon and her husband Wyatt (both were among the Bohannon slaves from Kentucky) were freed, but they continued to stay with the Swains and kept the Bohannon name.

No record of marriage exists for Mary and Wyatt in Red River County. It is possible that they may have already been married when they moved from Kentucky to Texas with the Bohannons. By 1895, Wyatt seems to no longer be listed in the various federal censuses and county land deeds. However, in the details of an 1895 deed of land just north of the T&P Railroad in Bagwell from William J. Swain to Mary and Wyatt, Wyatt's death is confirmed: "Wyatt Bohannon is dead and the said Mary Bohannon is still living and now resides on the said fifty acres."[48] After selling fifty acres of their land in Bagwell to Wyatt and Mary in 1895, the Swains had moved to Austin. Mary lived there until she sold it in 1907.

When the Howards settled in Bagwell around 1913, "Aunt" Mary Bohannon lived with Joe and Lottie Dennis.[49] Mary's occupation was left off the 1910 federal census. However, a local historian writes that "Mary Bohannon cooked for the affluent white folks in Bagwell in the early 1900s."[50] It is unknown whether she helped the Howards with cooking and such. She may have on occasion. Based on Robert's written account, she was acquainted enough with the Howards for young Robert to sit at her feet and listen to tales of her former life as a slave. Robert describes these stories in a letter:

> Old Aunt Mary had had the misfortune, in her youth, to belong to a man whose wife was a fiend from Hell. The young slave women were fine young animals, and barbarically handsome; her mistress was fren- ziedly jealous. You understand. Aunt Mary told tales of torture and unmistakable sadism that sickens me to this day when I think of them. Thank God the slaves on my ancestors' plantation were never so mis- used. And Aunt Mary told how one day, when the black people were in the fields, a hot wind swept over them and they knew that "ol' Misses Bohannon" was dead. Returning to the manor house they found that it was so and the slaves danced and shouted with joy. Aunt Mary said that when a good spirit passes, a breath of cool air follows, but when an evil spirit goes by a blast from the open doors of Hell follows it.[51]

The "fiend from hell" was Pauline Bohannon, the wife of Henry C. Bo- hannon. Apparently, Mrs. Bohannon was cruel to her slaves, and Robert got an earful about this as a child. Robert described Mary Bohannon as light-complected and attractive. Jealousy may have been the reason for Pauline Bohannon's ill behavior toward Mary.

In the same letter, Robert recalled several of Mary Bohannon's other stories:

> She told many tales, one which particularly made my hair rise; it oc- curred in her youth. A young girl going to the river for water, met, in the dimness of dusk, an old man, long dead, who carried his severed head in one hand. This, said Aunt Mary, occurred on the plantation of her master, and she herself saw the girl come screaming through the dusk, to be whipped for throwing away the water-buckets in her flight.[52]

This tale would certainly make the hair rise on any eight-year-old. Such tales were imprinted on young Robert's mind, and he would later use them as sources for several of his horror stories. Robert's most famous horror story, "Pigeons from Hell," was directly inspired by Mary Bohannon:

> Another tale she told that I have often met with in negro-lore. The set- ting, time and circumstances are changed by telling, but the tale re-

mains basically the same. Two or three men—usually negroes—are travelling in a wagon through some isolated district—usually a broad, deserted river-bottom. They come on to the ruins of a once thriving plantation at dusk, and decide to spend the night in the deserted plantation house. This house is always huge, brooding and forbidding, and always as the men approach the high columned verandah, through the high weeds that surround the house, great numbers of pigeons rise from their roosting places on the railing and fly away. The men sleep in the big front room with its crumbling fireplace, and in the night they are awakened by a jangling of chains, weird noises and groans from upstairs. Sometimes footsteps descend the stairs with no visible cause. Then a terrible apparition appears to the men who flee in terror.[53]

Though Robert changed some of the details in the story and added elements that made the tale more grueling and suspenseful, the gist of the story is still the same in his version of it. Stephen King declares that Robert E. Howard's "Pigeons from Hell" is "one of the finest horror stories of our century."[54] For that, Robert has Mary Bohannon to thank.

Mary Bohannon died on February 23, 1921, years after the Howards had moved away from Bagwell. She is buried in an unmarked grave on James Miller's land just off County Road 2111, about two miles northeast of Bagwell in what is now known as the Bagwell Cemetery.[55] Her influential tales, along with the piney woods area, can certainly be seen in several of Robert's other stories, such as "The House of Suspicion" and "Black Canaan," and they echo in some elements of "Kelly the Conjure Man" and his stories featuring Solomon Kane. Howard scholar Rusty Burke believes that they also make an appearance "in such early efforts as 'The Hyena' and 'The Hand of Obeah.'"[56] A Red River County historian also recognized the influence of Mary Bohannon on Robert:

> Mary was a story-teller, well versed in the legend and lore of her African heritage. She could not pass that lore to her own decedents since she seems to have had none who survived her. But she could and did implant those legends into the mind of an impressionable Robert Howard who, in turn, is said to have called upon them from time to time while creating his own unique form of literature.[57]

"Aunt" Mary was not the only African American in Bagwell to make an indelible impression upon young Robert. He also recalled a laundress named Arabella Davis, whom he described as "going placidly about town collecting washing." Robert claimed that Davis was a "black philosopher, if there was ever one." He remembered that she had a granddaughter who shadowed her wherever she went, carrying Davis's "pipe, matches and tobacco with as much pomposity as a courtier ever carried the train of a queen."[58]

On several occasions when Arabella Davis stopped to talk with Robert, she told him a few stories about her former slave life and her conversion to Christianity. Robert, most impressed with Davis's conversion story, conveyed it to Lovecraft:

> She often told of her conversion, when the spirit of the Lord was so strong upon her that she went for ten days and nights without eating or sleeping. She went into a trance, she said, and for days the fiends of Hell pursued her through the black mountains and the red mountains. For four days she hung in the cobwebs on the gates of Hell, and the hounds of Hell bayed at her. Is that not a splendid sweep of imagination? And the strangest part is, it was so true and realistic to her, that she would have been amazed had anyone questioned her veracity.[59]

Not much else is known about Arabella Davis, other than Robert's account of her.

Aside from his encounters with former slaves in Bagwell, it was there that Robert would also begin his education. He was seven when the Howards moved to Bagwell, and "free tuition for Texas schools did not begin until age eight."[60] Even so, it is highly likely that Robert's parents, especially his mother, would have ensured that by the time he entered first grade he could already read and write. A converted house with Victorian trim and a large L-shaped porch was used for the schoolhouse, which employed at least three teachers, two females and one male. The rooms in the house were classrooms designated for specific age ranges. Robert gave no account of the school in Bagwell, nor of any specific teachers or friends he may have had, except for one encounter involving a boy who was a playmate and an old woman whom the town considered to be a witch. Robert did not name either the playmate or the old woman, but he did explain that the old woman typically wandered around town, followed by several geese, and collected manure to fertilize her garden. Robert provides no details as to what his playmate did or said to this woman, but something occurred because she cursed him. Robert claimed that a few weeks after the woman cursed his friend, he died.[61]

By January 1915, the Howards had packed up and left Bagwell. Bagwell, however, never left Robert. He took his experiences of the town, its people, and their stories with him.

From birth to Bagwell—the first eight years of his life—Robert E. Howard experienced unrestricted freedom, which he would seek for the remainder of his life. Robert was raised and influenced not only by his parents but also by Texas. From one end of the state to the other, he experienced her people: pioneers, settlers, immigrants, small-town folk, and even former slaves. He experienced Texas expansion, various growth booms, Texas history, and a variety of tales. This freedom and these experiences would occupy his mind, fuel his desires, and permeate his writing until his final breath.

CHAPTER THREE

Cross Cut and Burkett

Robert and I were very close friends . . . in elementary school.
He read a lot and had a great imagination.

AUSTIN NEWTON, LETTER TO L. SPRAGUE DE CAMP
(CIRCA 1978)

On January 25, 1915, Dr. Howard brought his horse to a stop, stepped down from his buggy, and climbed the steps to the Brown County courthouse in Brownwood, Texas. He had arrived to register his medical credentials. At the time, the Howards lived in Putnam, Texas (Callahan County), north of Brown County. In 1915, rumors circulated that the T&P Railway would be laying tracks close to Putnam. As was their custom, the Howards may have moved to Putnam based on these rumors. While in Putnam, Dr. Howard was probably working with or learning from Professor J. H. Surles. Professor Surles ran the "largest drugless sanitarium in North Texas for several years."[1] Surles had recently taken charge of the Milling Sanitarium in Putnam and provided alternative medical therapies to new clients.

In those days, a handful of licensed western doctors used alternative methods, many of which were more commonly practiced in the East. Most western professional practitioners considered some of these alternative methods mere hokum, primarily because they thought of them as unscientific. At the time, the Western medical industry was beginning to regulate the practice of medicine and frowned upon some of these methods. However, most alternative methods used in Dr. Howard's day were biomedical practices that are used more commonly today. Dr. Howard was an advocate of alternative medical practices and often used them. Although it is uncertain how long the Howards were in Putnam, or whether they were there because of Professor Surles, it is certain that they moved from Putnam to Cross Cut sometime around January 29, 1915, which was just a few days after Dr. Howard's trip to the Brown County courthouse.[2] As was customary, Dr. Howard registered his medical license with that county.[3]

But why Cross Cut? This was perhaps the most unusual move the Howards made in those early years. In 1915, Cross Cut was tiny, and the area would not experience its first oil boom for another five years. Dr. Solomon Chambers, the family doctor in Cross Cut, was a good friend of Dr. Howard's. Dr. Chambers very likely urged him to move to Cross Cut, since he provided services within a fifteen-mile radius and was probably overwhelmed and in dire need of help.[4] If the rumors about the T&P Railway were true and Dr. Howard was in fact learning new methods from Professor Surles in Putnam, settling in Cross Cut also kept the Howards in close proximity to new opportunities in the area.

Nine-year-old Robert was still in school when the Howards arrived in Cross Cut. At the time, the town had a small school building with three teachers who taught various grades, and Robert was soon enrolled. Eventually he met Austin Newton, a kid his age, and the two became good friends. The Newton and Howard families also became close friends while they all lived in Cross Cut. In fact, Dr. Howard was the attending physician at the birth of Austin's younger brother, Howard, who was named for the doctor.

On June 11, 1915,[5] the Howards rented the Pentecost house from an E. DeBusk, who, according to land deeds, had bought the land and house in May of that same year.[6] The R. W. Pentecost family had lived in Cross Cut for approximately thirty years but decided to move to southern Arizona.[7] Their house (which is no longer standing) was a two-story farmhouse with several one-story rooms added onto the back. It sat about one hundred yards north of the Cross Cut cemetery.

As the Howards settled into a daily routine in Cross Cut, they became more involved in the community. The tiny town had two churches: Methodist Episcopal (ME) and Baptist. The Howards may have attended both but spent more time at the ME church. And yet, during at least one evening service, Dr. Howard preached at the Baptist church.[8] Religious studies had always been an interest of Dr. Howard's, and at one time he had seriously considered preaching as an occupation. Dr. and Mrs. Howard were quite involved with their church. On one Saturday evening, "Dr. Howard gave the young folks a party" at their home. It was reported that "all present [had] a nice time."[9] More than likely, this was a gathering for the youth from their ME church. On a different evening, "the ladies of the ME Church entertained at the home of Dr. Howard."[10] This event was hosted by Mrs. Howard for her ladies' church group, most likely because the size of their house made it easier to host social gatherings there.

Mrs. Howard enjoyed these social activities. During this period, the Howards were known to invite several friends and other families to their home. On numerous occasions, Dr. Solomon Chambers traveled with Dr. Howard and regularly visited the Howard home with his family in tow. Mrs. Howard would prepare a tasty meal, and the Howards would entertain. Another of Mrs. Howard's close friends in Cross Cut, Zettie Newton, made frequent visits, bringing her son Austin.

Austin and Robert were inseparable. With Robert sporting a Bowie knife that his father carried and Austin packing a Civil War cap-and-ball pistol that belonged to his uncle, the boys would roam the countryside, engaged in high adventure for hours on end. On occasion they would play at the creek and get muddy catching fish. As an adult, Austin Newton proclaimed that young Robert was a voracious reader and had a wonderful imagination. The two boys would spend some of their time acting out adventure stories that Robert concocted. They also played cops-and-robbers or cowboys-and-Indians with several of the other local boys.[11] At some point between living in Bagwell and moving to Cross Cut, Robert had developed a strong interest in boxing. It is uncertain how he acquired this interest—perhaps from boxing bouts he heard on the radio or boxing magazines he discovered in a drugstore. Whatever kindled his interest in boxing, by the time the Howards lived in Cross Cut, Robert had a profound passion for the sport. Austin Newton confirmed this when he revealed that when he first met the Howards, Robert was already studying the sport and its fighters. Austin and Robert sparred at times, both with and without gloves. One afternoon the two were bare-knuckle sparring. In an opportune moment, Robert managed to land a strong left jab to Austin's Adam's apple, sending the boy to the ground. That blow "ended the sparring for that day. But sparring continued to be one of our main past times," Newton recalled later.[12] Boxing would be critical for Robert as a young adult attempting to break into a variety of writing markets. His knowledge of the sport enabled him to create memorable boxing stories and detailed fight scenes that leapt off the page. Besides giving his stories an unprecedented energy, his interest in boxing also helped feed his passion for reading. Whenever Robert developed an interest in a subject, he typically sought numerous books or articles about it, and as a result he acquired a substantial book collection over the years.

Books were scarce in Cross Cut and the surrounding area, but the Howards managed to find them. Robert's passion for books and stories stemmed from his mother's practice of reading fiction and poetry to him in his formative years. However, in small Texas farming towns, a boy who spent most of his time reading often drew suspicious glares. Most nine- or ten-year-old boys were busy with their chores and learning skills that would enable them to eventually take over their family's farm. Robert was the child of a medical doctor without a farm or land to work, so he spent much of his time with his nose in a book, feeding his imagination, a habit that earned him a reputation and set him apart from the other boys. While young Robert was not an outcast, he was viewed as different or odd. Regardless, Dr. and Mrs. Howard continued to buy him books, and Mrs. Howard encouraged her son's imagination. The attitude of the locals, both young and old, toward his intellectual passions and activities may have caused a gradual change in Robert's behavior toward the people around him. He did not dislike people—indeed, he would carry on conversations with complete strangers—but he became prudent about whom he would let into his immediate circle.[13]

In the summer months, when Dr. Howard was away making house calls, Mrs. Howard occasionally pulled Robert from his books to play catch in the yard. Other times Austin and Robert would hang out in town at the drugstore. The summer months in Cross Cut also brought in "tent revivals," an assortment of religious revivals, usually of the Christian fundamentalist variety. These revivals were held so frequently that Cross Cut built an open-air tabernacle, which doubled as a picnic area for the townspeople. The music at these revivals was lively and vigorous, accompanied by exuberant hand-clapping and shouting. Austin Newton recalled:

> The sermons were always "hellfire and damnation" sermons with a sweating minister, screaming at the top of his voice, interspersed with many "hallalulias" [sic] "amens" and "yea verilles" [sic]. These were evangelical meetings and they were always bringing someone to God. In some groups there were seizures and speaking in tongues, which, of course, meant an unknown tongue. They rolled around on the ground during their estacy [sic]—hence the name "holy roller."[14]

Several of these revivals must have left an unforgettable imprint on the mind of young Robert. Coupled with his research on domestic and foreign religious rituals, these ritualistic religious experiences were often incorporated into various stories throughout his writing career.

While the Howards lived in Cross Cut, Dr. Howard developed a strong reputation in his profession. He was a consummate extrovert who loved being able to help people. Dr. Howard also loved hearing their stories, but more than that, he loved telling his own stories. Because he was the family doctor for so many people, the community of Cross Cut held him in high regard as their doctor and as a friend. His reputation was far-reaching, as he practiced medicine not only in Cross Cut but also in several surrounding communities, such as Burkett. Throughout this period, the Howards owned two horses and a buggy, and it is reported that Dr. Howard made all his Cross Cut house calls in that buggy.[15] During these same years, Dr. Howard studied in medical schools to update his credentials and improve his practice. From late June to early July of 1917, he traveled to New Orleans and attended four weeks of medical laboratory lectures.[16] His trips to New Orleans continued until 1921.[17] During these trips, Dr. Howard attended both Tulane University and Loyola University for postgraduate courses in advanced medical research. He also obtained an eyes, ears, nose, and throat certification.[18] On one of the longer trips, Dr. Howard brought along Mrs. Howard and thirteen-year-old Robert. This trip was extremely beneficial for Robert.

Most likely the Howards traveled on the Atchison, Topeka, and Santa Fe (AT&SF) passenger train from Brownwood, Texas, to Lampasas, through Temple to Houston and then on to New Orleans.[19] They arrived in New Orleans on March 10, 1919.[20] New Orleans was reeling from a series of brutal murders. The *New Orleans Times-Picayune* reported the capture of an ax-wielding predator who had been breaking into people's homes and killing his victims. Newsboys loudly proclaimed the man's capture as they ran up and down the streets of New Orleans selling their papers. These events would linger in young Robert's mind for years. Sometime between 1925 and 1928,[21] he wrote an essay, later titled "In His Own Image,"[22] that provided a few details about the "ax-man" of New Orleans:

> I remember strolling down a narrow street one day when the town was electrified by the shout of the newsboys: "They've got the ax-man!"
> The dirty ragged newsboys came scampering down the streets like

wisps of grass blown before the wind. They seemed all animated by an urge of motion for they scudded along screeching at the tops of their voices, scarcely stopping to make sales.

And it was momentous news they bore. For months the fear of the menace known as the ax-man had laid over the city like a fog. The morning I arrived in New Orleans, the morning papers were full of the latest atrocity, committed across the river among towns which so crowd the river bank that they are separated only by boundary posts.[23]

According to Robert's essay, the ax-man had broken into a house and killed an entire family, including a child who was only a few months old. These events were reported in the local New Orleans newspapers and in syndicated newspapers across the country. The family was reported to be Italian immigrants Charles and Rosie Cortimiglia and their two-year-old daughter Mary. In reality, Charles and Rosie survived the attack, but their daughter was killed. A grocer named Lorlando Jordano heard the Cortimiglias screams and ran across the street to investigate. Upon entering their home, Jordano saw Charles on the floor bleeding profusely, while Rosie was on the porch with a serious head wound clutching her dead child. Rosie later falsely testified that Lorlando Jordano and his son Frank were the perpetrators. She admitted two years later that she gave false testimony owing to spite and jealousy.[24]

In addition to details about the ax-man and his arrest, "In His Own Image" provides minutiae about Robert's experience of New Orleans and its people. By this time in Robert's life, he had witnessed new settlements in desolate Texas areas, oil and land booms, and listened to the firsthand accounts of Native Americans, pioneers, and former slaves, among a variety of others. And yet New Orleans showed him an entirely different ambiance. In 1919, the city and its people resembled something out of a Dickens novel, including Victorian attire and architecture. Within only a few blocks, Robert could see the dilapidated apartments of the poorest slums alongside upscale restaurants, hotels, and homes. The contrast did not escape him.

The Howards stayed "just four blocks from the boundary of Story-ville, New Orleans' notorious red-light district. And while the prostitution that was Storyville's raison d'être had been officially shut down in the fall of 1917, by no means had the district been shuttered."[25] If young Robert took the opportunity to roam in that direction, he would have seen "dance halls, cabarets, and restaurants which plied their trades legally."[26] And despite the fact that New Orleans was one of the first southern cities to enforce the Volstead Act, which established rules for various types of prohibited beverages,[27] Storyville continued operating its saloons and gambling halls. When the laws of prohibition were officially enforced against those establishments, New Orleans responded with speakeasies.

In New Orleans, the Howards rented rooms in a boardinghouse at 1904 Canal Street. It was owned by three sisters named Camille, Delphine, and Marie Durel. Robert described them as "gentlewomen of the old school, living in semi-seclusion and striving to maintain the standards of a faded aristocracy, and reconcile their natures with the necessity which forced them to run a rooming house."[28] It has been suggested that these three ladies "served as the inspiration for the Blassenville sisters" in Howard's horror story "Pigeons from Hell."[29] One of the sisters (perhaps Camille, because census records indicate that she was the owner of a boardinghouse) appeared as young Robert's landlady in his essay "In His Own Image."[30]

Canal Street typically bristled with activity from the quaint family-owned restaurants, barber shops, small local businesses, and vintage Victorian two-story homes, where people sat on window seats in open windows, reading or observing passersby. Moreover, the Tulane Graduate School of Medicine, where Dr. Howard attended postgraduate classes, was located in the Hutchinson Building at 1550 Canal Street, within walking distance from the Howards' rooms at the boardinghouse. While Dr. Howard attended classes, Mrs. Howard and Robert spent their afternoons exploring the nearby neighborhoods. They discovered a public library at 2940 Canal Street, just a few blocks in the opposite direction of the Hutchinson Building. They spent many afternoons indulging their passion for books and reading by perusing the shelves of this library. The place was a virtual treasure trove for young Robert. It was here that he would make a critical discovery while thumbing through a history book. Robert described this discovery in a January 1932 letter:

> I spent a short time in New Orleans and found in a Canal Street library, a book detailing the pageant of British history, from prehistoric times up to—I believe—the Norman conquest. It was written for school-boys and told in an interesting and romantic style, probably with many historical inaccuracies. But there I first learned of the small dark people which first settled Britain, and they were referred to as Picts.[31]

This discovery of the Picts would eventually yield Robert's character Bran Mak Morn, who is the primary character in several of Robert's stories, including one of his more popular and critically acclaimed adventure fantasy short stories, "Worms of the Earth."[32] In this story, Robert declared, he "looked through Pictish eyes, and [spoke] with a Pictish tongue!"[33] The Picts played a prominent role throughout Robert's writing output and appeared "in no fewer than thirty stories, poems, and fragments, from *The West Tower* (probably written circa 1922–1923), a Steve Allison fragment, to *The Black Stranger*, one of the last Conan stories, probably written in 1935."[34]

The Romance of Early British Life: From the Earliest Times to the Coming of the Danes by F. G. Scott Elliot is believed to be the book Robert discovered in the Canal Street public library.[35] Two chapters are devoted to the Picts' arrival in the British Isles, their means of hunting and farming, their language, and other details about how they lived. They are described as "short, with brown or black hair and eyes; they have a whitey-brown or sallow complexion, and their heads are relatively long."[36] Elliot's exposition is grossly and comically exaggerated: he derisively depicts the Picts as archaic and staunch savages. Furthermore, he characterizes their existence in Britain as an inconvenience to its history but explains that they played a necessary role in the development of a better civilization.

In several of his own stories, Robert utilized Elliot's cycle of civilization's destruction of barbarism followed by civilization's demise and descent back into barbarism. Robert did not adopt Elliot's pejorative attitude toward the Picts and felt sympathetic toward them. In fact, compared to Elliot's depiction, Robert's Picts are more warlike, aggressive, and powerful, with an honorable history. He explains this portrayal in a letter to Lovecraft:

> I had always felt a strange interest in the term [Picts] and the people, and now I felt a driving absorption regarding them. The writer painted the aborigines in no more admirable light than had other historians whose work I had read. His Picts were made to be sly, furtive, unwarlike, and altogether inferior to the races which followed—which was doubtless true. And yet I felt a strong sympathy for this people, and then and there adopted them as a medium of connection with ancient times. I made them a strong, warlike race of barbarians, gave them an honorable history of past glories, and created for them a great king—one Bran Mak Morn.[37]

Bran Mak Morn appears (or is mentioned) in several of Robert's stories and poems and would prove to be a fan favorite. Robert made him the *ne plus ultra* of his Picts. All this considered, the trip to New Orleans yielded high dividends for Robert's eventual writing career.

In late 1917 (or possibly early 1918)—almost a year prior to the How-ards' family trip to New Orleans—Dr. Chambers retired from practic-ing medicine in Cross Cut. Once retired, he moved his family to Galves-ton County to try his hand at farming. For a brief but pleasant vacation, the Howards took a train to visit the Chambers family in February of that same year. It was probably on this trip that Robert fell in love with the ocean. As an adult, he returned to Galveston and the Gulf of Mexico for leisurely trips. Although in various letters he called the town old and dingy, he adored its oleander blooms.[38] The Chambers stayed in Galves-ton County for a relatively brief time, about six years. In 1924, Dr. Cham-bers moved his family back to Cross Cut, bought land, and farmed for the rest of his life. Both families remained close until Dr. Howard's death in 1944.

In April 1918, a few months after the Chamberses relocated to Galves-ton County, the Howards moved from Cross Cut to Burkett, Texas, pos-sibly because Dr. Chambers had left Cross Cut.[39] Or they may simply have been on the move once again because of Dr. Howard's proclivity for wandering. Whatever the reason, Dr. Howard was able to continue practicing medicine in Cross Cut when needed because Burkett was only eight miles southwest of Cross Cut.

Burkett was established in the early 1860s when a small group of farmers and ranchers settled the land on the Pecan Bayou. The town was named for its first postmaster, William Burkett, in 1886. Its devel-opment was slow but steady. Eventually several businesses, a grocery store, a thriving drugstore, a blacksmith, and a school were established. The school in Burkett that Robert attended was built in 1911. "It was a four room frame building. It had two rooms at both the north and south ends, but since there had never been more than two teachers at Burkett, the south side was just one large room with a large stage across the east side."[40] Like many small Texas towns, Burkett was a close-knit commu-nity. To bolster its community spirit, the town had a picnic area near Pe-can Bayou where people gathered to eat, socialize, and host revivals.

Several months after the Howards moved to Burkett, on June 1, 1918, they purchased a house on two and a half acres of land from C. E. and Mary J. Burns. The deed included four consecutive payments of $200 each, beginning the first day of December 1918, with a final payment on

April 1, 1919.[41] The land was fenced, included a barn, and was located close to Pecan Bayou. Two months after this purchase, on June 5, 1919, Dr. Howard traveled to the Coleman County courthouse and registered his medical credentials.

At this age, Robert was well acquainted with frequent location changes. In Burkett, he simply picked up where he had left off in Cross Cut. He did, however, remain friends with Austin Newton, since Cross Cut was close enough for the Howards to continue their visits with the Newton family. While in Burkett, Robert befriended Earl Baker, a boy who was a year or two older. The Bakers were probably already friends with Dr. Howard before the Howards moved from Cross Cut to Burkett. The proximity of the two towns made it possible for Dr. Howard to make house calls in Burkett while living in Cross Cut. Because of Dr. Howard's reputation, the Howards were popular in Burkett, though a few thought that Robert's bookish and imaginative behavior was a little unusual. Even so, Alma Baker King, Earl Baker's older sister, recalled that Robert "had a mind that wouldn't quit [and] very advanced ideas."[42] Earl Baker recalled that Robert was a deep thinker who loved to box, collect swords and knives, read adventure stories, and spar with his friends.[43]

The Bakers owned a farm about a mile outside of Burkett where Calvin Baker, Earl's father, raised a few horses. Young Robert was taught to ride horseback at the Baker farm. He developed a penchant for horse riding and continued to ride into his middle teen years. When Earl and Robert were not horseback riding, throwing knives at tree stumps, or roaming the pastures, the Howards entertained the Bakers for lunch or Sunday evening meals.

Since the Howards had purchased a house in Burkett and grew close to its townspeople, it appeared that they might finally settle down. However, on October 15, 1918—after a mere four months as homeowners—Dr. Howard sold the house and land to Etta Brady, turning a profit of $400. But instead of moving, the Howards rented the house from Miss Brady for a year. After a while, Dr. Howard's nomadic spirit prodded him to explore new horizons. On October 24, 1919, the family packed up their things and relocated ten miles north to the slightly larger community of Cross Plains.

CHAPTER FOUR

The Birth of a Writer

Robert, I believe that some day you will be one of our major writers. Develop your talent.

CROSS PLAINS HIGH SCHOOL ENGLISH TEACHER (PROBABLY DORIS PYLE), UNSIGNED NOTE IN THE MARGIN OF ROBERT E. HOWARD'S STORY "PICTURES IN THE FIRE" [CIRCA 1921]

It is written in the Howard family Bible that Patches—Robert E. Howard's dog—was born Christmas of 1917.[1] Patches was probably a gift from Robert's parents for his twelfth birthday in 1918. Whatever the circumstances for the playful canine becoming a family member, the Howards were living in Burkett, Texas, when they got him. Robert and Patches eventually became inseparable. As an adventurous boy, he was already used to roaming the Pecan Bayou and countryside around Burkett alone or with friends, so it made sense for Patches to tag along with young Robert on many of his excursions. On one such occasion, the boy and his best friend stumbled upon Mrs. T. A. Burns, the postmistress of Burkett and a close neighbor of the Howards. Mrs. Burns recalled the occasion in an article for the *Cross Plains Review*:

> 'Tis early one Spring morning, accompanied only by current magazines. We take off across a nearby pasture for a walk, stopping occasionally to pluck an anemone or some other dainty pastel hued blossom which mother nature displays soon after the first robins return.
>
> After a time we find ourself seated upon a rock, lost in musings, with the only disturbance a tinkling cow bell down by a wooded section near the water hole or the twitter of birds as they flit to and fro

among the branches of an oak above us. Finally becoming so absorbed in reading we are unaware of any approach until a big black and white dog wearing a collar bounds down from a ledge of rock behind, startling us. The kind look in his eyes assures that he is at least friendly, when almost immediately a call "Come Patches, come Patches" is heard and looking up in direction of the voice we see a lad of about ten years crossing fence wearily. . . . Patches in the meantime, seems to be investigating a small cave under a huge rock. As his master approaches our position and politely announces, "I'm Robert Howard, [I] am sorry if we frightened you. Patches and I are out for our morning stroll. We like to come here where there are big rocks and caves so we can play 'make believe.' Some day I'm going to be an author and write stories about pirates and maybe cannibals.

"Would you like to read them?"

Assuring him that we would, he calls to Patches and they are soon out of sight over the crest of the nearby hill, where-up we resume musing and reading.[2]

The exact date of this event is uncertain. Mrs. Burns mentioned that Robert looked like he was around ten years old, but this is unlikely since we know Patches was born Christmas of 1917, when Robert was eleven and living in Burkett. It is more likely that he was either twelve or thirteen when he and Patches encountered Mrs. Burns. The significance of this account is that it reveals Robert's desire at such a young age to be a writer. Chances are that he was already trying his hand at the craft by age ten or eleven.

Around this same time, according to Robert, he created his first character, Francis Xavier Gordon, also known as El Borak. He was "the hero of 'The Daughter of Erlik Khan' (*Top-Notch*), etc. I don't remember his genesis. He came to life in my mind when I was about ten years old."[3] Considering Robert's early experiences, it is no surprise that El Borak is a gunfighter from El Paso, Texas, who has traveled the Far East, spending most of his time in Afghanistan. Texas and the western expansion in the United States were replete with stories about gunfighters and their exploits. And of course, El Borak never stayed in one place for too long. Even though Robert created El Borak when he was about ten, the character would not see the printed page until 1934.

In September 1919, Dr. Howard made a short trip to Cross Plains, approximately ten miles northeast of Burkett, to look at available property. J. M. Coffman, one of the first settlers of the community, was selling one-quarter of his land from the Steele Addition, atop a hill overlooking Turkey Creek. Dr. Howard bought the property for $1,500. With an initial down payment, he signed four promissory notes at $250 each as payments on the property. The final payment was to be made on or before the date falling four years after the initial down payment. Shortly thereafter, the Howards moved again.

The first people to settle the region around Cross Plains were German pioneers in the 1870s. They set up log-cabin-style homes near Turkey Creek and began farming right away. The Comanche who were native to this area had been driven north by the Texas Rangers, and buffalo had become increasingly scarce in the region. Occasionally, Comanche would return to the area, wreaking havoc on these early settlers. "Prior to 1877, the scattered settlers in Callahan County had to transact any official business, such as recording deeds, obtaining marriage licenses, and the like, either in Taylor County or Eastland County courthouses."[4] Local trade took place in larger towns such as Abilene and Fort Worth. By the turn of the century, the number of settlers on Turkey Creek had increased. The community had several merchant shops, a drugstore, a much-needed corn mill (established in 1877), and a post office and had even had telephones installed. However, anyone who wanted flour had to haul it by oxen and cart from Fort Worth. Turkey Creek had no formal elected government and no organized streets.

Around this same time, rumors circulated that the Texas Central Railway Company (TCRC) was building a line through Callahan County; with connecting lines from the Intercontinental Railroad to smaller communities and settlements, trade and travel would become easier. The news motivated several communities to move their settlements closer to railway service depots or tracks, and Cross Plains was no exception. By early 1910, the TCRC was negotiating contracts with groups of investors to build railway lines and a depot in proximity to the settlement on Turkey Creek, eventually agreeing upon an area on higher ground just northeast of the Turkey Creek settlement. The area would remain in Callahan County, but the townspeople on Turkey Creek needed to relocate if they wanted to be near the railway.

Word spread far and wide that on January 12, 1911, Callahan County was auctioning land just east of Turkey Creek near the new railway tracks and depot. "People came from miles around in buggies and autos for the great land auction. The train was scheduled to arrive at 10:15, but because of the overloaded conditions, it was late. Prospective buyers were stuffed into the cars with standing room at a premium—some even rode on top of the coaches."[5] Crowds of thousands gathered to buy land for residences and businesses. An elected city government was established after the auction, the town quickly incorporated, and Cross Plains became an official town where it still stands today.

Between 1911 and 1919, Cross Plains grew exponentially. Public utilities were established, businesses boomed, and the railroad enabled trade in and out, regularly bringing new community members and commerce into town. By the time the Howards moved to Cross Plains from Burkett in October 1919, the town's population hovered between nine hundred and one thousand. Robert was thirteen when his family moved into their new home. Because they moved in the fall, he simply transferred from his former school in Burkett to a much larger school in Cross Plains. Even as the Howards remained friends with several families from Burkett, such as the Bakers, Robert began to make new friends in Cross Plains. This was relatively easy for him given that the Cross Plains school had over three hundred students. Among Robert's new friends from Cross Plains, three stand out: Dave Lee, who may have introduced Robert to the local icehouse beer and sparring; Lindsey Tyson, who would be Robert's roommate in Brownwood while he attended the commercial department of the Howard Payne Academy; and C. S. Boyles, who was the first to have a hand in publishing several of Robert's short stories.

The Cross Plains public school operated like a typical small public school in the early 1920s. Classes were separated by grade and age of students. "By 1921 the school had eleven teachers, electric light and natural gas heat and 335 students."[6] Robert grew to dislike the routine of school. Being restricted to classrooms for most of the day and following a specific curriculum stifled his sense of freedom. Having been raised in an openly explorative environment, free to read what he wanted, roam where he wanted, and see things that many kids who were raised in one place never experienced, Robert felt trapped and uncomfortable in a static classroom setting. He once described the loss of freedom he felt in a letter:

> I hated school, not because any particular tyranny was practiced on me—I wouldn't have stood for it, anyway—but simply because the whole system irked me. Sitting still in one place for hours at a time got on my nerves. Having to go and come at certain times irked me; I hated for my actions to be controlled by the ringing of a bell. The fact that these things were necessary had nothing to do with it. School, any way it is looked at it, was a restriction of my freedom.[7]

Had an open classroom environment been available when Robert attended grade school, he might have enjoyed public education.[8] Not even the traditional classroom environment, however, could stifle Robert's creativity. He was an average student in most of his classes, but he did excel in English and history and performed reasonably well in science. And despite his aversion to the rigid structure of the public school system, he maintained a passion for learning through his leisure-time reading. He also understood the value of books to research. "Things I have discovered to be of most use, I learned mostly without formal teaching. What little knowledge I have picked up in a rudimentary manner here and there was mainly the result of reading for amusement."[9] Robert shined when some teachers gave him the freedom to write essays of his choosing and, in doing so, probably contributed to his passion for writing.

All of the Howards were avid readers, but books were difficult to come by in their rural area. The best opportunities to purchase books came when the family traveled to Brownwood, San Antonio, Fort Worth, or any other larger city with bookstores. The Howards' home library became substantial over the years, especially considering where they lived. Robert noted that "my own library was generally the largest in the place I lived, but it was small. I generally was given a book on Christmas and on my birthday. Occasionally between times a book was bought. For the rest I borrowed whenever I could." When he was older, Robert ordered books through the mail from larger bookstores in New York City. The scarcity of books never stopped the Howards from seeking new places from which to buy or order books. When books were unavailable, magazines proved a nice alternative, especially in Cross Plains and Brownwood. Nevertheless, "magazines were even more scarce than books," Robert wrote. "It was after I moved into 'town' (speaking comparatively) that I began to buy magazines."[10]

In the early 1920s, Cross Plains had two drugstores, City Drugstore and Cozy Drugstore; additional drugstores would open by the late twenties. Higginbotham Brothers & Company owned a large general mercantile shop on Main Street in Cross Plains that sold building materials, appliances, groceries, and other sundries that probably included a small selection of magazines. While it is not known for certain, Robert is likely to have bought his first pulp magazine in 1921 from one of these drugstores or from Higginbotham's:

> I well remember the first [magazine] I ever bought. I was fifteen years old; I bought it one summer night when a wild restlessness in me

would not let me keep still, and I had exhausted all the reading material on the place. I'll never forget the thrill it gave me. Somehow it had never occurred to me before that I could buy a magazine. It was an *Adventure*. I still have the copy. After that I bought *Adventure* for many years, though at times it cramped my resources to pay the price. It came out three times a month then.[11]

This literary discovery played a pivotal role in Robert's writing, igniting a desire to use "some of his homework assignments as his first-ever professional submissions to *Adventure* magazine, which he credits as being the magazine that inspired him to write fiction."[12] At age fifteen, he did in fact submit a story to *Adventure*, titled "Bill Smalley and the Human Eye."[13] The story was rejected, but Robert, smitten with the prospect of becoming a professional writer, began searching for similar pulp magazines. *Adventure* had given him a thrill most likely in part because it published pirate tales, which, he excitedly told Mrs. T. A. Burns when he was younger, he intended to write.

Adventure introduced the budding apprentice to several writers whose works were influential: Talbot Mundy, Rafael Sabatini, and Harold Lamb. Other significant writers who influenced Robert's earlier (and later) works include William Shakespeare, Edgar Rice Burroughs, H. Rider Haggard, Jack London, and Rudyard Kipling. Burroughs, Kipling, and London in particular gave Robert the idea of the feral protagonist—a rugged individual who either begins in a primitive state or attempts to claim his individuality by stepping away from the trappings of civilization. Moreover, some of the protagonists of these other authors turn to barbarism either because of civilization's duplicity or, like Burroughs's Tarzan, because they are juxtaposed between the primitive and civilized in that they began life as a feral in a primitive environment, experienced civilization, and opted to return to their primitive roots. In either event, these protagonists have a remarkably dual nature. The ideals of these characters became staple motifs for several of Robert's own protagonists, as he readily admitted: "When I begin a tale of old times, I always find myself instinctively arrayed on the side of the barbarian, against the powers of organized civilization."[14]

Much of this literature depicting rugged individualists and feral protagonists (especially Burroughs's Tarzan) was "inspired by ideas of natural virtue derived from Jean-Jacques Rousseau's thesis that most of the evils afflicting mankind are not the result of heredity but of the perverting effects of civilization."[15] And while this Rousseauist theme did not permeate Robert's stories directly, Rousseau's philosophy imbued aspects of the politics, literature, and entertainment of Robert's time and place, influencing him in turn as a thinker and writer.

Although it is not known for certain, it is likely that Robert began writing poetry in his teen years. As he approached his young adult years, he took the craft of poetry more seriously. His poetical influences include British poets of the Romantic period (1784–1837), especially Samuel Taylor Coleridge, as well as poets from the Victorian Age (1837–1914), especially Alfred, Lord Tennyson, and Algernon Charles Swinburne. Other poets who influenced Robert's work include G. K. Chesterton, Edgar Allan Poe, Rudyard Kipling, Henry Wadsworth Longfellow, and Robert W. Service. Robert would have read these poets in school as well, since his English teachers probably taught poetry from the Romantic and Victorian periods. However, World War I had changed the cultural, social, and literary landscape of the United States and Europe. The period from the end of the Victorian age (1901) and the start of World War I (1914) ushered in literary Modernism, whose poets included A. E. Housman, William Butler Yeats, Ezra Pound, and D. H. Lawrence.

Most Modernist poets and publications had been "traumatized by the impact of World War I, were deciding that life was a waste land, and indeed it must have seemed to alienated intellectuals."[16] Under this influence, the form and style of poetry changed, rhyme and meter were abandoned, and free verse gained popularity. Poets from the Victorian and Romantic periods, who wrote in traditional forms of rhyme and meter, were losing favor, but not for Robert. He championed the traditional rhyme and meter of those writers in his own poetry, and it served him well when he incorporated that style into his prose. Much of his prose maintains a metric pace, or ebb and flow, reflective of Romantic and Victorian poetry. At the same time, Robert adopted the cultural and philosophical ideology of the Modernist period—the belief that life is a waste land—as well as the period's existential angst about civilization and its apparently corrupt behavior. These ideas were often highlighted in Robert's poetry and stories. And in fact, in his day, Robert witnessed such corruption through the actions of large corporations (especially oil companies) and the government.

In October 1920, at the age of fourteen, Robert handwrote an eight-page report on Samuel Taylor Coleridge for an English class; one page conveyed biographical information, and the rest of the report was a seven-page analysis of Coleridge's poem "The Rime of the Ancient Mariner."[17] The teacher was more impressed with Robert's analysis (he got an

A) than the biographical portion (he got a B). A good friend of Robert's later reported that after two readings of Coleridge's poem, he already had it committed to memory.[18] The fact that Robert committed "The Rime of the Ancient Mariner" to memory is a pretty clear indication of the influence on him of the poem and its author.

During Robert's high school education, Cross Plains High School stopped at the tenth grade. If a student had ambitions to attend college, it was necessary to finish high school at the nearby high school in Brownwood, Texas. Dr. Howard claims that Mrs. Howard wanted her son to have a career in business.[19] Such an ambition meant that Robert needed to finish his high school education in Brownwood, giving him the option, should the need arise, to go to college. So, in the fall of 1922 the Howards moved their son to Brownwood so that he could complete the eleventh grade (which was the final year of secondary education in those days). At sixteen, Robert, of course, did not live by himself. It was arranged that he would live with his mother. "The Howards secured rooms in the home of Mrs. Alice Day at 316 Wilson Street, across Austin Avenue from Howard Payne College and just down the road from Brownwood High."[20]

This move would open up a whole new world for young Robert. He met new friends with similar literary interests, he discovered new authors and new books, and unlike Cross Plains High, Brownwood High had a school newspaper. More than likely it was in Brownwood that Robert discovered different pulp magazines besides *Adventure* at the local newsstands. One such pulp magazine was *Weird Tales*, which introduced Robert to several different genres, including weird horror and weird fantasy fiction. Around this same time, sixteen-year-old Robert created one of his more celebrated characters, Solomon Kane. Robert wasted no time taking his already written stories and submitting them to these new pulp magazines. If he could get one story published, surely he could get another published, and then another. So, while Robert obeyed his parents and attended Brownwood High School for his final year of high school because they wanted him to attend college, a career in writing was foremost in his mind.

CHAPTER FIVE

Tattlers *and* Yellow Jackets

Bob couldn't stand anybody telling him what to do. He was the most fiercely independent fellow you ever saw; that's the reason why he didn't go to college.

LINDSEY TYSON, IN A 1978 INTERVIEW WITH THE DE CAMPS

When Robert and Mrs. Howard moved to Brownwood, Texas, the town's population hovered around eight thousand, making it eight times larger than Cross Plains. Aside from Abilene to the northwest, Brownwood was the largest town within a one-hundred-mile radius of Cross Plains, and living in a larger town would provide multiple benefits for Robert. Brownwood had more newsstands than most everywhere else he had lived, and therefore a substantially larger selection of magazines. It also had a bookstore and a large Carnegie public library. Robert would make good use of all these resources. Brownwood also had two colleges, so the population of young adults was relatively high, bringing to the area a flurry of various activities to engage these young people. Robert would make new friends and participate in various activities, but he spent much of his time reading and writing.

Since the year before the year he spent at Brownwood High School (BHS), Robert had been submitting short stories to magazines. BHS would prove beneficial to him as an aspiring writer, if for no other reason than that it was the first place where he was measurably successful as a writer. BHS functioned as a "feeder" high school for students from all the smaller towns around Brownwood who wanted to go to college— in other words, students who, like Robert, attended eleventh grade at

BHS because their own high school stopped at tenth grade. That being the case, Robert was able to reunite with old friends—like Austin Newton from Cross Cut—while he also made new friends. Two of these new friends, Truett Vinson and Tevis Clyde Smith Jr. (who went by Clyde), would eventually become some of Robert's closest friends. Each had similar literary tastes and writing aspirations.

Once the school year started, T. C. Boyles Jr., Robert's friend from Cross Plains, joined the staff of the BHS school newspaper, *The Tattler*. The two may have discussed writing or swapped stories while attending school in Cross Plains. Whatever the case, Boyles was aware of Robert's talent, so it is possible he asked Robert to write a few stories for the school paper.[1] This was an opportunity to be published and find an audience that Robert did not have in Cross Plains. Robert went to work, and by the fall of the first semester he had submitted two stories to *The Tattler*: "'Golden Hope' Christmas" and "West Is West." Both were published on December 22, 1922. The local newspaper, the *Brownwood Bulletin*, ran an article featuring details about Robert's work and declared, "'"Golden Hope" Christmas' is the title of the better of the two stories, telling briefly of the career of an old-time desperado. The little story is well written and the theme is well chosen."[2] This article made the wider population of Brownwood aware of Robert's stories, giving them an opportunity to pick up that issue of *The Tattler*. The recognition for his hard work bolstered Robert's confidence and allowed him to see his efforts beginning to pay off, even if only at the local level.

Robert was sixteen when he wrote these two stories. The *Brownwood Bulletin* was correct in declaring "'Golden Hope' Christmas" the better of the two. Both are clearly amateur works, but they show great promise, especially considering Robert's age. Both stories are good examples of a budding writer using settings and motifs that are familiar to him from experience. The stories are general realistic fiction with western motifs. Robert utilized his research, the pioneer tales he had heard growing up around Texas, and his experience as a child riding horses in Cross Cut. "West Is West" is a kind of literary amalgamation, an experiment with various literary elements, including a brief smattering of Elizabethan English, an obvious Shakespearean influence. At the beginning of "West Is West" are several instances of alliteration, and toward the end Robert shifts from the earlier Elizabethan English to a more colloquial dialect. The attention and praise Robert received for these two stories probably solidified his desire to pursue a career as a writer. In fact, when writing the review, the *Brownwood Bulletin* reporter interviewed Robert about his career ambitions, and he expressed a desire to pursue "journalism as his life profession."[3]

Robert's close friend Truett Vinson was the same age as Robert, had a strong interest in politics, and was a socialist at the time. He frequently read works by Upton Sinclair and introduced Robert to the *Little Blue Book* series.[4] Truett was also the son of a Baptist minister who eventually opened a furniture store in Brownwood. For a spell, Truett maintained a small mail-order bookstore from which both Robert and Robert's other close friend, Clyde Smith, made regular purchases. Clyde was two years younger than Truett and Robert and met Robert through Truett. When Robert began Brownwood High School, Truett and Clyde were already friends. In fact, the two had an organization called the All-Around Club, "which meant that a group of boys banded themselves together to have a literary program, followed by a game of sandlot—or in this case front yard—football."[5] The point of the club was to discuss politics, literature, and such.

Clyde read Robert's two stories in the December 1922 issue of *The Tattler* and was impressed. Knowing that Truett was already acquainted with Robert, Clyde asked Truett to introduce him to Robert. Since Clyde had created the *All-Around Magazine* in the early spring of 1923, he wanted to become acquainted with Robert with an eye to soliciting stories for the magazine. Interestingly, according to Clyde's account, Robert left an odd impression on him when they first met:

> It was a day much like today—cloudless, pleasantly warm—proba-bly in early April, if not late March, 1923 that I asked Truett Vinson if he knew Robert E. Howard. We were on the school grounds at Brown-wood High, and Truett said, "Yes, there he is now." I told Truett that I'd like to meet Bob, and he called Bob over, introducing us to one an-other. We shook hands, if it could be called that, for Bob extended a limp palm and executed what was known as a "dishrag shake." I hadn't wanted him to break the bones in my hand, but I was a bit surprised at such a greeting, though I soon found out that he was warmhearted, and we became good friends before the school term ended.[6]

Though Clyde seemed a bit unimpressed when first introduced to Rob-ert E. Howard, an impressive friendship soon developed and lasted for the rest of Robert's life.

As Clyde mentioned, he was introduced to Robert several months into the spring 1923 semester at BHS. In January, when Mrs. Howard and

Robert returned to Brownwood from the winter break, Robert was still reeling from the attention garnered by his two stories. So he geared up to submit more. In the meantime, he continued to submit stories to various magazines like *Adventure*, *Argosy-Allstory*, and *Weird Tales*.[7] All three magazines rejected his stories, but while these were setbacks, he was not deterred. At this point, Robert primarily focused his attention on the pulp market, having already submitted to several "slicks," though without any success. He revealed his intention to focus on the pulp market in a conversation with Clyde: "'I'll never make the slicks,' he said. 'I'm not that kind of writer, but I'll make the pulps, and I intend to make them from here in Texas. I'm going to prove that a man doesn't have to live in New York to sell his stories.'"[8]

During the 1920s and 1930s, there were three types of magazine markets for writers: literary, slicks, and pulps. Literary magazines included high-end publications such as the *Atlantic Monthly*, *Esquire*, *Harper's*, and *The New Yorker*. The slicks were popular magazines such as the *Saturday Evening Post*, *Collier's*, *Ladies' Home Journal*, and *Cosmopolitan*. These magazines had glossy smooth pages, thus the name "slicks." And then there were the pulps, so called because the pages of these magazines were made from cheap wood-pulp paper.[9] A relatively talented writer had a greater chance of getting published in the pulps. The slicks paid substantially more than the pulps—as much as $1,000 or more for stories, whereas the pulps paid a penny a word or less. Very few writers who cut their teeth on pulp magazines managed to publish stories in the slicks or break into the literary magazine market. The writers who did cross that divide also eventually wrote novels and plays and won prestigious literary awards.[10] The pulp magazine market became Robert's sole focus in 1923.

In the meantime, *The Tattler* was more than eager to publish more stories from the aspiring writer, and Robert was eager to let them. On February 15, 1923, *The Tattler* ran one of Robert's detective stories, "Aha! Or The Mystery of the Queen's Necklace." The story features Hawkshaw, a famous detective, who was "inspired by a popular comic strip of the day, *Hawkshaw the Detective*, whose main character, Hawkshaw and his helper, the Colonel, are themselves loose adaptations of Sherlock Holmes and Watson, though with a humorous bent."[11] Robert lifted the characters straight from the comic strip and used them to create a tongue-in-cheek mystery story. Sax Rohmer's character Fu Manchu, who appeared in several of Robert's letters in which he poked fun at Sherlock Holmes, may have also had some influence on Robert's story.[12]

Gus Mager created *Hawkshaw the Detective*, a comic strip that ran in newspapers across the country between 1913 and 1922. During that period, Robert read the comic strip in the newspapers, as did many of the readers of *The Tattler*. When *The Tattler* published "Aha! Or The Mystery of the Queen's Necklace," *Hawkshaw the Detective* was on a publishing hiatus.[13] In its absence, the student body at BHS probably enjoyed seeing the characters being used again, in this case to highlight the tongue-in-cheek tone of the story. Although Robert's story was the work of a young writer borrowing characters from a well-known source, the story demonstrated that he was gaining a solid grasp of narrative pacing. The story had a steady pace and just enough content to control the scenes and maintain the reader's attention. The story also had a few clever plot twists at the end.

A few weeks later, on March 1, *The Tattler* published another of Robert's stories, "Unhand Me, Villain!" This story is a humorous romance, and like "Aha! Or The Mystery of the Queen's Necklace," the narrative pace is steady and in a twist at the end Hawkshaw appears to save the day. Both these stories were well received by the BHS students. In fact, on March 15, *The Tattler* featured Robert and the four stories they had published to date, reminding their readers that the *Brownwood Bulletin* had complimented him on his earlier efforts. *The Tattler* went on to compare Robert's writing style to those of O. Henry, Bret Harte, and Mark Twain. In addition to this write-up, this issue of the school paper featured "The Sheik," another story of Robert's.

While Robert was busy writing stories for *The Tattler*, Truett and Clyde were working on launching their newly developed *All-Around Magazine*. Both boys lived close to the Howards' boardinghouse, making it easy for Robert to pay them regular visits. Clyde's healthy interest in newspaper journalism as a career led him to purchase a small hand-operated printing press to print the *All-Around Magazine*:

> One day, in the early twenties, a delivery truck pulled up to our house and unloaded a shipment of merchandise from Meriden Connecticut. The shipment included one Kelsey Printing Press, and part of the equipment necessary for a small shop. Every nickel possible began to go for type, and supplies, and before long, The All Around Magazine, a small amateur paper, made its appearance.[14]

At the time, Truett also wanted to pursue writing as a career, so he became the magazine's assistant editor. As the three boys' friendship deepened, it was soon discovered that each had an interest in sports, especially Clyde and Robert. Before long, football and boxing had become the focus of some of their conversations, and eventually Clyde and Robert put on gloves and sparred.

By March 1923, the first issue of the *All-Around Magazine* was released. Truett and Clyde initially handed it out to their friends and later provided subscriptions to those who were interested. Clyde indicated that the magazine's "circulation was about 15."[15] Since it never seemed to exceed that number, the *All-Around Magazine* became one of the rarer collectors' items in Howard fandom. The first issue included a piece by Truett Vinson titled "A Tenderfoot's Hike," a short humorous story about three gents going on a hike and running into a series of mishaps, picking up chigger bites along the way. Truett also contributed a short piece, called "Astronomy," and Clyde offered a poem titled "The Lure of the North." The *All-Around Magazine* was not the most propitious platform for the aspiring writers, but in the end they had fun putting each issue together.

The second issue (April 1923) included "Texas," another piece from Truett. Truett also placed an ad for the Vinsons' furniture store, and Clyde contributed "The Last Up," a brief baseball story. On one of the last pages of the April issue is a small section called "Wiselets," written by a new contributor, Herbert Klatt of Hamilton, Texas. Klatt, another aspiring writer, eventually became a part of this circle of Brownwood friends through regular correspondence and one meeting. Klatt was an acquaintance of Truett's through the Lone Scouts of America. Founded by W. D. Boyce, Lone Scouts of America was a scouting organization formed in 1915 for boys in isolated rural areas who had no opportunity to join the Boy Scouts of America, the larger and better-known scouting organization. The Lone Scouts of America would merge with the Boy Scouts of America in 1924. The Lone Scouts of America had its own magazine, *Lone Scout*. Both the All-Around Club and its magazine were probably the result of Smith's and Vinson's Lone Scout activity. In fact, the *All-Around Magazine* was intended to be a "tribe paper" similar to the Lone Scouts' magazine.[16] With the date for BHS graduation approaching, Robert finally contributed to the *All-Around Magazine*'s May/June 1923 issue. Robert and Clyde collaborated on an unfinished tale titled "Under the Great Tiger." In addition to his contribution to the *All-Around Magazine*, Robert continued submitting works to other publishing venues.

During this time and into his mid to late twenties, Robert also wrote a substantial amount of poetry. "Toward the end of his senior year, Howard entered a poem in the Baylor College for Women's poetry contest."[17] Baylor College for Women eventually became the University of Mary-Hardin Baylor, located in Belton, Texas, just southwest of Temple. "Howard won Honorable Mention for his entry, which was probably 'The Sea,' as that poem was published in the school's United Statement in the spring of 1923, just before the winners were announced in May."[18]

Robert also won the Winnie Davis Chapter of the UDC (United Daughters of the Confederacy) Medal for best paper: "What the Nation Owes the South." It is not known for certain, but it is possible that Robert submitted this work directly to his landlord, Alice Day, who was a member of the UDC. She may have informed Robert about the contest, having already read his work in *The Tattler* or the *Brownwood Bulletin*. After announcing him as the winner, the UDC presented him with the medal at his class of 1923 BHS graduation ceremony. This medal-winning essay was then printed in the *Brownwood Bulletin* on May 26, 1923. A month after graduation, one of his poems, "The Sea," appeared in the June 29, 1923, issue of the *Cross Plains Review*. In May and June of that year, at the age of seventeen, Robert was being showered with awards and recognition for his work. As in the past, such recognition further fueled Robert's desire to pursue writing as a career.

In the summer of 1923, while other high school graduates were planning summer vacations or applying for colleges, Robert hit the streets looking for work. The accolades he had received for his writing were admirable, but his work was not paying him a living wage. Initially, he resisted any sort of arduous menial labor—because such work looted most of the time he hoped to devote to writing—but as the years passed his resistance waned. Even so, Robert managed to keep writing. In an effort to make a paying job coincide with his desire to write, sometime over the summer he began freelancing for the *Cross Plains Review*, writing up oil field reports. At first, he was assigned fewer of these reports than he had hoped. Needing more money, he told his friend Clyde in an August 24, 1923, letter that he was hoping to get additional work at the post office in Cross Plains.

Shortly after graduation, Robert moved back to Cross Plains and began corresponding with his good friend Clyde. The two maintained this correspondence for the rest of Robert's life. In the beginning, they discussed books they were reading and the latest movies they had seen, and they shared crazy stories and poetry. Some of these letters are hilarious. Often Robert expressed his frustrations about jobs and his attempts to get published. Through correspondence with both Clyde and Truett, Robert became acquainted with two other aspiring local Texas writers, Herbert Klatt and Harold Preece.

Sometime in August 1923, Robert began working at a tailor shop selling and delivering clothes. Even at his young age, this job was physically taxing and took up most of his time. He revealed to Clyde, "I walk from five to fifteen miles a day, no exaggeration, soliciting clothes and delivering them and when I'm not doing that I wash and clean clothes." Apparently, the tailor shop paid Robert commissions, probably based on sales of clothing. Robert mentioned that he earned around $40 per month, sometimes more. "Not an overly pleasant occupation, but I like it alright."[19]

Despite the hours he spent working for the tailor shop, Robert managed to write and submit "The Iron Terror" to *Cosmopolitan*.[20] This would be the last known story he ever submitted to the slicks. He was seventeen at the time. "The Iron Terror" is a clever early-twentieth-century science fiction story that utilizes a wonderful mixture of mystery, suspense, and action. For its day, it was cutting-edge, especially given the advanced nature of the science he writes about (for example, a remote-controlled robot). Even so, the story was rejected. Submitting that story to *Cosmopolitan* was perhaps not the wisest choice: the competition included high-caliber writers such as Sinclair Lewis, Theodore Dreiser, and W. Somerset Maugham. With some solid editing, however, "The Iron Terror" would have been good enough to easily fit into the array of fiction that *Weird Tales* published at the time, and Robert might have breached professional publication sooner if he had submitted it there.[21] In the fall of 1923, Robert submitted two short stories, "The Mystery of Summerton Castle" and "The Phantom of Old Egypt,"[22] to *Weird Tales*, which, under their original management, rejected both. He may have written these stories earlier for teachers at Cross Plains High School.[23]

Dr. and Mrs. Howard were eager for their son to begin college, but Robert did not share their enthusiasm. Despite his parents' prodding, he was unwilling to surrender his freedom at this point in his life. Ironically, however, he was willing to sacrifice his freedom working menial jobs. Perhaps he reasoned that this kind of work was the lesser of two evils and simply chose to postpone college and continue to work. At this point in Robert's life, whether he realized it or not, he was racing against time. He either had to achieve a viable level of income as a writer or give that idea up and settle for a conventional job. And even though his parents supported his efforts as a writer, they were not convinced that writing was a sustainable way to earn a living.[24] For them, college was the most viable option for Robert to earn a steady income, with a business degree. Robert was hoping to keep a job and in his spare time write and get published until the income from writing matched or exceeded the income from his job. The idea of being his own boss was quite appealing, and he knew as a paid writer he could have that kind of freedom. He later admitted as much in a letter to a colleague: "I took up writing simply because it seemed to promise an easier mode of work, more money, and more freedom than any other job I'd tried. I wouldn't write otherwise."[25]

When the fall semester began at BHS and Howard Payne College, Robert continued to work at the tailor shop in Cross Plains. His friends and former BHS classmates Claude Curtis and C. S. Boyles had both been on the editorial staff of *The Tattler* and would become the senior editor (Curtis) and associate editor (Boyles) of Howard Payne's school newspaper, *The Yellow Jacket*. Within days of the beginning of the first semester, Boyles solicited stories from Robert, who was more than eager to publish in *The Yellow Jacket*. It may still have been just a local publication, but as a college newspaper, it was a step up from *The Tattler*.

"Before there was a *Yellow Jacket*, there was the *Prism*. From the fall of 1915 to the spring of 1923, the *Prism* was responsible for bringing the students at Howard Payne College news from the school, the community, and the world."[26] The paper changed its name to *The Yellow Jacket* in 1923, just prior to Curtis and Boyles becoming its editors. Under them, the paper maintained the same responsibility to report school, community, and world news. And while Boyles asked Robert for stories in the early fall of 1923, it took Robert six months before submitting something to *The Yellow Jacket*. It is possible that his job at the tailor shop caused the delay. In fact, Robert was so busy during this period that he wrote Clyde only about once a month. Amid all this, news spread in October 1923 about the death of a classmate from BHS, Lee Roy Guthrie, from a self-inflicted gunshot wound through his heart.[27] Although it is not known how well Robert knew Roy Guthrie, he did mention the suicide in an October 5, 1923, letter to Clyde. Roy's suicide had a lasting effect on Robert and led him to consciously consider and defend such an option. Clyde confirmed this in an article many years later in which he wrote that Roy's suicide "had an impact on him [Robert], and, as the years went by, he became more constant in defending the right of self destruction, dropping hints of the value of such an ending."[28]

By February 1, 1924, Cross Plains High School had established its own newspaper, the *Progress*, and Robert submitted several works to it, among them a poem titled "The Maiden of Kercheezer" and a short humorous piece titled "Rules of Etiquette." The following month, *The Yellow Jacket* published a "Letter of a Chinese Student" and then a second "letter" by the same title on May 2, 1924.

> These two "Letters" from the *Yellow Jacket* archives, both apparently "lost" until now, have escaped the notice of Howard scholars for a couple of reasons: first, they were published during the 1923–24 school year, the year before Howard enrolled in HP's [Howard Payne's] commercial school for the first time; and, second, both are unsigned.

The two letters were apparently identified as Robert's work because of a "short notice appearing at the end of the second 'Letter.'"[29] Both are humorous pieces written from the perspective of a Chinese student's first-time experience of different cultures and people of other cultures (India, America, etc.). Robert pokes fun at dancing, history, and cultures in the letters. They were contributed to *The Yellow Jacket* "on account of the personal friendship toward certain members on the staff."[30]

Robert maintained his story output at the local level but was still unable to even get his toe in the door professionally. The menial jobs continued. In an April 1924 letter to his friend Clyde, he lamented, "I'm still working at the tailor trade and I haven't made very much money lately as another shop has been put in and three tailor shops are too many for a town this size."[31] Shortly after writing this letter, Robert lost his job at the tailor shop and ended up bouncing from one menial job to another until June, when he got a job heaving freight at the local depot.[32] Despite the time he had to spend jumping from job to job, Robert managed to write and submit two more stories to professional magazines: "The Fightin' Dumbbell" (to *Sport Story*) and "44-40 or Fight" (to *Western Story*). Both were rejected.

From 1921 to 1924, Robert had submitted eight stories to a variety of professional magazines with no success. The only publishing success he had experienced during these years was at the local level. It is likely that these professional rejections were distressing him, and he may have been questioning whether he had the ability to make it as a writer. But however great his disappointment over these rejections, his stubborn determination was greater. Refusing to give up, he marched forward, even though he knew that his failure at breaking into magazine markets and the difficulty of making a living in the Cross Plains job market meant that something had to change.

By the summer of 1924, Dr. and Mrs. Howard were pressing their son once again to turn his attention to college. During that summer, Robert continued working temporary jobs, but "with meaningful employment nowhere in sight, it was decided that [Robert] would return to Brownwood in the fall to attend classes at the Howard Payne Academy."[33] It should be noted that Robert took classes through the commercial department housed in the Howard Payne Academy building. The commercial department offered certificates to high school graduates who did not necessarily want or need a four-year college degree. It was a separate entity from the Howard Payne Academy (which offered a high school education) and Howard Payne College (which offered a four-year college degree). As it happened, Lindsey Tyson,[34] Robert's younger friend from Cross Plains, began his senior year of high school at the Howard Payne Academy for the 1924–1925 school year. The Howard Payne Academy, sponsored by Howard Payne College, was established "to function like today's junior colleges and was separate from the actual college; it even had its own building on the campus."[35] Moreover, for high school students in Brownwood and the surrounding rural areas, the Howard Payne Academy offered a complete high school education and accommodated high school students from rural areas who wanted to complete their final year, just as Brownwood High School had done for Robert.

Robert had been friends with Lindsey Tyson from the time the Howards moved to Cross Plains. The two boys, along with a few other friends in Cross Plains (Dave Lee, Tom R. Wilson, Bill Calhoun, and Winifred Brigner), explored the creeks and hills of the Cross Plains area. When they got older, Lindsey and Robert attended football games together and the annual Cross Plains picnic, and on several occasions they hitch-hiked to Fort Worth and Dallas to watch prizefights. In fact, according to Lindsey, "[Robert] and I used to do a lot of boxing, . . . we'd beat each other for an hour or so when we was [sic] young fellows."[36] Lindsey moved into a boardinghouse at 417 Austin Avenue in Brownwood toward the end of that summer of 1924 to attend Howard Payne Academy. That same semester Robert returned to Brownwood and moved into the same boardinghouse. This would be the first and only time Robert lived apart from his parents.

Wanting to keep school to a minimum number of hours, Robert took classes through the commercial department to study for a commercial business certificate, which could typically be completed in about a year. This program offered students a certificate in business administration, with classes in shorthand, typing, and bookkeeping. Even though Robert was back in school, his mind remained on writing. The upside was that since he was back in Brownwood, it was more convenient for him to submit stories to *The Yellow Jacket*. After the 1923–1924 school year ended at Howard Payne College, "C. S. Boyles moved away to Sweetwater, Texas, and was married before the next summer appeared. Curtis, however, was reelected to the top spot on the paper and was happy to publish Robert E. Howard's work."[37] And Claude Curtis did just that in the September 24, 1924, issue of *The Yellow Jacket* with Robert's story "Halt! Who Goes There?"

The boardinghouse at 417 Austin Avenue was a large two-story home that housed college students during the fall, spring, and summer terms. According to Lindsey Tyson, he moved into the boardinghouse first, then Robert moved in, and the two soon roomed together. This makes sense given that it would have saved Robert money to share a room. In those days, Lindsey remembered, Robert's focus was mostly on his desire to become a writer. "He was the hardest worker I ever saw," said Lindsey. "He'd write all day and all night and maybe all the next day." That semester when they lived at the boardinghouse, Lindsey recalled, there were times when Robert stayed up for days doing nothing but writing. "He wouldn't go to bed, maybe, two days and a night. Maybe longer. . . . I'd go to bed and go to sleep, and he'd just keep typing."[38]

There is no doubt that Robert was driven. Being back in school seemed only to further fuel his desire to get professionally published. Robert discussed books and writing with Lindsey and expressed his desire to be published in the pulp magazines. Lindsey recalled Robert telling him that he just needed one breakthrough to get started in the industry. "That was the hardest part, to get started."[39] So Robert kept working into the small hours of the night, hammering away on his typewriter. Later that fall, his efforts finally produced success.

During this period from the early to mid-1920s, Robert continued to hone his poetry writing skills and he produced quite a number of poems. It was also during this time that Tevis Clyde Smith introduced Robert to the British World War I poets.[40] Both were duly impressed by some of these poems and in their correspondence discussed these poets' merits and influences upon their own works. In these early years, a large portion of Robert's poetry maintained the rhymes and rhythms of the classic Romantic and Victorian poets. Although Robert did not particularly

care for free verse poetry, he shared with Clyde in their ongoing correspondence several free verse poems he had written.

Probably because of his mother's passion for poetry and her practice
of reciting poems to him throughout his formative years, Robert grew to
be a true poet at heart. He would eventually write over seven hundred
poems, though only a few dozen were published in his lifetime. Poetry
served Robert well. He had a natural ability to make his prose sound poetic, with his distinct cadence and word choices. As the years passed and
he continued to write both prose and poetry, his poeticism was keenly
enhanced and gave his prose a signature style like no other writer's.

CHAPTER SIX

Pulp Fictioneer

I must confess that the main motive for establishing Weird Tales
was to give the writer free rein to express his innermost feelings in
a manner befitting great literature. I feel Lovecraft, Howard and
Smith came close to reaching that eminence.

JACOB CLARK HENNEBERGER, LETTER TO JOEL FRIEMAN,
OCTOBER 20, 1968

Weird Tales, the pulp magazine from the early 1920s read avidly by the young Robert E. Howard, called itself "The Unique Magazine" and was the brainchild of Jacob Clark Henneberger, a fan of Edgar Allan Poe and strange tales. An English professor named Captain Stevens had helped sow a passion in Henneberger for Poe's works. In a letter, Henneberger recalled his experience studying under Captain Stevens: "As a lad of 16 I attended a military academy in Virginia. The English department was headed by one Capt. Stevens, a hunchback who was a rather chauvinistic chap in that he favored Southern writers." Henneberger continued: "One entire semester was devoted to Poe! You can imagine how immersed I became in him."[1] Apparently, Captain Stevens's students were also offered classes on "Rossetti, Dowson, Swinburne, Ambrose Bierce, Hart Crane, Baudelaire and many others who were influenced by Poe."[2] Reading these authors inspired Henneberger enough to make him want to be a writer.

Later Henneberger earned $5 per column for articles on the events at the college he attended in Lancaster, Pennsylvania. Soon after, while living with his brother, Henneberger worked briefly for a newspaper in Portland, Oregon, writing a sports column. By 1919, he had "landed a job in Indianapolis with a weekly newspaper owned by the perennial candidate for President on the prohibition ticket." It was at this job that Henneberger met "a map and atlas publisher who employed college students to sell their products during the summer months."[3] Through this contact, Henneberger established the Rural Publishing Corporation in Chicago. He pitched to various financial creditors the idea of a national magazine aimed at college undergraduates called *The Collegiate World*. "This magazine attracted many embryonic writers, but few advertizers [*sic*] with the result that a sizable debt [was] incurred."[4] The magazine lasted until 1923 and racked up a debt of $30,000. By focusing on collegiate athletics, it would temporarily garner most of its attention from the student body of each school it featured in the magazine. This, of course, limited its monthly readership. In the end, *The Collegiate World* was a failure. Though Henneberger did not realize it at the time, this failure set him on a course that eventually led him to create several successful magazines.

With creditors pressing him to make good on his debts, Henneberger scrambled to figure out how he might salvage *The Collegiate World*. While pondering different ideas from his creditors, the headmaster of a "self-help college located just south of Chicago" visited Henneberger in his Chicago office to submit an article about his school.[5] This headmaster told Henneberger that he liked the magazine and especially enjoyed the magazine's college humor section. Shortly thereafter, Henneberger pitched to his creditors the idea of changing the name of *The Collegiate World* to *College Humor* and focusing the magazine's content solely on humor. "Despite the objections of two backers who used several pages in the magazine to advertise summer work for students, the printer and [Henneberger] won out and within a few weeks the new publication was on the press."[6] The first printing of fifty thousand copies sold so well— at the handsome price of 50 cents each—that an additional fifteen thousand copies were printed. *College Humor* was a smashing success and sold out every month for an entire year. This new magazine platform was such a successful cash cow that Henneberger began another magazine, *Detective Tales*, and hired Edwin Baird, a writer and a crime and mystery aficionado, to edit it. Besides *Detective Tales*, Henneberger also created *Weird Tales* to publish strange stories from popular authors who had told Henneberger that they wished a market for such stories existed.

> I had talked with such nationally known writers as Hamlin Garland, Emerson Hough, Ben Hecht and other writers then residing in Chi-

cago. I discovered that all of them expressed a desire to submit for publication a story of the unconventional type but hesitated to do so for fear of rejection. Pressed for details, they acknowledged that such a delving into the realms of fantasy, the bizarre, and the outre could possibly be frowned upon by publishers of the conventional.[7]

At the time, no other magazine offered its writers or readers a fictional diet solely of unconventional ("weird") fantasy and horror fiction. Frank Munsey's magazines *Argosy*, the *All-Story*, and the *Cavalier* offered some science fiction (or weird) stories, but these kinds of stories were not the sole focus of his magazines. By focusing exclusively on fantasy, weird, and startling horror fiction, *Weird Tales* set a precedent that the publishing industry frowned upon and preemptively considered doomed to failure. Since Henneberger already employed Edwin Baird as the editor for *Detective Tales*, it made financial sense to also make Baird the editor for *Weird Tales*. This was not necessarily the best option for Baird or for *Weird Tales*, however, since Baird was not a weird or horror fiction fan. In fact, he considered supernatural fiction, at best, subpar.[8] It is possible that Baird protested the new assignment, feeling that his attention was being divided between *Detective Tales*, which he enjoyed, and *Weird Tales*, which he did not. In any event, Henneberger hired Farnsworth Wright, a music critic for syndicated newspapers, and the author Otis Adelbert Kline to assist Baird with editing.[9]

In March 1923, the first issue of *Weird Tales* hit newsstands across the country. The cover price was high for a new pulp fiction magazine at 25 cents. The first issue had twenty-four stories and featured one serial work by Otis Adelbert Kline. Serials would be a trend for *Weird Tales* from its first issue in 1923 until 1940.[10] With no interior artwork, the first issue of *Weird Tales* had a rather bland look. This would change in subsequent issues, however, and eventually the magazine's artists would become nearly as popular as its writers.

With Baird's attention divided and his despondency about being responsible for *Weird Tales* continuing, trouble ensued. In the beginning, *Detective Tales* "was undistinguished and had a rocky start, almost folding after its fourth issue."[11] Several factors were responsible for the lackluster start, the most important being that *Detective Tales* published only local Chicago writers. Moreover, when he first floated the idea for *Weird Tales*, Henneberger may have thought that he had received assurances from several well-established writers—Garland, Hough, and Hecht—

that they would submit unconventional fiction to *Weird Tales*. However, these authors never appeared in the magazine.[12] And even though Henneberger loved weird fiction and horror stories, it has been suggested that he "founded *Weird Tales* not out of some altruistic goal of fostering artistic weird literature but largely in order to make money by featuring big-name writers."[13] This may have been at least partially true if Henneberger actually did attempt to recruit well-established writers in an effort to keep *Weird Tales* financially stable. But his passion for horror and weird fiction was such that the prospect of providing readers with a venue for that kind of story was probably his primary reason for starting *Weird Tales*. Of course, not getting the support he had hoped for from Chicago writers could have been a setback for the magazine.[14] And even though *College Humor* was quite successful, it was not making enough money to cover his mounting debts for both *Detective Tales* and *Weird Tales*. With creditors nipping at his heels, Henneberger had an important decision to make.

Throughout these serious financial setbacks with *Detective Tales* and *Weird Tales*, Henneberger maintained his belief in the idea of a magazine focused solely on unconventional fantasy and horror. After serious consideration, Henneberger risked everything and sold *College Humor* and *Detective Tales* to J. M. Lansinger, his partner at Rural Publishing Corporation. He then used the money to pay off his debt and chose *Weird Tales* as his mainstay publication. Since Lansinger, as a condition of the sale, had kept Edwin Baird as the editor for *Detective Tales*, Henneberger either needed a new editor for *Weird Tales* or needed to create a new magazine.

Prior to the sale of *College Humor* and *Detective Tales*, Henneberger had encountered H. P. Lovecraft's work in the amateur magazine *Home Brew* and thoroughly enjoyed his stories. In the first few months after *Weird Tales* had begun publication, Lovecraft submitted five stories simultaneously.[15] Edwin Baird did not care too much for Lovecraft's work and had made certain demands upon his stories.[16] Henneberger, however, had made sure that everything Lovecraft submitted got published.[17]

Of the five stories Lovecraft submitted, *Weird Tales* published "Dagon" first, in its October 1923 issue, and the other stories followed in subsequent issues. Henneberger, perhaps uncertain about the future of *Weird Tales* and impressed with Lovecraft and his stories, offered Lovecraft the position of editor for a potential new high-grade magazine. In a letter of March 18–19, 1924, to his aunt, Lillian D. Clark, Lovecraft explained:

But it is from Henneberger that the startling thing came—the thing
which has aroused vast excitement in this placid and newly-founded
house-hold. This honest but uncouth worthy writes that he is making
a radical change in WEIRD TALES, and that he has in mind a brand
new magazine to cover the field of Poe–Machen shudders. This magazine, he says, will be "right in my line," and he wants to know if I would
consider moving to Chicago to edit it![18]

Lovecraft gave the idea considerable thought, but he eventually turned
down the offer, for various personal reasons. This new magazine idea
never came to fruition, and Henneberger continued with *Weird Tales*,
hiring staff member Farnsworth Wright to be its new editor. This single decision by Lovecraft may have saved *Weird Tales*. It certainly pushed
the magazine forward. With Wright in place as editor, Henneberger
hired William Sprenger, a savvy businessman, to oversee the magazine's
finances. Although Sprenger had no real interest in unconventional fiction, over the long run he was a relatively good fit for *Weird Tales*. Henneberger then established Popular Fiction Publishing, Inc., and handed the
reins of the magazine over to Wright. Some of the stories Wright published during his career with *Weird Tales* were rubbish, but others were
quite good.

Despite the sale of *College Humor* and *Detective Tales* to pay off a large
debt, *Weird Tales* temporarily remained on financially shaky ground in
1924. In hopes of limiting certain costs, the magazine published a single
issue dated May/June/July 1924. This was followed by a three-month hiatus from August to October to regroup and raise more funding. Considering the circumstances, *Weird Tales* should have folded during this
period, but it managed to survive. The staff at the magazine understood
the uniqueness of their publication. Wright himself once declared: "That
there is a real field for such a magazine as *Weird Tales* is evident from the
letters that continue to pour in asking that the magazine return to the
news stands."[19]

With committed support from its readers, *Weird Tales* moved forward, and a new issue edited by Wright hit newsstands in November
1924. The initial goal of seeking only "big-name" or well-established
writers changed with Wright. "This magazine will print the finest weird
fiction that it can get, regardless of whether the authors are known or
unknown." Moreover, Wright told his readers, they were the reason the
magazine existed. "This is your magazine, and anything you have to say,
either in praise or in blame, will be listened to with eager attention."[20]

Broadening the scope of story submissions and catering to the tastes of the magazine's readers were wise moves on Wright's part. These changes also issued an open invitation to the likes of Robert E. Howard. His writing had reached a level by 1924 that might gain the notice of the new staff at *Weird Tales*. He just needed direction and a clever angle.

Robert first discovered *Weird Tales* in 1923, and he probably subscribed to the magazine eventually, if for no other reason than to avoid missing an issue at the newsstands. His submission of "Spear and Fang," as we examine in this chapter, seems to indicate, owing to the dates of submission and early responses to editorial comments on certain issues, that he was a subscriber. If he did subscribe to *Weird Tales*, it is not known whether he had the magazine mailed to his boardinghouse in Brownwood or whether it was sent to his house in Cross Plains and then delivered or mailed by a parent or friend to Brownwood. Robert probably received the December 1924 issue of *Weird Tales* in early November. As with most other magazine subscriptions, *Weird Tales* subscribers received their issues a month or so in advance.[21] Robert had submitted two stories to *Weird Tales* in 1923, but both were rejected by Edwin Baird (see chapter 5). During Farnsworth Wright's editorial tenure, however, the fall of 1924 would be a turning point for Robert, or so it seemed.

From its inception, *Weird Tales* included an editorial and a readers' section called "The Eyrie" where readers could voice their opinions about each issue's contents. Making his debut with the November 1924 issue of *Weird Tales*, Wright used "The Eyrie" in this issue and the next one for an editorial about the magazine's history, its upcoming stories, and the importance of its readers, while also essentially providing an open invitation to new writers to submit stories. In the December 1924 issue, Wright declared:

> We get plenty of manuscripts dealing with fights between dinosaurs and pterodactyls on the one hand and cavemen on the other, but we send them all back because these creatures had disappeared from the earth before the first great anthropoid apes rose to the stature of manhood, according to the records of the rocks as read by the geologists. But Neandertalers [*sic*] and Cro-Magnons existed side by side, and waged relentless and savage warfare against each other.[22]

In this editorial, Wright essentially revealed to the readers and writers the idea for a story that *Weird Tales* had an interest in publishing. A recent article indicates that Robert probably read the editorial and wrote

"Spear and Fang" as a response to Wright's suggestion. For decades it has been assumed that Robert's submission of "Spear and Fang" to *Weird Tales* was no different from how he submitted all his previous stories. As it turns out, this is likely not the case. In the opinion of Howard scholar Patrice Louinet, "'Spear and Fang' is certainly not one of Howard's best tales."[23] But the context of Wright's editorial clarifies why *Weird Tales* would have agreed to publish what would have otherwise been considered just another average story destined, most likely, for the "reject" pile.

If Robert needed any more incentive to sit down and write the tale, the continuation of Wright's editorial would have provided it:

> Our learned friends among the anthropologists tell us that the legend of ogres dates from cavemen tribes. The Neandertalers [*sic*] were so terrible and primitive and brutish, they tell us, that the Cro-Magnon cavemen never interbred with them, but killed them without mercy. And when a Cro-Magnon child strayed alone from its cave, and a cannibalistic Neandertaler stalked it, that was the end of the child; but the memory of those brutish and half-human people remains in our legends of ogres; for the Cro-Magnons were not exterminated by the nomadic tribes that afterwards entered Europe and peopled it, but intermarried with them, and retained some of their legends.[24]

Wright goes on to declare:

> How would you like a tale of the warfare between a Cro-Magnon (say one of the artists who painted the pictures of reindeer and mammoths which still amaze the tourist) and one of those brutish ogres, perhaps over a girl who has taken the fancy of the Neandertaler; and the Cro-Magnon artist follows the Neandertal man to his den, and. . . . But we have no room to tell the story in "The Eyrie." We wish one of our author friends would write it for us.[25]

It is most reasonable to think that Robert read Wright's editorial and, excited by the story possibilities, almost immediately sat down at his typewriter to write "Spear and Fang." In fact, a simple cursory reading of "Spear and Fang" reveals a striking and uncanny similarity between Wright's suggested story line and Robert's story. The similarities between the ideas in Wright's editorial and "Spear and Fang" could hardly be merely coincidental. And of course, "Wright accepted the tale because he had, in a way, specifically requested it."[26]

Even though Robert was in the middle of his winter term, he ignored his schoolwork and worked instead on "Spear and Fang," keeping everything in mind that Wright mentioned in his editorial. Once he finished, he mailed the story—probably by early November—and waited. A few weeks later, shortly before Thanksgiving, Robert received a letter from *Weird Tales* accepting his story for publication.

It is important to note that unlike better-established pulp magazines and the slicks, *Weird Tales* paid on publication, not on acceptance.[27] So acceptance of "Spear and Fang" was merely a promise to publish it, and Robert would have to wait to see the financial fruits of his labor. Robert's roommate Lindsey Tyson, who was with Robert when he opened the letter from *Weird Tales*, recalled that Robert was so happy that he told Tyson he was going to thank God, then knelt by his bed and said a silent prayer.[28] Robert's happiness was certainly warranted, especially considering the extensive time and effort he had put into writing and submitting stories. Even so, his actions following the news from *Weird Tales* were a bit premature. Under the assumption that this was the break he had so diligently been working toward, Robert "dropped out of the commercial school, apparently in the middle of the winter term, and returned to Cross Plains shortly thereafter."[29]

His behavior was imprudent, to say the least, and his parents were probably stunned at the sudden decision. In an effort to convince them that he made the right decision, Robert may have shown them the letter from *Weird Tales*. Regardless of their possible insistence that he remain in school, he stayed back at home and "began to write in earnest."[30] By December 1924, he had submitted two more stories to *Weird Tales*: "The Lost Race" and "The Hyena." On January 7, 1925, Robert received another acceptance letter from *Weird Tales* for both stories, once again promising payment upon publication. Reeling from excitement, he probably showed his parents this new acceptance letter to reinforce his argument that he need not return to the commercial department at the Academy.

Robert's timing with *Weird Tales* was impeccable. The magazine was looking for new writers, and he had stories to submit. Shortly after he received the second acceptance letter, Robert submitted "In the Forest of Villefère," which *Weird Tales* eventually accepted, once again with the promise of payment upon publication. By now, however, with merely the promise of payments from *Weird Tales*, Robert was once again forced to find a job.

In March 1925, Cross Plains was in the middle of an oil boom that provided multiple avenues of employment. Robert took advantage of these opportunities and returned to grinding out oil reports. He wrote to Clyde Smith: "I'm writing oil news for a bunch of papers now, *Record, News* and so on. Five bucks per column."[31] He also wrote oil reports for his local newspaper, the *Cross Plains Review*. Soon he was so busy writing these reports that he had little time to do anything else, not even travel. He lamented to his friends in Brownwood: "I've tried for weeks to come over there, but you have no idea the amount of work there is. Lots of times I've worked until nine o'clock at night, principally on oil reports, and am a way behind on them now."[32] To his frustration, these reports plundered most of his creative writing time as well.

By June and July 1925, the oil boom in Cross Plains was at its apex. A wide assortment of sordid types had moved into town, some seeking legitimate employment opportunities, others having been sent by large corporations to nab a share of the wealth. A large oil well inside the town limits produced four hundred barrels, and every "big company in Texas has men in town and leases are changing hands so fast it makes you dizzy," Robert reported. The oil boom kept him so busy, he told Smith, that "these guys don't wait to hire me, they fight over the typewriter, figuratively speaking."[33]

Robert made good money on his oil reports, but driven to make more money still until his checks arrived from *Weird Tales*, he also began working as a public stenographer. Six months after "Spear and Fang" had been accepted by *Weird Tales*, and with summer approaching, the promise of publication had not come to fruition. Robert must have been feeling a certain amount of frustration and impatience, partly over how much time he was sacrificing working menial jobs he cared nothing about, and partly because of how long it was taking to see his stories in print. He may have started to question *Weird Tales'* intentions, and therefore his own success. To escape work and the stress of not hearing from *Weird Tales*, Robert planned a brief trip to Brownwood in early July of 1925 to see his friends Vinson and Smith. Prior to his arrival, and as an act of reprisal for a prank Robert had played on Smith a few weeks earlier, a scheme was concocted to trap Robert in an awkward situation with Smith's girlfriend, Echla Laxson, who was in on the prank. The prank would backfire on Smith, however, and a grisly truth about Robert would surface.

There are two primary sources for the 1925 Brownwood prank: Robert's semiautobiographical novella *Post Oaks and Sand Roughs*, written in 1928,[34] and several letters written by Robert to Clyde Smith afterward to clean up the mess, so to speak.[35] The cause of the prank on Robert was Robert himself. Close to a month prior to the Brownwood trip, Robert jokingly created a "legal letter" on stationery letterhead from Paul V. Harrell's legal offices, where he worked as a public stenographer. The letter was a fake summons for Clyde Smith to appear in court for allegedly raping a sixteen-year-old girl.[36] This was a stout joke, to say the least. "It is not known how his friend responded to [Robert's] joke, but Clyde decided to pull a joke of his own a month later."[37]

Robert traveled to Brownwood on Friday, July 10, 1925, and stayed with Smith that evening. The next morning Smith and Robert went to pick up Echla Laxson on the pretense that Laxson had thoroughly enjoyed Robert's work in *The Tattler* and wanted to meet him.[38] When they arrived at her house, she was waiting for them on the curb, "a slim passionate brunette, seventeen, with much more first hand knowledge of the world than was good for her."[39] It was at this point that Smith and Laxson activated their prank. "Smith had previously arranged for Laxson to flirt with his girl-shy friend, hoping, no doubt, to watch him squirm at the attention."[40] If the details from *Post Oaks and Sand Roughs* are accurate, Robert "knew instinctively that he was going to be subjected to some ordeal or humiliation" for the earlier "summons" prank.[41]

Anticipating retaliation, Robert intended to turn the tables on Smith and Laxson. Soon after Laxson and Robert were introduced to one another, Robert began flirting with her. Laxson sat between Smith and Robert in the car, and a few minutes after they drove away from the curb, she turned to Robert and asked, "Why are you afraid of women?" Not missing a beat, Robert laughed and then leaned in and kissed her. "The kiss took him [Robert] by surprise. He had not intended to bring matters to a point so quickly. But her eyes were close to his, her lips were lifted as she spoke, and he acted instinctively."[42] Apparently, even though Laxson was caught off guard, she accepted the kiss, perhaps in an attempt to maintain her composure and continue with the prank. But Robert did not stop with a single kiss: he continued to flirt, she played along, and "they then proceeded to make out for the duration of the ride."[43] Smith initially laughed at the whole situation, but after returning home, Robert received a letter from Truett Vinson indicating that Smith was quite upset.

The fallout from the attempted prank was short-lived but very melodramatic. Letters of apology were exchanged, explanations were made, and an aspect of Robert's personality surfaced that at the time ought to have been taken more seriously. In Robert's last letter regarding the prank, he confessed to Smith: "I see, have already seen, your point of view and I want to tell you that I acted damn cheap." As he continued the letter, Robert's words and the emotions he expressed became increasingly sensational. "Truett said my letter was like the product of a soul close to the bottom of its rope. How close, and in what manner, neither of you dream."[44]

Given the fact that Robert had been doing drudge work for almost seven months and had yet to see any of his stories appear in *Weird Tales*, he probably felt stressed and disheartened. How much stress he felt is anyone's guess, but his letter to Smith was more than a mere apology. It was also a cry for help. It is difficult to determine how much of the letter is Robert blowing the entire situation out of proportion, possibly to elicit sympathy, and to what degree he was serious, at least at the time, about taking his own life. Robert was known to exaggerate not only his emotions but certain facts of the circumstances when the opportunity arose. And he may have done just that in this case. In Rusty Burke's opinion, "While it's possible [Robert] was feeling some stress over the failure of his writing career to take off like he'd thought it was going to, getting acceptances but then no publication, I don't think it contributed any more to his response to Clyde & Truett's little joke than his normal thin-skinned nature did."[45]

Burke may be right. Nevertheless, the letter reveals Robert's personality in ways that ought to be considered. He explains his circumstances, expresses his disdain for the drudgery of his jobs, and says that he thinks he is a failure. This is probably a reference to the delay at *Weird Tales* in publishing his stories and his possible doubts about their intentions. In the middle of this lament to Smith, Robert confesses:

> I sat [in the law office where he worked] and my life passed before me in a long chain. The whisky had cleared from my head and I was perfectly clear-minded. Really, I had not taken a drink that day. I saw myself as I had always been, a failure. Battering against a high steel wall and only pulping my hands; clambering nearly to the top of accomplishment, until the rungs of desire gave way beneath my clutching fingers and hurtling me down again.

Even if Robert was looking for sympathy, he was also certainly demoralized to a certain extent; every minute siphoned off his day by those menial jobs took him away from what he desired most. The success and freedom he so desperately wanted was just beyond his grasp, and he thought that not attaining it was a serious failure. "I sat and thought. My thoughts ran, shall I live and continue to be a failure, to grind my life out and at last pass on, a failure, among failures *or*?" Robert never answered the "or" question, but his next comment confirms the implication: "I really never expected to leave that office when I entered it, alive."[46]

The letter then takes an abrupt turn in mood and tone. Robert admits that he could not end his own life because of a "vicious stubbornness that won't let [him] admit defeat."[47] Then the letter ends with "a segue to how hard he's been working and how little he's been eating (as if Clyde needed *more* reasons to feel sorry for him), and then a kind of casual, 'Here's what I tried to do about that letter to Echla, but oh well' ending."[48] Here we see, in a single letter, the intensity of Robert's emotions and the swiftness of his mood swings. Although he may have been grandstanding, as his friends admitted he was prone to do, this letter indicates that he was certainly suffering from stress and perhaps some kind of depression.

Aside from the hyperbole and melodrama in Robert's letter, the underlying issue is his suicidal feelings. Confessing a desire to kill oneself is a serious matter. If anything, this portion of his letter indicates that Robert had no qualms about taking his own life, or at least about admitting that he would do so under certain circumstances. It is easy to imagine that had he failed as a writer and been forced to continue doing menial work to survive, the utter loss of the freedom he desired could have driven him to an early self-inflicted death. This seems to be the confession between the lines of his letter to Smith, even if on the surface he seemed only to be looking for sympathy. But of course, for the time being, he did not follow through.

Soon after the Brownwood debacle, "Spear and Fang" finally appeared in the July issue of *Weird Tales*, and by August everything was back to normal, almost as if nothing had happened. In August 1925, with "Spear and Fang" in print, Robert received his first check from *Weird Tales*, for a meager $16. That same month *Weird Tales* published "In the Forest of Villefère," and soon afterward he received a second check, for $8. In two months, Robert made $24 as a writer. This was hardly a living salary. But even though he was forced to continue in his menial jobs, Robert felt that he was on the verge of being a paid writer. *Weird Tales* had also not yet published "The Lost Race" and "The Hyena," so more checks were sure to come.

According to *Post Oaks and Sand Roughs*, Farnsworth Wright returned "The Lost Race" to Robert, requesting changes. Wright told Robert that the story "left too much to the imagination and left some important facts unexplained." But Wright "professed himself ready to take the story if the changes and additions which he suggested were made."[49] It is not known how long it took Robert to make the changes, but the interruption did delay the story's publication.[50]

By now, Robert had become acutely aware that he needed to write more stories. In the summer of 1925, he was working on "Wolfshead," the story that would eventually give him the real publishing break he had worked so hard to achieve.

CHAPTER SEVEN

The Other Side of the Counter

*Clerking in a store is about the worst job you can have. So I
decided the only way I could get out of working for a living was to
start writing.*

ROBERT E. HOWARD TO NOVALYNE PRICE ELLIS, IN ELLIS,
ONE WHO WALKED ALONE (1986)

R obert E. Howard finished writing "Wolfshead" sometime in
early September 1925 and submitted the story to *Weird Tales*
that same month. It was the last story he submitted that year.
The following month *Weird Tales* accepted the story with the standard
terms: payment upon publication.

Up to that point, "Wolfshead" was the longest story Robert had submitted for publication. More than most of his previous stories, "Wolfshead" demonstrated his potential prowess as a writer. The language of
the story also contained less of what has been called Robert's "archaic
tang."[1] Words such as "quoth," "nay," "aye," "mayhap," and "ye" were less
pervasive in "Wolfshead." Robert had odd feelings about the story and
told Clyde Smith, "I'm not altogether sure I wasn't off my noodle when I
wrote it. I sure mixed slavers, duelists, harlots, drunkards, maniacs and
cannibals reckless."[2] Regardless of his feelings about the story, *Weird
Tales* liked it.

In August 1925, after several summer courses, Clyde Smith graduated from Brownwood High School. After a brief rest, he started classes
at Daniel Baker College in Brownwood. Within a few weeks of the fall
semester, Smith was "elected to the editor position of Daniel Baker College's student paper, *The Collegian*."[3] And in short order he solicited sub-

missions from Robert, as he had done when he edited *The Tattler*. In the early fall of 1925, Robert visited Brownwood. According to Smith, they spent time at the Carnegie public library, where Robert roamed the shelves, selecting books. Since books were scarce in rural Texas, trips to the public library were paramount for Robert, especially when he needed to consult sources he did not have in his own personal library. Reminiscing about this trip to the library, Smith had this to say about Robert's reading and research habits:

> He scanned through some of them, and read others more thoroughly, eager to get their contents, keeping up with, at the same time, trends in the pulp fiction field, as well as reading everything connected with boxing, from *The Police Gazette* to *The Ring*, for he was well balanced in his interests, and enjoyed some sports as much as literature.[4]

Robert's former roommate Lindsey Tyson also confirmed that Robert "was the fastest reader you ever saw. He'd read a book just as fast as he could turn the pages . . . [and] tell you everything that was in it." Tyson noted that "they didn't teach speed reading then, but he was the champion. He was the best."[5] By all accounts, Robert also had a near-eidetic memory. He could read a passage from a book once and recite it almost verbatim, even years later. This ability was instrumental when he was researching sources for his stories and was especially useful one time when he had to rewrite an entire story ("Wolfshead") from memory. Robert did not brag about his ability to speed-read and retain large portions of what he read, but his friends were duly impressed and bragged on his behalf.

Robert returned home from Brownwood to a letter from Farnsworth Wright, who informed him that Clyde Smith had written to *Weird Tales* about one of Robert's recent stories. Robert immediately sat down and wrote Smith, on October 9, 1925. He told his friend about the letter from Wright, who had quoted Smith as saying that Robert's story "In the Forest of Villefère"—which was Robert's first published, genuinely weird story—"went good with the readers" and who had added, "Personally I think it was a gem."[6] Any other compliments Wright received about the story never made their way to "The Eyrie," however, because all the praise lauded on Murray Leinster's story "The Oldest Story in the World," which appeared in the same issue, overshadowed any compliments for "In the Forest of Villefère."

Tucked away in the August 1925 issue of *Weird Tales*, "In the Forest of Villefère" is brief (just over 1,350 words) and features a werewolf. Taking a theme from the story, *Weird Tales* had added the subtitle: "If the Werewolf is Slain as a Man, His Ghost Haunts the Slayer."[7] This idea reappeared in "Wolfshead." In fact, "In the Forest of Villefère" is a precursor for "Wolfshead." Both stories feature the character De Montour of Normandy, and both involve a werewolf. Moreover, each story contains newly created elements of werewolf lore that had not been used in this kind of literature prior to these stories: "If a werewolf is slain in the half-form of a man, its ghost will haunt its slayer through eternity. But if it's slain as a wolf, hell gapes to receive it. The true werewolf is not (as many think) a man who may take the form of a wolf, *but a wolf who takes the form of a man!*"[8] Interestingly, both these stories were published prior to the first major werewolf novel, Guy Endore's *Werewolf of Paris*; published in 1933, this book has been the cornerstone of the legendry and lore of werewolves, from its initial publication to the present day.

Only a few werewolf stories had been published in *Weird Tales* prior to Robert's. The most notable, "The Werewolf of Ponkert" by H. Warner Munn, was the cover story of the same issue in which "Spear and Fang" appeared. Munn's story was inspired by a letter that H. P. Lovecraft wrote to "The Eyrie" in the March 1924 issue in which he had suggested a story written from "the point of view of the wolf and sympathizing strongly with the devil to whom he has sold himself."[9] One reader, James March Jr. of Sellyville, Indiana, wrote to *Weird Tales* about Munn's story, which appeared in "The Eyrie" of the September 1925 issue. Explaining why "The Werewolf of Ponkert" was his favorite story in the July issue, March explained that it "is something different. Up to this time we have had hints, shadows and glimpses of werewolves. In this story, we see them from a direct angle. In other words, we almost live with the 'hated things' as we read, which makes this story all the more realistic."[10]

It is possible that Robert read this comment in "The Eyrie," but it is *impossible* that it was the catalyst for his two stories, since "In the Forest of Villefère" was published one month prior to the September 1925 issue of *Weird Tales* and written earlier that year. By then, Robert had already written and submitted "Wolfshead" to *Weird Tales*. March's letter does, however, indicate that readers were craving such stories. Robert fed their cravings as one of the few early writers in *Weird Tales* to provide werewolf stories.

By casting "Wolfshead" as a first-person narrative, Robert wrote that story in a very different vein. The story is set in a Portuguese colonial castle on the west coast of Africa. The protagonist, who witnesses the events as they unfold, feels sympathy for and provides aid to the were-wolf in "Wolfshead"—who is De Montour, the protagonist from "In the Forest of Villefère." Incorporating the same idea from "In the Forest of Villefère" that, if a werewolf is slain in the half-form of a man, its ghost will haunt its slayer through eternity, Robert unwraps this idea further in "Wolfshead." These two stories raise the question: with these stories, did Robert create a new element of werewolf lore?

Historically, it seems that this is the case, which speaks volumes about Robert's ingenuity within the weird and horror genres. Creating unconventional stories and subverting genres (by, for example, mix-ing genres, tropes, and other literary elements in a single story) would be staple features of Robert's work.[11] Eventually he would use elements of previous fantasy and realist fiction to construct a new species of fan-tasy; Robert would clearly put his own stamp on this new form of fan-tasy fiction.

In December 1925, *Weird Tales* informed Robert that "Wolfshead" was slated to be the cover story for an upcoming issue. During its prep-aration, on January 20, 1926, Robert received a letter from Farnsworth Wright declaring, "I hope you have a carbon copy of WOLFSHEAD. If so, will you please forward it to me at once by special delivery."[12] This re-quest put Robert into a panic since, at the time, he had not used carbons when he wrote his short stories. According to Wright's letter, the artist (E. M. Stevenson) had yet to send the manuscript back to Wright, and *Weird Tales* was desperately trying to keep its print schedule from fall-ing behind. In a frantic reply to Wright's letter, Robert confessed, "I have no carbon copy of 'Wolfshead.'" "I certainly hope the mss. is not lost, but am today beginning to re-write it from memory. Kindly let me know whether the story is lost immediately upon receiving this letter. If nec-essary, I can mail you the re-written ms. within twelve hours from the time I hear from you."[13] Robert then scrambled to do just that: rewrite the manuscript from memory. The original manuscript that Wright was waiting for from Stevenson did eventually make its way back to the *Weird Tales* offices. Wright paid Robert an extra $10 for his trouble in re-writing the story.[14]

"Wolfshead" was the cover story for the April 1926 issue of *Weird Tales*. The readers enjoyed the story, and it received a strong number of votes as one of the better stories for that issue, as confirmed in the June 1926 issue: "Again it is the weirdest story in the issue that wins your votes for first place: *The Outsider* by H. P. Lovecraft; but this is closely pressed by *Wolfshead*, Robert E. Howard's medieval adventure story."[15] An ardent fan of Lovecraft's work, Robert probably did not mind "Wolfshead" coming in a close second to Lovecraft's "The Outsider." Lovecraft admitted years later that "Wolfshead" caused him to take serious note of Robert as a new up-and-coming writer for *Weird Tales*:

> I first became conscious of him [Robert E. Howard] as a coming leader just a decade ago—when (on a bench in Prospect Park, Brooklyn) I read *Wolfshead*. I had read his two previous short tales with pleasure, but without especially noting the author. Now—in '26—I saw that *W.T.* had landed a new big-timer of the CAS [Clark Ashton Smith] and EHP [E. Hoffmann Price] calibre. Nor was I ever disappointed in the zestful and vigorous newcomer. He made good—and how![16]

Shortly before the publication of "Wolfshead" as the cover story in the April issue, *Weird Tales* sent Robert the "advance sheets" for the story. According to *Post Oaks and Sand Roughs*, Robert read them and became so despondent that he went out and got a job as a drugstore soda jerk.[17] Although his emotions may have been exaggerated for fictional effect in this account, Robert did, in fact, get a job as a soda jerk at a Cross Plains drugstore.

Given Robert's presentation of events in *Post Oaks and Sand Roughs* and the names given the characters in the story, the Cross Plains Drugstore is most likely the drugstore where he worked. It was owned and operated by a Dr. Robertson, a retired physician. In fact, in a small ad placed in the *Cross Plains Review* on January 1, 1926, Robert's father, Dr. Howard, and his colleague Dr. Young announced that they had moved their offices into Dr. Robertson's Drugstore (the Cross Plains Drugstore). Although in *Post Oaks and Sand Roughs* Robert explains that "Gus Robinson [Dr. Robertson], manager of a local drugstore, approached Steve [Robert E. Howard] with a proposition for working behind the soda fountain," it may have been that Dr. Howard, now working out of the drugstore, told his son about the available soda jerk position.[18] However Robert discovered the job, and to his eventual regret, in the early spring of 1926 he became a soda jerk.

Robert labored at the drugstore during the pinnacle of the Cross Plains oil boom. According to *Post Oaks and Sand Roughs*, he "worked seven days out of the week, from ten in the morning to closing time, which was anytime between ten at night and two in the morning."[19] While these hours may be slightly exaggerated—again, for fictional effect—there is some evidence that his hours were long enough to keep him from writing as much as he wanted. From early spring to at least the late summer of 1926, Robert wrote very little prose and seems to have turned his attention to poetry. Three of these poems were published by Clyde Smith in *The Daniel Baker Collegian*: "Illusion" and "Fables for Little Folks" in the March 15, 1926, issue, and "Roundelay of the Roughneck" in the April 14, 1926, issue. During this period, Robert wrote only seven letters to Smith, owing to his long work hours, but his May 7, 1926, letter contained more poems that he had managed to write when he could grab a moment. Two of those poems were published in the May 25, 1926, issue of *The Daniel Baker Collegian*, "Futility" and "Tarantella." Robert wrote dozens of other poems during this period, but none appeared in a professional publication until *Weird Tales* published "The Ride of Falume" and "The Song of the Bats" in the fall of 1926.

While Robert and his friend Clyde Smith had exchanged poems in earlier letters, for some reason Robert sent more poetry to Clyde during this time than at any other time in their entire correspondence. It was a time when his confidence in his work was weak. Clerking at the drugstore was perhaps the worst job Robert ever had, and the hard work involved and taxing hours may have brought on bouts of depression in Robert, who was severely enervated. At one point he admitted to Clyde:

> I'm a failure. Ha ha ha ha ha ha! Rich ain't it? All day I've tried to write poetry. I've worked. Hell, how I've worked. Changing, revising, aw hell! My stuff is so infernally barren, so damnably small. I read the poems of some great author and while they uplift me, they assure me of my failure. Hell, hell, hell. My soul's a flame of divine fire, a god's voice and damn me damn me damn me, I can't give it a human, worldly voice. No wonder most poets drink themselves into the gutter and out again and into the mire.[20]

His lack of confidence, however, did nothing to dampen his desire to write verse. He also had no qualms about submitting his verse to various publications. At one point he even submitted his poetry to Benjamin F. Musser, the editor of *Contemporary Verse*. In a July 1929 letter to Clyde, Robert indicated that Musser had enjoyed his poems even though he had never heard of Robert E. Howard and could not find Cross Plains on a map. Musser told Robert that his poetry was superb and offered suggestions for improvement. Although he enjoyed Robert's work, Musser indicated that his magazine had no room for additional verse. Apparently, Musser's praise did little to bolster Robert's confidence. In the same letter to Clyde, Robert called his poetry junk. Clyde and Musser disagreed. Still, Robert continued to write poetry. Over the years, he created a large collection of poetry, including sonnets and ballads. But by the early 1930s, he had made the practical and financially driven decision to turn his back on verse and put all his attention on prose.

The drugstore job was greater drudgery to Robert than writing oil reports and working as a stenographer. At least in those two jobs he was not dealing with the public. Even so, while working behind the counter serving up fountain drinks, Robert claims that he "became acquainted with, and sometimes friendly to, whores, bootleggers, gamblers, dope fiends, and yeggs, besides the general riff-raff drillers, tool dressers and roustabouts." He probably also served drinks to businessmen, salesmen, and drifters arriving in town to chase various opportunities. "A boom town drugstore is an ideal place to study humanity."[21] In fact, Robert's experience at the drugstore would serve as ground zero for many of his future characters. He admitted that his most famous character, Conan the Cimmerian, was an amalgamation of "the dominant characteristics of various prizefighters, gunmen, bootleggers, oil field bullies, and honest workmen."[22] Robert may have encountered several of these sordid characters when he worked at the drugstore.

Being heavily taxed, physically and mentally, by his job, and with *Weird Tales* delaying publication of several stories he had submitted a year or so earlier, Robert knew that something had to give. When the summer of 1926 ended, he decided to go back and finish his bookkeeping certificate. This had to be a difficult decision, especially considering his recent spate of successfully published stories. Nevertheless, Robert approached his parents with a proposed deal, which Dr. Howard later described to one of Robert's fellow pulp writers and friends, E. Hoffmann Price:

> Once, when he commenced to try and break into the [writing] game, he came to me and said, "Dad, I want to break into the writing game. Will you feed me for two years? If by then I can't make it, I will take out and go with the casing crew." I said, "Son, take 2 years, 5 years, 10 years. Be at ease, you are at home and will always be at home with your mother and dad."[23]

The accuracy of the details in Dr. Howard's letter to Price is anybody's guess. Robert did return to school in the fall of 1926 to finish his certificate in bookkeeping. And he did so with the idea that afterward he could continue for a period to try to make his living at writing. If he failed in the "writing game," he would then get a conventional job. Novalyne Price Ellis, Robert's girlfriend in the midthirties, remembered a similar plan of Robert's in her book *One Who Walked Alone*. "Clyde Smith told me that when Bob finished school and decided to write full-time, he asked his parents to give him a year. If at the end of that year, he had not sold anything, he would give up his dream of being a writer."[24]

Clyde Smith recalled that Robert's father was leery of his son's desire to be a writer. "This precarious living worried Dr. Howard, who suggested newspaper work, a suggestion which received a cool brushoff."[25] Lindsey Tyson remembered that Dr. Howard "didn't think that [Robert would] make it [as a writer], you know." According to him, his father "wasn't much encouragement" to Robert.[26] Despite Dr. Howard's reluctance and possible doubt that Robert could make a living as a writer, he agreed to the deal. Emotionally and physically spent, with no spare time to write, Robert eagerly quit the drugstore and went back to school in the fall of 1926.

Since Tyson was enrolled at Howard Payne for the 1926–1927 school year, Robert decided to move back in with his old roommate at 1214 Main Avenue. Back at the commercial department at the Academy, the door was once again open for him to submit stories to *The Yellow Jacket*, which was more than happy to receive his submissions. *The Yellow Jacket* published two of his stories right away, in the October 27, 1926, issue, "After the Game" and "Sleeping Beauty." Having written so much poetry while he worked at the drugstore, Robert submitted several of these poems to *Weird Tales*, which accepted two of them, "The Ride of Falume" and "The Song of the Bats."[27] Most importantly, now that he was back in school, Robert had spare time to write stories again. That fall, he began working on "The Shadow Kingdom," which featured a new character, Kull of Atlantis. This story marked a new era for Robert and a categorical shift in his writing.

When Robert returned to the commercial department at the Academy, he "needed 16 units to get his bookkeeping diploma, 10 of which he probably got credit for from his high school work (literary course). That left one unit each for the following classes: Bookkeeping, Commercial Law, Business English, Business Arithmetic, Penmanship, and Typewriting (according to the 1926–27 catalogue)."[28] That fall semester, Robert took two classes, bookkeeping and typing. Despite his resistance to authority and his disdain for the rote nature of school, Robert enjoyed J. E. Basham, the head of the business college, whom Tyson remembered as a "kindly old man."[29] Robert did well his first semester, receiving Bs in both of his classes.[30] The fall term ended in late November, on the twenty-fourth, and the winter term began five days later, on November 29. During that hiatus, Robert received notice from *Weird Tales* that "The Lost Race," which he had submitted back in December 1924, would finally be published in the January 1927 issue. There was hope on the horizon. When it did finally publish "The Lost Race," *Weird Tales* paid Robert $30.

"The Lost Race" shows Robert dipping into his knowledge of Picts and medieval Celtic folklore, mythology, and history. Some of the history and folklore for this story may have been gleaned from G. E. Scott Elliot's book *The Romance of Early British Life*. In truth, considering the time Robert spent at the Brownwood public library and in visits to several bookstores, it is more likely that he had also read other books about Picts and Celtic folklore and history. What is intriguing about "The Lost Race" is that Robert taps into a historical vein of traditional European folklore and history similar to the influences on J. R. R. Tolkien, C. S. Lewis, and G. K. Chesterton via William Morris and George MacDonald. As far as we know, however, Robert never read Morris or MacDonald, and his publications preceded those of Tolkien and Lewis. Set in Britain, the fantastical folklore of "The Lost Race" becomes evident when Robert's protagonist, Cororuc, a Briton soldier on a reconnaissance mission, is captured by "little people"; no taller than four feet, they happen to be a certain kind of Pict and are the source of Gaelic folklore. Once captured, Cororuc is taken into their timeless world, where he begins to understand their true origin:

> Little he [Cororuc] knew that he was gazing on one of the mysteries of the ages. That the tales which the ancient Gaels told of Picts, already warped, would become even more warped from age to age, to result in tales of elves, dwarfs, trolls and fairies, at first accepted and then rejected, entire, by the race of men, just as the Neandertal monsters resulted in tales of goblins and ogres.[31]

Here Robert is referring to the Picts he discovered as a boy in a New Orleans public library. But these Picts are different, as Robert's protagonist recognizes: "'I have fought Picts in Caledonia,' the Briton protested; 'they are short but massive and misshapen; not at all like you.'" The leader of these elvish or dwarf-like Picts responds, "'They are not true Picts,' . . . 'Look about you, Briton,' with the wave of an arm, 'you see the remnants of a vanishing race; a race that once ruled Britain from sea to sea.'"[32]

"The Lost Race" is a clever commingling of an adventure story in the vein of H. Rider Haggard, one of Robert's formative influences, with a different breed of Pict. Robert blended Haggard's lost world or lost persons motif with Celtic history and folklore to make an idiosyncratic adventure story. Moreover, he had begun writing "The Lost Race" while still a teenager, in 1924. It should be noted that "The Lost Race" is technically not a work of weird fiction. Even so, Robert did feature a character in the story, Berula, a chief of the Alban Picts, who is a type of shapeshifting wolf, framed in the story as a historically early kind of werewolf.

After the 1926 fall term ended, Robert remained in Brownwood for the winter term. During these months, Mrs. Howard wrote her son two letters: one on December 9 and the other on January 4. In the latter, out of concern for his well-being, she declared, "There are several cases of measles in Brownwood, and if you begin to feel bad, ache, or feverish or anything, go to Dr. Fowler, Bailey, or Snyder, or any of these men, & let them go over you to see what your trouble is."[33] Mrs. Howard's concern was warranted. The outbreak of measles worsened to an epidemic, and it soon affected the Powells, who owned the boardinghouse where Robert and Tyson lived. Here is Tyson's account of Robert's response:

> While we were there an epidemic of measles got started, the Powells we were living with had a baby girl who got the disease. The Howards heard about the epidemic and came to take Bob home as he had never had the measles. Bob said this time I dam [*sic*] sure will have this stuff, he did not want to go. He went into the bathroom that the little girl had been useing [*sic*] picked up a glass that the child had probably been useing, [*sic*] drank out of it, rubbed a towel over his face that he thought she had probably been using.[34]

According to Tyson's letter, soon after Robert drank from the glass and rubbed his face in the towel, he came down with a severe case of the measles. As for the Powells' daughter, "one Nelda June Powell, aged 16 months, [she] died on March 1, 1927."[35] There is no explanation from any source for why Robert reacted so defiantly to the epidemic. It is possible that he was merely acting out against his parents' authority (especially his father's). There had been times when they butted heads, as his friend Clyde Smith had witnessed.[36] Robert was sick for two months, lost his winter term tuition, missed his classes, and did not resume school until the spring, on March 1, 1927.

The spring term was uneventful. Robert took one class—bookkeeping—and managed to get another story, "The Reformation: A Dream," published in the April 21 issue of *The Yellow Jacket*.[37] That May, *Weird Tales* published one of Robert's poems, "The Song of the Bats," paying him $3.50. Over the years, *Weird Tales* would eventually buy and publish more than thirty of his poems. By the early summer of 1927, Robert had finished writing "The Shadow Kingdom" and set it aside to finish the last two classes he needed to get his certificate. He finally graduated from the commercial department at the Academy on August 3, 1927. With school behind him, Robert now had at least one year to prove to his parents, while they supported him, that he could earn his living as a writer. He determined to avoid taking a job as a bookkeeper. As he told his roommate Lindsey Tyson, "if anybody thought that [I] was going to tie [myself] down to any grubby job of bookkeeping etc., they were crazy."[38] With utter determination, Robert dedicated all his time and energy to writing and submitting stories.

CHAPTER EIGHT

A New Species of Fantasy Fiction

*One of the most astounding literary phenomena of this century is
Robert E. Howard (1906–1936) who, despite the disadvantage of
living his entire short life in or near the dusty little village of Cross
Plains, Texas—over a thousand miles from any of his literary
peers in the genre of fantastic fiction—nevertheless produced a
considerable body of inspiring fantasy epic prose and poetry.*

RICHARD L. TIERNEY, *TIGERS OF THE SEA* (1979), 11

The Shadow Kingdom" was a defining moment in publication
history because it helped lay the foundation for a new species
of fantasy fiction. Robert began writing the story in the fall
of 1926, periodically setting it aside to work on other pieces (mostly poetry), then revisiting it. He wrote the bulk of the story during his final semester and summer term in 1927. The timing of that story's completion
was fortuitous, since Robert was entering a period when he could focus
all his attention on writing. At this stage in his writing career, he began
to experiment with his fiction. Robert was proud of "The Shadow Kingdom," and he told Clyde Smith, "I enjoyed writing it more than any piece
of prose I ever wrote."[1]

Wanting to be certain that her son was cared for, Mrs. Howard offered some of the financial support that she and Dr. Howard had prom-
ised as part of their agreement with Robert. Being a doctor in a rather
small community of poor farmers, Dr. Howard was occasionally paid
for his services in the form of meat or produce instead of cash—and
probably more often after the Great Depression reached the area. So
Mrs. Howard bought much-needed clothes for her son, and shortly af-

ter he graduated from the commercial department, she financed his trip to San Antonio with his friend Truett Vinson.[2] While in San Antonio, Vinson sent a postcard to Harold Preece, a friend who lived in Austin. Vinson knew Preece through the Lone Scouts organization and had been corresponding with him for several years. The postcard had a color picture of the Alamo on the front and was postdated August 20, 1927. It read, "Bob and I will be in Austin Monday morning. Will call you up."[3] This was the first time Robert met Harold Preece, and the first time Vinson met him in person. Robert and Clyde Smith had only ever heard about Preece through Vinson. When the three of them met in Austin at the Stephen F. Austin hotel, a friendship developed, and from that came a relatively long period of correspondence and other meetings between Robert and Harold Preece.

When Robert arrived home from his trip, he sent "The Shadow Kingdom" to *Weird Tales* and then, without waiting for the response, began working right away on another story featuring his new character, Kull of Atlantis. The result was "The Mirrors of Tuzun Thune." While the two stories were in the same fantastical vein, their narrative pacing was substantially different. "The Shadow Kingdom" ebbs and flows with dialogue and has elements of mystery, intrigue, and action, culminating in several swashbuckling sword duels designed to put readers on the edge of their seats. "The Mirrors of Tuzun Thune" has a steady, metronomic pace. The story is more introspective and soul-searching, and Robert waxes far more religiously philosophical. The pace of the narrative matches Kull's introspection, allowing the reader to participate in his thought process. The orphaned Kull was raised as an Atlantean barbarian, but he is "a thinking man's barbarian."[4] He is prone to brooding and uses his mind as often as he uses his sword. Even so, Kull has a talent for getting himself into harrowing and almost inescapable situations. In these moments, a mighty Pict, Brule the Spear-slayer, is there to save him. Robert frequently incorporated Picts into his adventure fantasy stories, especially his Kull and Conan tales. And of course, Bran Mak Morn, the mighty and last king of a diminishing race of Picts who have already slipped deeper into barbarism, is featured in several adventure fantasy stories.

Beginning with "The Shadow Kingdom" and "The Mirrors of Tuzun Thune," Robert progressively began "rewriting history in the guise of fiction."[5] Within that scope, he eventually built different worlds: "The world of Kull, set one hundred thousand years in the past, is effectively a secondary world despite its earthly settings."[6] This development of world-building would culminate in Howard's Conan stories. Notably, unlike Solomon Kane and El Borak, whom Robert created when he was younger, Kull was created and developed almost at the same time Robert first committed the character to the page. When readers are introduced to Kull, he is the king of Valusia, not through primogeniture or any form of familial heritage, but by virtue of brute conquering strength. In these first two Kull stories, a group of serpent priests ("The Shadow Kingdom") and an individual sorcerer ("The Mirrors of Tuzun Thune") attempt to remove Kull as king of Valusia, either by death or through entrapment.

These initial Kull stories set a precedent for what was to come. Both stories are bathed with fantastical elements such as the use of magic, shape-shifting serpent people, sorcerers, ghosts, various creatures, and mystical places ("The Mirrors of Tuzun Thune"). Moreover, Robert would repeat the religious and philosophical elements of these stories in a few of his Solomon Kane and Conan the Cimmerian stories.

Weird Tales published "The Shadow Kingdom" in the August 1929 issue, and the following month it published "The Mirrors of Tuzun Thune." Readers' responses, especially to "The Shadow Kingdom," were overwhelmingly positive. The initial editorial on the piece in "The Eyrie" of the October 1929 issue declared, "It is the consensus of our readers that the August WEIRD TALES was a little bit better than any previous issue of the magazine. *The Shadow Kingdom*, by Robert E. Howard, evoked enthusiasm that in some cases bordered on delirium."[7] Both the readers and writers of the magazine wrote the editorial staff to compliment Robert:

E. Hoffmann Price, whose weird orientales have been much admired by readers of this magazine, thus comments on *The Shadow Kingdom* in a letter to the editor: "That is a story for you! Weird, fantastic, but peopled with real men who think and act as we conceive the thoughts and acts of men. And good fighting stuff. Howard very nicely refrained from slowing his combat stuff by technicalities of the sword. As it is, one gets into the spirit of the thing and supplies the cut, thrust, *parade* or *riposte* necessary to the scene: the reader can fight it out according to his own school of swordsmanship. Weird enough and then some; and savage and hairy-chested! Good character portrayal, too. None of the dummies that pirouette through some stories, using stilted, supposedly archaic language, and moving in response to the author's obvious string-pulling. All of which leads you to believe that I like it. Correct. I do. And all the rest of the issue is mighty good reading."[8]

Even Abraham Merritt, a popular writer of fantastic fiction who frequently published short stories and novellas during this period in Frank Munsey's magazines *All-Story*, *Argosy All-Story*, and *Argosy*, wrote *Weird Tales* and declared, "*The Shadow Kingdom* is told beautifully."[9] According to the votes of *Weird Tales* readers, there were no close seconds to "The Shadow Kingdom" in the August 1929 issue. Little did the readers, writers, and Robert himself know, but this story would initiate a new fantasy fiction subgenre, which Robert would develop and define through subsequent stories.

Shortly prior to publication of Robert's two Kull stories in *Weird Tales* in 1929, he began submitting stories in other magazine markets. He knew that to publish consistently at a level that would make him a comfortable living and give him the much-desired freedom he sought, he had to publish in other markets. That would require writing a variety of stories. In fact, prior to the publication of "The Shadow Kingdom," Robert broke into three other magazine markets with successful submissions to *Ghost Stories*, *Fight Stories*, and *Argosy*.

Ghost Stories, published by the Macfadden Group between 1926 and 1932, focused on ghost stories written in a kind of true-confession style. *Argosy*, one of the better-paying popular magazines, and its various iterations (*The Golden Argosy*, *The Argosy*, and *Argosy All-Story Weekly*) were published by Frank A. Munsey and later by Popular Publications (from 1942 to 1978). It ran from 1882 to 1978. Although it published a modicum of weird and fantasy fiction, *Argosy* focused on general fiction, adventure stories, and some western stories. *Fight Stories*, published by Fiction House between 1926 and 1952, was the first pulp magazine devoted entirely to a single sport: boxing. Established in response to the growing popularity of the sport, and possibly inspired by the success of *The Ring*, a boxing magazine that began publishing in 1922, *Fight Stories* published fast-paced, exciting, action-packed boxing stories. Of the three, *Fight Stories* would be the most lucrative for Robert.

It was at this stage in his writing career that Robert first published a boxing tale, "The Apparition in the Prize Ring,"[10] in the April 1929 *Ghost Stories*. This story develops a phantasmal motif that could, technically, qualify it to be considered a kind of weird supernatural story. However, the boxing theme is too pervasive to allow this story to be categorized as anything other than a boxing story with a simple but effective phantasmal or supernatural twist. In fact, mixing genres may have been Robert's intention, since he was trying to breach other markets: with its various tropes and motifs, he could easily submit a story like "The Apparition in the Prize Ring" to numerous magazines.[11] This was a clever approach that served him well. And *Ghost Stories* apparently liked the phantasmal element of "The Apparition in the Prize Ring" enough to publish it.

For an extended period (1929 to 1932), *Fight Stories*, alongside *Weird Tales*, would be a stable source of much-needed income for Robert. He initially submitted "The Pit of the Serpent" to *Fight Stories*, and it was published in its July 1929 issue. Another boxing story, "Crowd-Horror," was published in the July 20, 1929, issue of *Argosy*, the pulp magazine Robert had submitted stories to for years without success.[12] Neither of these stories had the same sort of strange elements found in "The Apparition in the Prize Ring."

In the fall of 1927, shortly after Robert submitted "The Shadow Kingdom" to *Weird Tales*, he began writing a story titled "Solomon Kane" (hereafter called "Red Shadows," the title later given to it by *Weird Tales*). This story not only marked the character's debut but would ignite a series of tales featuring the dour Puritan vindicator. A total of seven Solomon Kane stories were published in *Weird Tales* from 1928 to 1932. These stories demonstrated that Robert was fine-tuning his practice of blending tropes and motifs. As in the tales of H. Rider Haggard and Talbot Mundy, the core environment of the Solomon Kane stories is the exotic African jungle.

Solomon Kane is an action adventure character in several Howard stories that incorporate vampires, zombies, and mojo, a kind of African dark voodoo magic. The moral ambiguity and retributive nature of Solomon Kane make him a truly interesting character, and readers consistently requested more of him in the pages of *Weird Tales*. Robert did an admirable job of utilizing his early teenage literary influences (such as Arthur O. Friel, Rudyard Kipling, and Rafael Sabatini) in the Solomon Kane stories, while keeping his own voice, style, and unconventional writing practices at the forefront.

"Red Shadows" was another landmark work in fantasy fiction and is one of the best examples of how Robert was attempting to expand his markets. His use of adventure mixed with a late medieval character, an African jungle setting, swashbuckling sword duels, and a strong undercurrent of the fantastic elevated the story to a level of distinction far beyond other stories of that publishing era. Robert admitted to Clyde

Smith, "I wrote this story for *Weird Tales* originally and then decided to try my luck with *Argosy-All Story*, just as it was."[13] After he submitted the story to *Argosy-All Story*, the associate editor, S. A. McWilliams, in a letter dated February 20, 1928, rejected it for all the reasons just mentioned for its originality.

> In some ways this story is very good, and in others it is rotten. I think you may have the stuff if you get steered right, & for that reason [I] am going to hand out the why & wherefore, in detail, that the story was turned down.
>
> It starts out as a period story and finally changes into a modern & medieval African jungle story. You can't mix periods and atmospheres like that. Stick to one or the other. Your story is disconnected partly because of that same wandering from one period to another.
>
> There is too much that is unfinished or unexplained and too much that is miraculous. For instance, it would seem rather incredible to a reader that the Wolf [Le Loup] would not return [to] the secret passage of the cave & attempt to recover part of his loot. Then, there is absolutely no connection between the first & second parts. In one jump you change from the middle ages to Eugene O'Neil [*sic*] jungle stuff. With no explanation save a vague intimation that there has been some kind of pursuit. If there has been such a chase or hunt, you can't omit it from your story.
>
> The stuff pulled by the shaman is good. But you can't let it go as an unexplained miracle. Unexplained miracles are easy to write, but the reader soon tires of them. What the readers want, and, incidentally, is hard to write is miracle stuff which can be explained to them by one means or another. One thing more—as a general rule conversation and descriptive matter should not be included in the same paragraph.
>
> You seem to have caught the knack of writing good action and plenty of it into your stories. If you guard against the faults I have outlined, I believe your stuff will be saleable and will be interested in seeing some of it. Good luck.[14]

After McWilliams's critique and suggestions, Robert did not submit a rewrite to *Argosy-All Story*. It is likely that he did not agree with some of McWilliams's remarks. Robert did, however, admit to Clyde Smith that he appreciated McWilliams's candor and the time he took to detail why the magazine rejected the story. In fairness to "Red Shadows," McWilliams's misunderstanding of the setting and time frame were likely

due to the lack of mention in the first two parts of the work of any setting. But the conflict, the protagonist (Solomon Kane), his mission, and
the antagonist (Le Loup) are all well explained in a fashion that does a
nice job of sinking its hook into the reader. Especially riveting is the oft-
quoted line that ends part 1: "Men shall die for this."[15] This is something
McWilliams should have noticed, but he was focused on peripheral elements of the first two parts of the story: the missing settings and the
time frame.

The fact that, stylistically, "Red Shadows" was decades ahead of its
time may have been one reason why McWilliams took issue with certain aspects of the story. The setting in those first two parts of the story
is not important. How Robert develops the conflict and how he sets the
stage are significantly more critical. The narrative technique of having
the setting jump around—as it does in "Red Shadows" between parts 1,
2, and finally 3, where readers end up in the jungles of Africa—eventually became pervasive decades later, especially in film. Also, contrary to
McWilliams's complaint, the time period of the story remains the late
seventeenth century. Finally, McWilliams's complaint about unexplained
miracles is answered by how clearly Robert establishes N'Longa as a sha-
man (magic man). He also incorporates into the magic some local cus-
toms and invented beliefs to justify N'Longa's magical acts. Knowing
that this is another technique that was ahead of its time suggests that
McWilliams was expressing his own need to have the magic explained to
him, masked as concern for the reader.

By part 3, the reader has been given a distinctive setting—Africa.
From there the story advances the chase that was introduced and developed in part 2, leading to sword duels, N'Longa's use of supernatural sorcery, and Solomon Kane executing his retributive justice upon the antagonist. Despite his various qualms, McWilliams did appreciate Robert's
action scenes, which Robert excelled at his entire writing career. The one
thing Robert most likely gleaned from McWilliams's letter was his admission that Robert had what it took to be a published author. So instead
of rewriting the story for *Argosy-All Story*, he submitted it to *Weird Tales*,
and Farnsworth Wright accepted it as written, changing only the title (to
"Red Shadows," as mentioned) and promising to pay Howard $80 upon
publication.[16] Wright also made it the cover story for the August 1928
issue.

Between *Weird Tales* and *Fight Stories*, Robert managed to make
good on his 1927 agreement with his parents. By 1929, he was making
a living wage as a writer and had achieved the freedom—at least from

loathsome menial work—that he had desired for so many years. He continued to break literary ground—varying his techniques, mixing tropes, writing excellent action scenes, and developing weird characters and creatures. Only one more Kull story would be published in his lifetime, "Kings of the Night," which centered on another soon to be popular protagonist, Bran Mak Morn. And in 1930 a shifting magazine market would shift Robert's fictional direction as well.

By the middle of 1930, another magazine began accepting Robert's work: *Oriental Stories*. The brainchild of Farnsworth Wright and published by Popular Fiction Publishing, *Oriental Stories* was a spin-off of *Weird Tales*. The purpose of *Oriental Stories* was to give readers adventure and fantasy stories set in the East (and in some cases the Middle East). Some of Robert's more historically driven works would be published in *Oriental Stories*.[17] When some readers responded to these stories with complaints about the liberties Robert was taking with certain aspects of history, he responded in turn by developing his own period of "history," which he called the Hyborian Age. It was a denizen of this age, Conan the Cimmerian, whom Robert would introduce to the literary world.

Unlike many modern fantasy tales, the Hyborian Age is not set in another world apart from our own. Rather, the Hyborian Age is set on earth in a prehistoric time, before recorded history. This setting allowed Robert to do as he pleased with the "history" of the story. Along with Kull, Solomon Kane, and Bran Mak Morn, Conan the Cimmerian—who became his most popular character and remains so to this day—helped establish Robert E. Howard as one of the cornerstone progenitors of a new species of modern fantasy fiction.

CHAPTER NINE

Friends and Letters

Wright recently sent me a letter from W.T. author Robert E. Howard, praising my "Rats in the Walls" & giving incidental remarks on early Celtic Britain. Howard seems to be a rather erudite person—& I am dropping him a line.

H. P. LOVECRAFT TO CLARK ASHTON SMITH, JUNE 23, 1930 (IN SCHULTZ AND JOSHI, EDS., *DAWNWARD SPIRE, LONELY HILL: THE LETTERS OF H. P. LOVECRAFT AND CLARK ASHTON SMITH*, 2017)

It seems obvious to declare that friends were important to Robert E. Howard. Friends are important to us all. What is perhaps less obvious is how important some of Robert's friends were to his fiction. Robert had a coterie of friends in Cross Plains with whom he spent time, and two stood out among the others: Lindsey Tyson and Dave Lee. After Robert's untimely death in 1936, it was discovered that Robert wrote a last will and testament leaving all his assets to his close friend Tyson. The two had traveled together to amateur boxing matches and prizefights, and on several occasions they sparred and drank together at the icehouse in Cross Plains.

The Cross Plains icehouse has been a topic of much speculation and discussion for several decades, but little is known about the activities that took place behind its walls. In one of his letters to Clyde Smith, Robert declares, "Dave [Lee] was saying the other night, when he and Pink [Lindsey Tyson] and I were sitting around drinking beer in the ice house, for me to get you and Truett over here Saturday and we'd throw a party in his shack, that night."[1] This was in 1930, at the height of Prohibition, but with the amount of bootlegging in the area—around isolated creeks and in out-of-the-way places[2]—the fact that one could get a cool beer at the icehouse is not surprising. In a different letter, Robert tells a story about another icehouse:

> Yet when I look for the peak of my exultation, I find it on a sweltering, breathless midnight when I fought a black-headed tiger of an Oklahoma drifter in an abandoned ice-vault, in a stifling atmosphere laden with tobacco smoke and the reek of sweat and rot-gut whisky—and blood; with a gang of cursing blaspheming oil-field roughnecks for an audience. Even now the memory of that battle stirs the sluggish blood in my fat-laden tissues. There was nothing about it calculated to advance art, science or anything else. It was a bloody, merciless, brutal brawl. We fought for fully an hour—until neither of us could fight any longer, and we reeled against each other, gasping incoherent curses through battered lips.[3]

This account, *if true*, more likely describes a prizefight (or amateur bout) that Robert witnessed, not a boxing match that he fought himself (as the letter indicates). Certain details ("We fought for fully an hour," "neither of us could fight any longer," "It was a bloody, merciless, brutal brawl") indicate that this might have been a prizefight Robert witnessed. That it took place in an *abandoned* "ice-vault" probably eliminates the Cross Plains icehouse as the site of the fight.[4] More than likely this account is simply a tall tale. Robert was known for telling a few tall tales to exaggerate a situation, stress a point, or even concoct a completely fictional account of purported events for dramatic effect.

It is possible that Robert sparred or participated in some type of brief boxing bouts at the Cross Plains icehouse; in fact, there is some evidence for this.[5] But full-blown boxing matches are not likely to have taken place there. Robert's passion for boxing certainly shows in his boxing fiction, and he shared this passion with his friends. If anything, this letter is a nice example of how his mind worked when he wanted to spin a yarn (or a tall tale).

Besides the friends he grew up with in Cross Plains, Robert's life can generally be neatly divided into two groups of friends and correspondents: his friends in Brownwood, including Harold Preece of Austin and Herbert C. Klatt of Aleman, Texas, in one group; and the Lovecraft circle of correspondents in the other. Though Robert was already writing stories before he entered his final year of public education at Brownwood

High School, his friends in Brownwood were significant, helping him to develop not only his craft but also his reading repertoire. His friendship with Tevis Clyde Smith (through Truett Vinson) led to his publication in the local school newspapers that Smith edited (*The Tattler*, *The Yellow Jacket*, and *The Collegiate*). That relationship was critical for Robert's early amateur writing career, since all these school newspapers helped him refine his craft and functioned as stepping-stones to professional publishing.

All of Robert's Brownwood friends were aspiring writers, including Harold Preece and Herbert Klatt. Klatt was in a far more precarious living situation than Robert, Truett, and Clyde. Klatt lived in Aleman, a community eight miles southeast of Hamilton that was even more rural than Cross Plains. The son of a poor farmer, he aspired to be a journalist, but given his location and lack of any substantive source of income, his odds of success were quite slim. Klatt had become acquainted with Robert, Clyde Smith, and Truett Vinson through his involvement with the Lone Scouts organization, his predominant social outlet. After he graduated from high school, he kept busy on his family's farm— so busy, in fact, that he hardly had time for anything else. Since farming was his sole means of employment, his pay was room and board. His lack of cash stifled any desire he may have had to build a personal library or to travel. And while he could ride one of the family horses (or later drive their truck) to Hamilton to visit the town's Carnegie public library, his rural isolation limited his only consistent source of reading material to the Lone Scouts' publication, *Lone Scout*.

Despite his isolation and straitened circumstances, Klatt was driven by a sheer desire to write, and through the Lone Scouts, he did publish in various locales around the United States. He wrote articles for *Semi Weekly Farm News*, *Southland Farmer*, and various local newspapers, including the "Lone Scout Report" for the nearby *Hamilton-Herald-Record*. Robert and Klatt began corresponding sometime in 1925, discussing books and magazines they had read and essays and fiction they had written. They met only once, for a day and an evening shortly after Christmas 1925. Klatt managed to travel to Brownwood, and all the boys (Howard, Vinson, Smith, and Klatt) drove to (Ben) Stone Ranch, Smith's uncle's place, for an evening of drunken romp and fun. In the short time they knew one another, Robert had a greater impact and influence on Klatt than Klatt did on Robert. However, Klatt did introduce Robert to the works of O. Henry. And Robert included Klatt (as the character Hubert

Grotz) in his semiautobiographical novel *Post Oaks and Sand Roughs*. Unfortunately, Klatt's dream of being a journalist never materialized. He died on May 10, 1928, from pernicious anemia at the age of twenty-one.

It was through Herbert Klatt that Truett Vinson became acquainted with Harold Preece. Preece, another Lone Scout, began corresponding with Vinson through the *Lone Scout* "Messenger Department." In those early days, Preece was an aspiring writer, and of all Robert's Texas friends, Preece would be the most successful at the writing game besides Robert. When Robert, Vinson, and Preece initially met in Austin, Robert and Preece connected almost immediately. They began corresponding in late 1927 or early 1928.[6] The two discussed favorite films, books, and writers, as well as Preece's interest in Celtic and Gaelic folklore and history. Between late 1927 (or early 1928) and 1932, their letters about Celtic and Gaelic folklore and history were critical to Robert's fiction during this period. Robert already had a healthy interest in Celtic history and folklore, as evidenced in his story "The Lost Race." His correspondence with Preece certainly heightened his interest in Gaelic history as well. It also spurred him to write some very well received historical fiction that incorporated that same history.

During this midpoint of his twelve-year writing career (between 1928 to 1932), Robert focused much of his attention on writing and publishing historical fiction.[7] Two influences were mainly responsible for his focus on historical fiction: Farnsworth Wright's development in the early 1930s of the new magazine *Oriental Stories*, and the Celtic and Gaelic folklore and history discussed in Robert's correspondence with Harold Preece. Wright invited Robert to submit to *Oriental Stories* in the late spring of 1930.[8] Robert's historical fiction output at the beginning of this period was slow, but the more letters he and Preece exchanged the more that output increased. A few years before Wright's invitation, Robert had confessed to Clyde Smith that he felt like his writing efforts were in vain (probably owing to slow sales and a limited medium):

> Here am I, with seven years [1921–1928] of hard work behind me and only some twenty five stories, articles and rhymes marketed to show for it. Here am I, slugging away at a cheap, little known magazine which may already be bankrupt, weaving fanciful and impossible tales and absolutely unknown outside that magazine's limited clientele. When compared to the clever, intelligent and gifted writers of today who have already reached their zenith, I admit there is little to my favor.[9]

One cannot help but notice the note of frustration in Robert's letter. In late 1928 and then especially in 1929 and beyond, his publication efforts would be more successful and his attitude would improve, at least for a time. In certain letters to H. P. Lovecraft, Robert claimed that he wrote simply to make money. While that is true to an extent, there was always beneath the surface of that claim a sense of Robert's desire to have his work stand out. He wanted to be more than merely a weird fiction author published in what he might have felt was a low-grade magazine with a limited number of readers. Coincidentally, it was during this period when he was corresponding with Preece, and shortly after he wrote this letter to Lovecraft, that Robert's writing took a turn toward historical fiction. Perhaps this change in his fictional output was partly a response to the frustration he had so openly expressed to Clyde Smith.

By 1930, with "The Voice of El-Lil," Robert's productivity in writing historical fiction showed a marked increase. "The Voice of El-Lil" is one of the best examples of Robert's use of history in a work of fiction. Robert himself admitted to his friend Clyde Smith, "I sold 'The Voice of El-Lil' to Farnsworth for $95.00 being about the first story I ever sold that I had to batter out by pure force of study."[10] To "batter out" this story, Robert relied on H. G. Wells's *The Outline of History*. "The Voice of El-Lil" incorporates El-Lil, Sumerian history, Sargon of Akkad, the Akkadians, and a small temple in Nippur erected to the god El-Lil, which may have promulgated the myth of the tower of Babel—all of which stems from *The Outline of History*.[11] Moreover, the way Robert used the history of the Sumerians is extraordinarily unique.

In "The Voice of El-Lil," Robert created a lost civilization (from Sumer) that had existed in the northern part of the Arabian Peninsula around 3000 BCE and placed it in the African jungles in the late 1920s. He developed its history and a reason for its migration to Africa. He also added adventure, sword play, and a weird element (strange gods) to the narrative. The story was published by Farnsworth Wright in *Oriental Stories* in its premier (October/November 1930) issue. Fellow pulp writer Wallace West declared, "*The Voice of El-Lil* and *Strange Bedfellows* also are out of the ordinary, the former being as good as H. Rider Haggard's best."[12] *Oriental Stories* would be a lucrative magazine for Robert and his historical fiction. Even though the magazine released only nine issues, Robert had a total of six stories published during its short run.

During this period, Robert and Clyde Smith collaborated on an action adventure story, "Red Blades of Black Cathay." Set in Asia during the late twelfth or early thirteenth century, the story features Genghis

Khan, the founder and first Khan of the Mongol Empire. Robert submitted the story to *Oriental Stories*, and it became the February/March 1931
cover story. The collaboration was well received by the magazine's readers. Henry S. Whitehead, a fellow *Weird Tales* writer, declared, "Con-
gratulations on the February–March issue of ORIENTAL STORIES. That
leader, *Red Blades of Black Cathay* is as good an action-adventure yarn
as I've ever read in my life, and both you and the authors are to be con-
gratulated. It is a real corncracker!"[13] This would be the only story Clyde
Smith published in a pulp magazine. However, he would go on to write
and independently publish several local histories, a few of which include
important biographical chapters about Robert.[14] In addition, during the
1960s and 1970s, Smith contributed articles about Robert to fanzines.

Robert's correspondence with Harold Preece spawned four stories
that appeared in several of the nine *Oriental Stories* issues.[15] Among
these, Robert created a character, Cormac FitzGeoffrey, around whom
he hoped to develop a fictional series for *Oriental Stories*.[16] If Robert
could establish a character popular enough for a series, it would ensure
continued publication in the magazine and provide him with a steady
stream of income. This was a good idea, especially since he had witnessed
other writers publish successful character-based series, but Cormac Fitz-
Geoffrey and Turlogh Dubh O'Brien—another character, Howard admitted to Preece, around whom he wanted to build a series of stories—would
not be the characters to generate a series. That spot eventually would be
occupied by Robert's most popular character: Conan the Cimmerian.

One of the most interesting aspects of this period in Robert's writing
career (1928 to 1932) is that he began to build worlds. He bridged stories
with characters and histories, developing a contiguous historical epic.[17]
This publication period ultimately steered Robert toward creating the
Hyborian Age by using elements of these histories to develop a whole
new age and peoples. Initially, Robert's fictional world-building began in
his 1926 story "Men of the Shadows," which was rejected by *Weird Tales*.
Using the "history" from "Men of the Shadows" coupled with his Celtic
and Nordic "races," and inspired by his discussions with Preece about
Celtic and Gaelic history, Robert developed new Gaelic medieval (Cru-
sades era) protagonists such as Turlogh Dubh O'Brien, Cormac Fitz-
Geoffrey, and Conan of the Reavers.[18] Robert was rewriting history in
the guise of fiction.[19]

The last extant letter between Robert and Harold Preece is dated November 24, 1930. It is uncertain why their correspondence ended. There
may be lost letters yet to be discovered, or they may simply have stopped

writing to each other owing to their busy schedules. Whatever the case, the letters stopped after 1930. Harold Preece went on to publish a slew of articles for various magazines from the mid-1930s to the mid-1970s. In August 1935, Preece published an article in *Opportunity: The Journal of Negro Life* titled "Confession of an Ex-Nordic." In this frank and transparent piece, Preece explains his transformation from being a prejudiced person, mostly toward blacks, to having an antiracist stance lauding blacks and their heritage, works, and plight. Long before the civil rights movement of the 1950s and '60s, this early article advocating antiracism launched a steady flow of such articles Preece wrote for publication in other African American magazines published in the 1930s and '40s, such as *The Crisis*. Preece was a socialist when he was corresponding with Robert, and he continued his socialist activity by publishing articles in *The New Masses* journal.[20] He was also recognized as an expert in regional Texas and Old West history.[21] Preece graduated from Texas Christian University and took some courses at the University of Texas at Austin. Like Robert's friend Clyde Smith, Preece published several articles in a couple of fanzines in the 1970s, most of which were accounts of his experiences with Robert.

Shortly before his correspondence with Harold Preece ended, Robert inadvertently began corresponding with fellow pulp writer H. P. Lovecraft. Robert's correspondence with Preece had motivated his research for his historical fiction and sent him in several different directions as a writer, improving his writing skills in the process. As important as that was, Robert's correspondence with Lovecraft and other pulp writers he met through Lovecraft would elevate Robert's output and skill even higher.

"The Rats in the Walls," which appeared in the March 1924 issue of *Weird Tales*, was one of Lovecraft's early stories. At the end of this story, he uses a Latin phrase, *"Magna Mater! Magna Mater!,"* followed by Gaelic verbiage.[22] After the story was published, Lovecraft wrote his friend Frank Belknap Long and confessed:

> That bit of gibberish which immediately followed the atavistic Latin was *not* pithecanthropoid. The first actual ape-cry was the *"ungl."* What the intermediate jargon is, is *perfectly good Celtic*—a bit of venomously vituperative phraseology which a certain small boy ought to know; because his grandpa, instead of consulting a professor to get a Celtic phrase, found a ready-made one so apt that he lifted it boldly from *The Sin-Eater*, by Fiona McLeod [*sic*], in the volume of *Best Psy-*

chic Stories which Sonny [Frank Belknap Long] himself generously sent! I thought you'd note that at once—but youth hath a crowded memory. Anyhow, the only objection to the phrase is that it's *Gaelic* instead of *Cymric* as the south-of-England locale demands. But as—with anthropology—details don't count. Nobody will ever stop to note the difference.[23]

As it turned out, when the story was reprinted in the June 1930 *Weird Tales*, Robert noticed the Gaelic and realized the error.[24] That same month Robert wrote a letter to Farnsworth Wright pointing out that Lovecraft's choice of language (via MacLeod's "The Sin-Eater") probably signaled that Lovecraft held to "[Edward] Lhuyd's theory as to the settling of Britain by the Celts."[25] At the time, Robert was immersed in researching Celtic and Gaelic history, languages, and folklore. Wright forwarded the letter to Lovecraft, who then responded to Robert. This letter has since been lost or destroyed. But Lovecraft's response resulted in a six-year correspondence between the two writers. These letters are essential to understanding Robert's growth as a writer, as well as his mentation and its evolution in his later fiction.

Robert was beside himself with excitement when Lovecraft replied to his letter. At the time, Lovecraft was one of Robert's favorite contemporaneous authors, and he was quite complimentary toward Lovecraft and his works: "I am indeed highly honored to have received a personal letter from one whose works I so highly admire." Robert further confesses, "I have been reading your stories for years, and I say, in all sincerity, that no writer, past or modern, has equaled you in the realm of bizarre fiction." Following his initial fan moment, Robert immediately explains why he thinks the Cymric peoples were the first to populate the British Isles. In great detail, he delineates examples to support his claim, citing sources and providing historical, geographical, and linguistic evidence. Robert humbly prefaces his detailed delineation with a claim that he has "scanty knowledge" of such things, but what he goes to write reveals that he has performed a high level of research.[26] In his reply, Lovecraft admits, "Your observations on Celtic philology & pre-history proved immensely fascinating to me, & wholly bely your modest claim of 'meagre' knowledge of the subject."[27]

Their initial correspondence—which lasted, on and off, a little over two years—primarily focused on the British Isles, its history, peoples, and languages, and Celtic and Gaelic folklore. Neither was a scholar on these matters, but their letters provide a good deal of insight about the historical and anthropological schools of thought of their day. In between the Celtic and Gaelic discussions, new discussions emerged about their regional histories. Robert waxed nostalgic about his childhood in Bagwell spent listening to Mary Bohannon's stories. In return, Lovecraft told Robert tales of regional historical witchcraft and Puritanism and the ghostly tales that circulated in and around his hometown of Providence, Rhode Island. Robert began reading authors whom Lovecraft recommended (many of them horror writers), and Lovecraft sent some of his own poetry and unpublished short fiction to Robert for his opinions and insights. As these exchanges increased, Robert's own fiction changed markedly.

Within a few months after their correspondence began, some of Robert's fiction gravitated toward different styles and genres. By 1934, his production of historical fiction began to wane. Between 1930 and 1934, he began writing horror stories and eventually westerns (some blended with horror motifs and tropes). Robert's westerns surfaced as his correspondence with Lovecraft gravitated toward Texas history and the Old West. Prior to corresponding with Lovecraft, Robert had incorporated elements of horror into his adventure fantasy fiction; for example, several Solomon Kane, Kull, and even Bran Mak Morn stories contained a certain number of horror elements. Some of Robert's earlier works, such as "In the Forest of Villefère" and "Wolfshead," were traditional horror stories that he wrote in an adventurous style with various weird elements. All of these stories are "marked by a creative exuberance that is sometimes only barely under control."[28] With all that in mind, the horror Robert initially created when he and Lovecraft began their correspondence contained elements he had never used before: cosmic creatures, otherworldly elements, and various occultlike elements such as lost books and nameless cults or peoples.

"The Children of the Night" was Robert's first attempt at blending Lovecraftian horror with his own adventure fiction. He probably wrote this story in the late of summer 1930, a couple of months into his correspondence with Lovecraft. In fact, in "The Children of the Night," Robert mentions Lovecraft's name and his story "The Call of Cthulhu" as a master horror tale, along with Edgar Allan Poe's "The Fall of the House of Usher" and Arthur Machen's "The Novel of the Black Seal."[29] Robert uses this name- and story-dropping in the tale to introduce readers to von Junzt's book *Nameless Cults*.[30] Robert's characteristic writing style, pace, energy, and action are still present, but the content is clearly like that of no other story he had written. "The Children of the Night" is an amalgamation of various elements from Robert's previous stories, with a few new ideas added. He incorporates ancestral memories (or reincarnation) into the story to cast one of his protagonists, after a blow to the head, into a past life. "The Children of the Night" is the first of three attempts (along with "The Black Stone" and "The Thing on the Roof") to develop stories using Lovecraftian elements. Of the three, "The Black Stone" is the most popular and generally considered the best-written.

Each of these stories is connected to the others through various elements, but the singular underlying connection is Robert's fictional character von Junzt and his book *Nameless Cults*. Originally known as the Black Book, it reveals hidden secrets and mysteries that allegedly drove its author mad. "The Children of the Night" introduces the book and calls its writer a madman. Details are gradually revealed between "The Children of the Night" and "The Black Stone"—such as the subsequent editions of *Nameless Cults*, the history of von Junzt, why he may have gone mad, and the various secrets of his book. In their correspondence, Lovecraft gave Robert permission to incorporate elements from his own stories into these stories. In turn, Lovecraft did the same with Robert's character von Junzt and the book *Nameless Cults*, as well as with Justin Geoffrey, another fictional character Robert created.[31] Lovecraft gave von Junzt his first names, Friedrich Wilhelm. It became a relatively common practice with Lovecraft and his fellow pulp writer correspondents: to exchange ideas and then incorporate them into their stories, developing what is now known as the Cthulhu Mythos.[32] Robert utilized aspects of this mythos in a number of his stories, experimenting with the mythos in several different genres.

Lovecraft was a boon for Robert and his fictional productivity, and their correspondence would last for the rest of his life. Through Lovecraft, Robert met many of his fellow writers from *Weird Tales* and other pulp magazines. These new contacts opened doors for him in ways he had never imagined, and they steered him toward new markets. Lovecraft gave Robert the addresses of the writer Wilfred Branch Talman; Bernard Austin Dwyer, who was another Lovecraft correspondent and a fan of *Weird Tales*; and the writer Donald Wandrei.[33] Of these three, Talman proved the most beneficial: Robert managed to get "The Ghost of Camp Colorado" published in the April 1931 issue of *Texaco Star* via his correspondence with Talman, who was the magazine's editor at the time. By the end of 1932, Robert had begun corresponding with August Derleth and Robert H. Barlow, and with Clark Ashton Smith by early 1933. His letters to Smith and Derleth were similar to those he wrote to

Lovecraft in that they exchanged poems and stories and discussed each other's work. Robert and Derleth also exchanged a fair amount of regional history. All these correspondents bolstered Robert's confidence and planted seeds for his literary harvest.

In September 1931, Lovecraft expressed his desire to visit New Orleans and Texas and finally get to meet Robert.[34] But as both men knew, income for writers, especially during the Great Depression, was often sporadic, and Lovecraft lamented to Robert that the cost of the bus fare was too great. Having adjusted to living on such small means for so long, Lovecraft was masterful at stretching every dollar he earned, and eventually he had saved enough for the trip. In June 1932, he traveled through the southeastern states, cut across Tennessee and Mississippi, and then traveled to New Orleans. Soon after his arrival, Lovecraft wrote to Robert and told him that he would be in New Orleans for at least a week.

At the time, E. Hoffmann Price, with whom Robert had been corresponding for some time, lived in New Orleans. Robert quickly sent Price a telegram providing the address where Lovecraft was staying. In the meantime, Robert scurried to find a way to travel to New Orleans, but he never managed to secure transportation. In a second letter from New Orleans, Lovecraft thanked Robert for telegramming Price, admitting that he knew Price lived there but was unable to find his address in the directory.[35]

There were several reasons why Robert was unable to make the trip. Shortly before Lovecraft traveled to New Orleans, and unaware that he was doing so, Robert attempted to buy an automobile. But Robert's bank in Cross Plains had collapsed, another victim of the Great Depression, and he had lost a good portion of his money. This loss, coupled with only fitful success in some publishing markets, had left Robert without disposable income at the time. He explained all this to Lovecraft in a July 13, 1932, letter and expressed his deep regret over not being able to make the trip. In despair, Robert told Lovecraft that in making every attempt to find a way to see him in New Orleans, he had not even been able to "secure a saddle-pony."[36] Had Lovecraft notified Robert of his upcoming trip prior to leaving for New Orleans, Robert might have had more time to prepare and secure some form of transportation. One can only imagine what treasures would have resulted from H. P. Lovecraft, E. Hoffmann Price, and Robert E. Howard spending time together in New Orleans.

Of all the *Weird Tales* writers, and particularly those in Lovecraft's inner circle, Robert had the opportunity to meet only one: Edgar Hoffmann Price. On April 8, 1934, Price, along with his wife Wanda, drove from Pawhuska, Oklahoma, to Cross Plains. At the time, because the Federal Bureau of Investigations and the Texas Rangers Frank Hamer and Maney Gault were in hot pursuit of Bonnie Parker and Clyde Barrow and his Barrow gang, most of the border crossings into Texas from Louisiana and Oklahoma were being watched by state and federal law enforcement. Driving south from Oklahoma into Texas, Price and his wife crossed the Red River in their Model A Ford. Price asked his wife to light up a cigar for him shortly after they crossed the river. The car, the place, the circumstances, and especially a woman lighting up a cigar were enough to bring officers stepping out into the road and forcing the Prices to stop their vehicle.[37] After revealing their identities, the Prices were released by the officers. They finally arrived at the Howards' house in Cross Plains later that evening.

Since the Prices had not established a particular time for their arrival, Robert was not home when they reached the Howards' house. But Dr. and Mrs. Howard made the Prices feel at home. Right away, Dr. Howard began bending Price's ear about *Weird Tales*' delayed payments to their writers and how frustrated this made Robert. Price also expressed his frustration at the delay and assured Dr. Howard that Robert was not the only *Weird Tales* author to whom money was owed. At the time, *Weird Tales* was suffering from the effects of the Great Depression. Financially, the magazine was struggling to keep its head above water, and checks to its writers and artists were beginning to bounce. This caused William Sprenger, *Weird Tales*' business manager, to inform Farnsworth Wright that all checks would have to be suspended for a period.[38] Price admitted that the most *Weird Tales* ever owed him for back stories was about $300.[39] The magazine owed Robert substantially more; estimates run from $800 to as much as $1,300. The Great Depression was also affecting Dr. Howard and his practice, and at that time Robert was helping with the medical expenses for the care of his mother. This is most likely why Dr. Howard expressed his concern to Price.

The next morning Price finally met Robert, whom he described as "tall, broad, towering—squarish face, tanned to swarthiness—deep chest, short, solid neck—a lot of man." He was also surprised at the "quiet friendliness" of Robert's voice.[40] Based on their correspondence, Price had expected a stronger, more bullish voice. Soon after breakfast, the two writers went for a stroll in downtown Cross Plains so that Price could get a much-needed haircut. On the way, in the middle of their conversation, Robert blurted out how proud he was that Price was visiting him. At the time of this visit, Price greatly admired Robert and his work, so the comment surprised him. Robert then admitted that the towns-people of Cross Plains did not think much of him. Price thought this odd, especially considering the number of Robert's fans who read his stories in various magazines. He could not understand why Robert even cared what an inconsequential small town thought about him, consider-ing how popular Robert was in the magazines. It dawned on Price that Robert may not have realized how successful he was at the time.

Price made two trips to see Robert, first in April 1934 and then in October 1935. During both visits, Price learned several revealing and interesting things. He found it interesting that Robert pronounced the word "wound," meaning an injury, in the same way one would say, "I wound the clock." Also, Robert stressed the *w* in the word "sword." Price did not care much for Robert's Conan stories, and during Price's first visit Robert said that he was growing tired of writing about Conan and had turned his attention to serious and comedic westerns. During Price's second visit, in October 1935, the third period of Robert's writing career was ending: he was writing mostly adventure fantasy and transitioning into working on westerns. Price thoroughly enjoyed Robert's comedic westerns and admitted that he thought those stories were some of Rob-ert's best.

In this transitional time, new markets, ones he had previously strug-gled to breach, were opening for Robert. When Price visited Robert, he got the impression that Robert wrote instinctively and impulsively. "A story was either right," Price reports Roberts telling him, "or else he'd throw it aside and start another."[41] There is some truth to this claim: at times Robert created admirable first drafts, even though edited manu-scripts have been discovered in all of Robert's papers and drafts. Robert splashed the various markets with a great number of stories, and over the decades unfinished manuscripts and fragmented stories have been dis-covered. Because Robert was attempting to earn an income as a writer, he wrote more and more often. Robert's writing practices led Price to be-lieve that Robert might have not had a solid grasp of magazine market-ing and publication. For example, if Robert sent out a Celtic story, absent of weird elements, to *Adventure* magazine and it was rejected, he may have concluded that the magazine's editor either did not care for him or thought his story was lousy.[42] Price assumed that Robert believed that if a single magazine rejected his first submission, that magazine's edi-tor thought the story was no good, causing a bias against him. Because of this, Robert assumed that other stories he later submitted were rejected based on this initial bias. There's possibly some truth to this based on Robert's insecurities as a young writer. But it is probably due more to Robert's early naive view of the magazine publication markets; the idea that the more places he submitted stories, the greater the chance one of those magazines would want to publish him, what Robert called "splashing the field." So instead of perfecting his stories, he simply tried a different magazine. This practice changed as Robert aged and matured. Price indicated that toward the end of Robert's life, his understanding of the industry was changing, along with his perspective on what made a story great. Some of this transformation came about because Robert hired Otis Adelbert Kline as his agent.

Shortly before the summer of 1932, Robert joined the American Fiction Guild (AFG). It is not known how he discovered the group.[43] Once he did, however, he alerted Clyde Smith in a May 1932 letter: "John Kelley of Fiction House [publisher of *Fight Stories* and *Action Stories*] is dead. I learned this through the bulletins of the American Fiction Guild, of which I am a member, and which seems to be a solid organization. I suppose you've received a request to join."[44] In the same month, Robert also told Lovecraft about the organization. "I've recently joined the American Fiction Guild, which looks like a pretty good thing. If you are not already a member, and would care to look into it, I'll have them send you some literature regarding it."[45] A year into his correspondence with fellow *Weird Tales* writer August Derleth, in December 1933, Robert wrote to him about AFG:

> By the way, are you a member of the American Fiction Guild? If not, we'd be mighty glad to have you join. The Guild is growing and I honestly believe that some day it will be a power in the land. We have a free market tip system, and our official organ is the Author & Journalist, which to my mind is the best publication of its kind extant. The present officers are: Arthur J. Burks, president; Erle Stanley Gardner, Albert Richard Wetjen, Frank Tinsley, Willard E. Hawkins, Sewell Peaslee Wright and Eugene Cunningham, vice-presidents; secretary, Ed Bodin; and Theodore Tinsley, treasurer. Membership, I believe, totals nearly 250. I'm enclosing an application blank in case you'd be interested.[46]

The AFG was opening unexplored doors for Robert. It was probably through either his association with the group or his correspondence with E. Hoffmann Price, or a combination of both, that he discovered Otis Adelbert Kline, a fellow *Weird Tales* writer, who was offering his services as an agent for writers through ads in *Author & Journalist*.⁴⁷ Price had used Kline's agency services on a couple of occasions in mid-1932.⁴⁸

Kline "had been a writer in the pulps in his own right, today most remembered for his Edgar Rice Burroughs-esque serial novels like *The Planet of Peril* (1929), *Jan of the Jungle* (1931), and *The Swordsman of Mars* (1933) for *Argosy*, but he was also an early contributor to *Weird Tales*, and anonymously edited the May-Jun-Jul 1924 issue."⁴⁹ He was able to sell most of what he wrote to various magazines, but it was not enough to sustain the lifestyle he desired.⁵⁰ To supplement his income, he decided to use the strong connections he had developed in the magazine industry and offer his services as an agent to other writers. In the late spring of 1933, Robert acquired Kline's agency services. The two worked out an agreement by which Kline would submit Robert's stories to markets other than *Weird Tales*, since Robert had already established himself at that magazine.

Robert and Kline probably began corresponding in late 1932 or early 1933, and "while much of the correspondence between [them] is no longer extant, the few letters that remain give an outline of their business relationship. Kline waived reading fees (a fee for reading a manuscript and trying to sell it) and worked on a straight commission: 10% of whatever the story sold for went to Kline."⁵¹ Through Kline's efforts, Robert garnered additional success in markets he had yet to tap.

The year 1932 was a transitional one for Robert's fictional output. In October 1931, he had submitted "People of the Dark" to a start-up magazine, *Strange Tales of Mystery and Terror*, which was "a companion to Clayton's *Astounding Stories* and was likewise edited by Harry Bates." *Astounding Stories* was one of W. M. Clayton Publishers' most popular pulp magazines and one of the more difficult pulp magazines for writers to break into during the pulp era. Wanting to tap into *Weird Tales'* success, Clayton Publishers offered *Strange Tales* as an alternative to *Weird Tales*. It "was the only magazine published as direct competition to *Weird Tales* that offered that magazine a serious challenge."⁵² *Strange Tales* was intentionally published for the *Weird Tales* audience. During the deepest part of the Great Depression, many *Weird Tales* writers would submit their work to *Strange Tales* to gain a felicitous stream of additional income. *Strange Tales* paid two cents a word—twice the *Weird Tales* rate. However, *Strange Tales* lasted only seven issues and never posed a serious threat to *Weird Tales*.

The Depression was hurting countless pulp magazines and their writers. Robert admitted as much to Clyde Smith in a May 1932 letter:

By the way, a friend of mine in Marlin [Texas] wrote [Harry] Bates, boosting my "People of the Dark," and he wrote her telling her that he guessed she could consider me as a new regular now—I hope he remembers that, and holds to it. God knows I need the money. Markets are cracking every day. The depression is beginning to lick the wood-pulps.[53]

"People of the Dark" was the first story in which Robert used the name Conan. Even so, its protagonist, Conan of the Reavers (who is also John O'Brien), is clearly not the same character as Conan the Cimmerian, whom he also developed in 1932.[54] There are, however, some striking similarities between the two characters: both wield a broadsword, and both are massively built, with large torsos, and have black hair. Of course, this same description fits various other Celtic and Gael characters Robert used in several of his historical adventure stories. What makes Conan of the Reavers interesting is that he "represents an important intermediary step between the Irish/Celtic characters of 1930–31 (Turlogh, Cormacs Mac Art and FitzGeoffrey, Cahal Ruadh O'Donnel, Donald MacDeesa, and of course "Spears of Clontarf" has a large cast of Irish warriors) and Conan the Cimmerian."[55] Robert uses the motif of ancestral memory (or reincarnation) from "The Children of the Night" in "People of the Dark" as well. This would make "People of the Dark" another stepping-stone in Robert's horror fiction during this period that stemmed from his correspondence with Lovecraft.

"People of the Dark" was accepted for publication by Clayton Publishers in January 1932 and then published in the June 1932 issue of *Strange Tales of Mystery and Terror*. In between the story's acceptance and publication, in February 1932, Robert took a trip to Mission, Texas, in the southernmost part of the state, near McAllen. Inspired by the area and its atmosphere, he penned the now-famous poem "Cimmeria." The first line begins, "I remember," echoing once again the ancestral memory motif he used in "People of the Dark."[56] This is further evidence of Robert's transition into his final writing period from the Celtic/Gaelic fiction of the middle of his career. From this point, Robert's fictional output shifted to fantasy adventure, and at its core was Conan the Cimmerian.

In the late spring of 1933, likely on the advice of Kline, his new agent, Robert also turned some of his attention to westerns and detective stories. He did not give up on writing horror fiction, but his output in this genre waned for a time. Even after this shift, Robert continued to be influenced in his writing by his correspondence with Lovecraft, not only in his Conan the Cimmerian stories but also in some of his westerns and subsequent horror stories.

Before long, Robert and Lovecraft began discussing the differences between barbarism and civilization. When and why their correspondence shifted in this direction is difficult to pinpoint, but Robert's dislike for Rome and its civilization seems to be the likeliest reason why they began to discuss the classical worlds of Rome and Greece. These discussions began relatively early; the topic of ancient Rome and Greece came up, if only briefly, as early as 1931. By August 1932, the barbarian versus civilization discussion had developed into a debate, as indicated in their letters "with a statement like, 'as for barbarism versus civilization.'"⁵⁷ Prior to this, in an April 1932 letter, Robert told Lovecraft, "I've been working on a new character, providing him with a new epoch—the Hyborian Age, which men have forgotten, but which remains in classical names and distorted myths." Robert continued: "Wright rejected most of the series, but I did sell him one—'The Phoenix on the Sword' which deals with the adventures of King Conan the Cimmerian, in the kingdom of Aquilonia."⁵⁸

Some of the ideas from both sides of the barbarian versus civilization debate made their way into Robert's fiction, especially his Conan stories. The debate itself lasted almost three years—that is, for nearly half of their entire correspondence. At times during their ongoing debate, Lovecraft was insolent toward Robert, who took it in stride, exhibiting a stoic patience with his interlocutor. Occasionally that patience crumbled, however, and Robert responded to Lovecraft's insolence with harsh sarcasm. They also brought to this debate their political discussion of 1930s fascism and socialism in Germany and Europe, and this was one area where Robert's patience could wane. By the mid-1930s, Howard "takes a sarcastic tone in referring to his friend's views on the merits of civilization, especially when referring to Lovecraft's sympathies with, and defenses of, Mussolini and the fascists." At some point in their correspondence the two had developed a comfortable enough rapport that Robert's initial relation to Lovecraft as an enamored fan of him and his work had shifted to a relationship of equal peers. In other words, "while Howard continues to express admiration for the other's literary efforts, it seems clear that he at last feels himself at least equal to, if not in some ways superior to, Lovecraft."⁵⁹

Other topics arose between the two writers throughout the six years of their correspondence. They often discussed the issue of freedom, which neatly tied into, especially for Robert, the barbarism versus civilization debate, as well as his reasons for writing. In a January 1934 letter to Lovecraft, Robert admitted:

> And just as I have struggled for a maximum amount of freedom in my own life, I look back with envy at the greater freedom known by my ancestors on the frontier. Hard work? Certainly they worked hard. But they were building something; making the most of opportunities; working for themselves, not merely cogs grinding in a soulless machine, as is the modern working man, whose life is a constant round of barren toil infinitely more monotonous and crushing than the toil on the frontier. He's not building anything. He's simply making a bare living.[60]

Robert disdained the conventional idea of the worker as a "cog" in the system, as he called it, merely doing the job assigned. And yet he had enormous sympathy for those forced into such a life. In some ways, the corporatized state of labor in his day fostered his romanticized view of frontier life and stoked his desire for freedom in his own life. Of course, he did achieve a semblance of freedom through his writing career, if only being a paid writer kept him away from menial jobs and at home doing what he loved. Although he would later sacrifice this freedom to care for his ailing mother, the idea of freedom—or individual liberty as best as it could be achieved—was critical for Robert. Without it, he felt that life was not worth living. This notion of freedom also speaks volumes about Robert's views regarding the ideal form of barbarism (and frontier life):

> In the last analysis, I reckon, I have but a single conviction or ideal, or whateverthehell [sic] it might be called: individual liberty. It's the only thing that matters a damn. I'd rather be a naked savage, shivering, starving, freezing, hunted by wild beasts and enemies, but free to go and come, with the range of the earth to roam, than the fattest, richest, most bedecked slave in a golden palace with the crystal fountains, silken divans, and ivory-bosomed dancing girls of Haroun al Raschid. With that nameless black man I could say:
> "Freedom, freedom,
> Freedom over me!—
> And before I'd be a slave,
> I'd lie down in my grave
> And go up to my God and be free!"

That's why I yearn for the days of the early frontier, where men were more truly free than at any other time or place in the history of the world, since man first began to draw unto himself the self-forged chains of civilization. This is merely a personal feeling. I make no attempt to advocate a single ideal of personal liberty as the one goal of progress and culture. But by God, I demand freedom for myself. And if I can't have it, I'd rather be dead.[61]

These ideals and thoughts are in fact the basis for many of Robert's characters, and principally for Conan the Cimmerian.

Closely tied to his discussion of freedom with Lovecraft was the topic of why each of them chose to sit at a typewriter and create stories for a living. Like many other writers, Robert E. Howard wrote to make money. The practical aspect of writing as a career was foremost in his mind. This was not the case for Lovecraft. He viewed writing as artistic expression, and getting paid was peripheral to his desire to create. For Robert, getting paid gave him a critical kind of freedom, at least from the menial jobs he so hated. The two writers would never see eye to eye on this issue. It should be noted that while Robert genuinely did write to get paid, and despite all his strenuous efforts to convince Lovecraft this was his sole reason for writing, if he were honest with himself Robert would ultimately have to admit that his writing to some degree was an art form. He had expressed a desire in the past to be known as a writer whose work would survive the test of time.[62] For that to be the case, Robert was aware that he had to maintain a strong sense of the artistic value of his work.

Despite their occasional differences and disagreements, Lovecraft's respect for Robert as a person and a writer was obvious. On several occasions, Lovecraft bragged about his Texas correspondent: "Robert E. Howard is a notable author—more powerful & spontaneous than even he himself realises." Lovecraft explained that "[Robert] tends to get away from weirdness toward sheer sanguinary adventure, but there is still no one equal to him in describing haunted cyclopean ruins in an African or Hyperborean jungle. He has written reams of powerful poetry, also—most of which is still unpublished."[63] In an April 27, 1935, letter to fellow pulp writer C. L. Moore, Lovecraft detailed Robert's abilities as a writer:

"Two-Gun Bob" will never be a hack because he puts so much of himself into his work—even his most ostensibly mercenary work. He is King Kull or Conan or Bran—or whatever may form the subject of any given tale. And not even what Clark Ashton Smith calls his "monotonous manslaughter" can spoil the vividness of his results. Nor do I know of anyone else who can throw such an aura of unholy, palaeogean antiquity about a lonely jungle ruin or a Cyclopean crypt beneath some mouldering, aeon-weighted city of horror & decay. Of all R. E. H.'s work I think I like the "Kull" stories most—though some of the newer things are fine. That "Queen of the Black Coast"—which appeared last spring or summer—flowered into sheer poetry in places.[64]

Based on Robert's lengthy descriptions of Texas and its history, Lovecraft also encouraged him to write about his region. "Most assuredly you must write that history of the Southwest. No one with your keen knowledge of the subject, and your positively genius-touched ability to 'put it over,' has any right not to!"[65] Elsewhere, Lovecraft told Robert, "I enjoyed tremendously your observations on the differences between East and West Texas—many of which confirmed what I had already thought." Lovecraft found that "the amount of variety within the state is impressive in the highest degree—and suggestive of the region's self-sufficient and almost imperial status. Every division of the US seems to be represented somewhere and in some way. Your remarks are a virtual treatise, and I wish they could achieve the permanence of print."[66] Toward the middle of the 1930s, Robert did in fact earmark a possible fictional (or even nonfictional) history of Texas and the western frontier.[67] But alas, beyond what he wrote in his letters, that account would go unwritten.

All of Robert's correspondence proved beneficial, in that it allowed him to express his philosophical, political, and religious views, which often could be discerned in his fiction. The letters of Robert E. Howard are quite engaging, and fantasy fiction fans and scholars alike have turned to them for helpful insights into his personal life and his writing career.

CHAPTER TEN

Novalyne Price

*A man of adventure. But a man in chains. A man shackled by his
own gentleness of nature. He was held firmly to a small town, to a
chair at a typewriter, bound by the chains of love and duty to an
old sick woman while he dreamed of another life, another time,
another exciting world.*

NOVALYNE PRICE, *ONE WHO WALKED ALONE*, 105

No one knew Robert E. Howard like Novalyne Price (Ellis),
who had a close relationship with him from 1933 to 1936.[1]
Novalyne's memoir about her time with Robert, *One Who
Walked Alone*, employs information from the journals she kept at the
time she knew him, including conversations she transcribed, events,
people, and the general atmosphere and attitude of that region of Texas
in the 1930s. The book provides a wonderful window into the life and
times of Cross Plains, its townspeople, Robert, and the Howard family. She reveals Robert's personality, mood swings, and political opinions, the current events of the 1930s, Robert's passion for history, his
writing habits, his relationship with both of his parents, and the Howard family dynamic. It is safe to say that *One Who Walked Alone* is the
best firsthand account covering the last three years of Robert's life. Tevis
Clyde Smith, who also wrote several personal accounts about Robert, declared, "I feel that the details which Novalyne recorded day by day present a vivid picture of Bob which will eagerly be received by her readers."
Smith further emphasizes, "This is her interpretation of the real man. If
the reader is surprised at some of her statements that person should be

assured that Bob was a very complex man and that Novalyne was well acquainted with him."[2]

Novalyne was twenty-five years old in the late spring of 1933 when Clyde Smith introduced her to Robert at her family's house and farm just outside of Brownwood, Texas. She and Smith had dated for a time, and in several of their conversations, Smith had revealed that Robert was a published author. Novalyne was an aspiring writer herself, so she was eager to meet an actual published author. Unlike most women at the time and in that area, Novalyne had adopted an early feminist perspective and had ambitions beyond being a housewife. After she graduated from high school, she worked various jobs to put herself through Daniel Baker College. Being young and a bit naive, she candidly reveals in her book her somewhat conventional expectations of what a writer (and therefore Robert) should look like:

> This man was a writer! Him? It was unbelievable. He was not dressed as I thought a writer should dress. His cap was pulled down low on his forehead. He had on a dingy white shirt and some loose-fitting brown pants that only came down to his ankles and the top of his high-buttoned shoes. He took off his cap and I saw that his hair was dark brown, short, almost clipped. He ran his hand over his head.[3]

Her thoughts about Robert's inauspicious appearance would occasionally be a point of contention when they began dating. And surprisingly, Robert often acquiesced to her expectations about his apparel and appearance.

In the summer of 1934, a year after she met Robert, Novalyne secured a teaching position at the Cross Plains high school. Enid Gwathmey, Novalyne's cousin, was head of the English Department and informed Novalyne about the job. In her interview with Nat Williams, superintendent of the Cross Plains schools, she revealed that at age fourteen she began teaching speech to junior high kids. She also had several years of experience giving private oratory and speech lessons to six students, making $18 per month. This extra income helped put her through college. Impressed with her experience, Williams and the board of trustees for the Cross Plains schools offered Novalyne the job. She was assigned to teach public speaking, English, and history. Her excitement about living in the same town as Robert almost dwarfed her excitement about the new teaching position.

Even though at this point in her life Novalyne's attention was primarily focused on a writing career, she had intentionally never mentioned that aspiration in her interview with Nat Williams. In *One Who Walked Alone*, Novalyne reports that "the prevailing attitude of the people throughout that section of Texas in the 1930s was discouraging to a beginning writer." Occupational expectations for younger people included clerking, bookkeeping, retail (at Higginbotham Brothers or Woolworths, for instance), teaching, farming, and such. "Sitting at a typewriter and writing stories indicated you were lazy, no-good, and were sponging off your poor old mother and grandmother."[4] That being the case, Novalyne learned to keep her writing aspirations to herself, especially in job interviews. Perhaps more than anyone else, she understood Robert's odd situation as a writer in Cross Plains. Many in town thought Robert was a ne'er-do-well, since he had no conventional job and still lived with his parents. Few realized that he was making a better living than just about everyone else in town. By the time she moved to Cross Plains, Novalyne had submitted her stories to several of the slicks, such as *Harper's, Collier's, Woman's Home Companion*, and the confession magazines, but had received only rejections. Being in the same town as Robert, she hoped to learn something from him about breaking into the writing game.

Novalyne spent the summer of 1934 settling into her room at the Hemphill boardinghouse in Cross Plains. She attended faculty meetings, met new people, and tried to acclimate herself to the small town. Meanwhile, her thoughts were on how she might connect with Robert. She soon discovered that making that connection was not as easy as she thought.

In 1934, Dr. Howard's office was located at Smith's Drugstore, directly across the street from Higginbotham Brothers, the general store. Novalyne's cousin Enid Gwathmey was a good friend of Mrs. Smith's, the owner of the drugstore. One afternoon while Novalyne and several other ladies were chatting with Mrs. Smith at the drugstore, Dr. Howard came out of his office and greeted them as he passed. Having never seen Dr. Howard, Novalyne inquired about him. A bit surprised, Mrs. Smith told her who Dr. Howard was, as if she should already know. Seeing this as an opportunity, Novalyne then asked Mrs. Smith if she knew Bob Howard.

As Novalyne tells it, her cousin Enid was alarmed at the question. Mrs. Smith nonchalantly answered that she knew a Robert Howard and then explained that Dr. Howard was Robert's father. With the subject of Robert introduced into their discussion, the other ladies exchanged suspicious glances. Novalyne explained that Robert made his living as a writer, as if that might assuage their misgivings. One of the ladies, Jimmie Lou, matter-of-factly stated that Robert was a freak. The other ladies agreed and chimed in, saying they had heard he was crazy. This was standard small-town gossip. At this, Novalyne became irritated and began defending Robert, explaining that she had already met him and thought he was nice. She then declared that she wanted to get better acquainted with him. The ladies offered her blank stares. Mrs. Smith shrugged her shoulders and told Novalyne that Robert was not very friendly; she only ever saw him talk to Dave Lee and Lindsey Tyson. Novalyne soon found out that these reactions to Robert were standard fare among most people in Cross Plains. But their opinion of Robert did not deter her from wanting to connect with him. Novalyne found the Howards' telephone number in the phone book at Smith's Drugstore and promptly called their house. The other ladies watched in stunned silence, startled by what they thought was her brazen behavior.

Though she did not realize it at the time, Novalyne's call to the Howard house would be her first encounter with the family gatekeeper, and thus a small glimpse of the Howard family dynamic. Mrs. Howard answered the phone and tersely explained to Novalyne that Robert was out of town, but she would let him know that Novalyne had called. After the call, Novalyne expected to hear back from Robert. She never did. In fact, she made several more attempts to contact Robert only to be told by Mrs. Howard that he was unavailable for various reasons. Novalyne soon realized that Mrs. Howard was not giving Robert her messages.

Frustrated, Novalyne took it upon herself to meet Robert by showing up at his house for an unexpected visit—the idea being that Mrs. Howard could not interfere if Novalyne was on their front doorstep and Robert was home. This incident, immortalized in the film *The Whole Wide World*, was Novalyne's first encounter with the entire Howard family.[5] It revealed an important aspect of Robert's writing habits. Novalyne described the moment in *One Who Walked Alone*:

> A thousand impressions impinged on my mind as I went down the walk. The house was average. A white frame house in need of paint. The walk was average. The yard was average, no better kept than the yards next door. Nobody here had done anything spectacular about

the place he lived in. I went up the steps and across the porch. I could
hear the sound of a typewriter and someone talking at the very top of
his voice. It sounded as if somebody were reading from a book while
someone else typed. I stood still at the door listening. Bob was writing
and talking at the top of his voice as he wrote.

Robert was in the habit of speaking his stories aloud as he typed them.
About this odd practice, he explained, "I find that if I talk them out—
hear the words as I put them down, the yarn goes a little smoother.
Sounds better when you read it."[6]

This was how Robert wrote stories for the better part of his writing
career. In fact, Mrs. Butler, the Howards' next-door neighbor, once com-
plained to Mrs. Howard about the noise Robert made. In a July 22, 1977,
interview, her son Leroy Butler, a friend of Robert's, reported that once,
when he returned home, he went next door to visit Robert. He found
Mrs. Howard to be less friendly than usual. He discovered sometime
later that his mother and Mrs. Howard had been in a quarrel. "I didn't
know what the quarrel was all about, until last year [1976], when I read
Jack's column about the neighbors complaining of [Robert's] typewriter
late at night."[7] The sound of the typewriter was probably compounded
by Robert speaking his stories out loud as he typed them.

On this surprise visit to the Howard house, Novalyne finally made
it past Robert's gatekeeper. This was also the first time she formally met
Dr. and Mrs. Howard. After brief greetings were exchanged, Robert
asked Novalyne to stay and chat for a spell, offering to drive her home
afterward. This first encounter with Robert in the presence of his parents, especially Mrs. Howard, furnished Novalyne with a solid idea of
how Mrs. Howard guarded her son. Both of Robert's parents guarded
their son while he worked, but especially Mrs. Howard, who was usually home for most of the day. When Novalyne asked Robert whether his
mother had given her messages to him, he replied,

> My family . . . they're damn good to put up with me staying around
> home writing all the time. Everybody in this town thinks I ought to
> be out working at some kind of job. That's hard on my family. And
> so I just tell them to hell with what people think. When I'm writing,
> I'm working. You know I'm working. To hell with everybody else. So
> when I get going on a yarn and somebody calls me, just tell them I'm
> working, or something like that. But I think you must have misunder-
> stood her.[8]

Robert had also instructed his mother to screen calls and answer the door while he was working. In 1934, Robert was twenty-eight, did not have a conventional job, and still lived at home. At the time, Novalyne did not fully grasp the dynamic between Robert's writing and Mrs. Howard's work as his gatekeeper. It was odd, however, that Mrs. Howard never gave Robert the option of returning Novalyne's calls, since she never relayed Novalyne's messages.

To some people in Cross Plains, Robert's writing work was altogether unusual. The town loved and admired Dr. Howard and his services, but, as Robert was aware, they blathered among themselves about his son. Novalyne knew why some people in Cross Plains did not understand Robert's job. She also knew why they behaved the way they did toward him. Only a few weeks before she met the Howards, Nat Williams, the superintendent of the Cross Plains schools, had lectured the teachers about their private lives and activities. Cross Plains schoolteachers were not allowed to play cards, drink, dance, or even go to picture shows. Novalyne, who was fairly progressive in her thoughts and ideas for a woman in those days, balked at these restrictions and thought them ridiculous. But she understood why the town of Cross Plains might have misunderstood Robert and his circumstances.

Novalyne later came to appreciate Mrs. Howard's role in Robert's life. In an interview in the late 1980s, she admitted that Mrs. Howard "was his guardian—she certainly kept young women from calling (*laughs*)—but she also helped, I think, to see to it that when he went in to the typewriter, he wasn't interrupted."[9] On occasion, Novalyne was warned by Clyde Smith that Robert was very attached to his mother and characterized him as tied to her apron strings. This notion bothered Novalyne and led her to hold Mrs. Howard in a certain degree of contempt.

When Novalyne began dating Robert, several things were already in motion. Robert was in the third stage of his writing career—producing adventure fantasy—but transitioning toward writing westerns. He had already created his most popular character, Conan the Cimmerian. By the fall of 1934, Conan was already a strong serial character in *Weird Tales*, which at that point had published ten of the seventeen Conan stories it would eventually publish. Robert was also in the middle of his correspondence debate with H. P. Lovecraft about the pros and cons of barbarism versus civilization. These preoccupations—the barbarian versus civilization subject and his character Conan—often permeated Robert's conversations with Novalyne.

In the fall of 1934, Robert was also a well-established writer, making a lucrative living. In fact, Novalyne thought that Robert made almost as much as Nat Williams.[10] Most importantly, Mrs. Howard and Robert had developed their strong symbiotic relationship by then. Besides guarding the front door and answering the phone to screen calls when he was writing, Mrs. Howard cooked and served Robert meals while he worked long hours. She also washed his clothes and cleaned up after him. Mrs. Howard made sure that Robert had the freedom he needed to focus on his work. In return, Robert took care of his mother as her health declined. He was adamant about the obligation he felt to look after her, especially since his father was away much of the time. For all intents and purposes, the relationship between Mrs. Howard and Robert was a kind of business partnership, and if something tried to interrupt that partnership, each of them—but especially Mrs. Howard—guarded the other as necessary.[11]

Novalyne experienced this symbiotic relationship when she first attempted to call the Howard house from Smith's Drugstore, as well as when she met Robert's parents at their home. When she and Robert left the house that first evening, they drove around for a spell. While they were out, Robert realized that he needed to give his mother her medicine. This bothered Novalyne; she had overheard him telling his mother that he would be back in time to give her the medicine. When she asked Robert why Dr. Howard did not give his wife her medicine, he answered, "It's my job. My dad is gone a lot of the time. When he's home he has to try to get some sleep. No telling when somebody will knock on the door for him to get up and go take care of a sick baby, man, or woman."[12] There was nothing unusual about this response. Dr. Howard was a small-town doctor, on call twenty-four hours a day, and he did spend long periods of time away, either seeing patients at his office or making house calls. Novalyne's frustration about Robert's solicitous care for his mother might have been due to a little jealousy.

On dates, usually automobile drives around the local area, Novalyne and Robert talked about civilization, history, and current events. She was enamored by Robert's passion for history and his ability to present the history of Genghis Khan through florid, captivating stories.[13] These kinds of topics, which Novalyne admitted she thoroughly enjoyed, made up the bulk of their discussions during the period when they dated, from 1934 to 1936. During this time, Novalyne sometimes found herself defending Robert from the opinions of certain townspeople. Unlike many in town, she had taken the time to get to know him. She tried to understand him, and she listened to him. Others in town, having made their quick assumptions about Robert, slandered him in conversation with one another.

Even Price's cousin Enid Gwathmey claimed that Robert was crazy and that his stories were inappropriate.[14] Other people in town gave Novalyne strange looks or sometimes made snide remarks about Robert. Novalyne received her share of verbal slings and arrows for merely dating Robert. To try to get people to realize that Robert was nothing like what they assumed from listening to silly rumors and seeing him around town doing odd things, she attempted to persuade him to attend social events and meet people.[15] Robert resisted. His awareness that people were ridiculing him behind his back would, of course, explain why he did not want to socialize with them.

After a while, Robert met Novalyne's mother and Mammy, her grandmother. She had talked to Robert about both of them, explaining that each had a certain history and personality. She felt dubious that Robert would be comfortable around them when they finally met, but he pleasantly surprised her. She explained: "I loved the way he was at ease when I introduced him to Mother and Mammy. He hadn't been that much at ease when I was introduced to him. With them, he was sure of himself. Poised."[16] Robert was immensely intrigued by Mammy, who was old enough to remember the Civil War. As they got to know each other, Robert became eager to see Mammy and would sit for hours to listen to her tell stories about the Civil War and other historical events, hanging on her every word. Understanding her rich history, Robert encouraged Novalyne to write stories about her Mammy's experiences.

On one of their excursions to Brownwood, Novalyne and Robert visited Dublin's Books so that he could purchase a history book. Since she loved books almost as much as Robert did, Novalyne looked forward to browsing the store's shelves. After visiting Dublin's Books, they window-shopped for a moment and then crossed the street toward Robert's automobile. As they crossed, Novalyne encountered a man she had known since childhood, and they exchanged greetings as they passed. When Robert inquired about the gentleman, Novalyne explained how she knew him and told Robert about the rumor that he was an illegitimate son of a prominent white man in Brownwood. Taking note of her words, Robert piped up and asked what she meant by a prominent white man. He understood the implication that the man was a mulatto.[17]

Robert's response sparked a heated conversation between them about this man and about African Americans in general. What ensued reveals much about Novalyne's and Robert's thoughts about race and racial tensions in the surrounding area. Hearing Novalyne talk so casually about this man disturbed Robert, and he got aggravated. She pointed out to Robert that he got aggravated only after finding out that the gentleman was not white, and that bothered her. Having exacerbated the situation, and in defense of the gentleman, Novalyne made an astounding claim: "At the end of the day when work is over, that man's white father . . . can go to the best restaurants in town . . . but that mulatto, his son, can't go in there by himself and sit down at a table and eat."[18] Novalyne declared that she thought the gentleman should have the same rights as his white father. Robert disagreed. Having never heard a woman say the kind of things Novalyne was saying, he warned her to not talk like that to anyone else but him.

To a certain degree, Robert was correct in warning Novalyne to keep these thoughts to herself. The racial ambience during that time and in that region, especially in the state of Texas, was hazardous and could be dangerous for those who opposed the established Jim Crow laws. And even though the Ku Klux Klan's political clout and activities had waned substantially since the late 1920s, there were still men who were part of that organization who occasionally made their presence known in an attempt to keep alive a general threat to anyone who questioned conformity.[19] Novalyne admitted that she thought Robert was surprisingly closed-minded about this issue, especially since he had been so open-minded about other issues.

Their conversation soon gravitated to white men secretly visiting the place in Brownwood known as "the flats," where African American women could be found for sexual encounters. Novalyne believed that if white men were willing to engage in that kind of conduct, risking pregnancy for the women involved, then those children should have the same rights as their white fathers. This position was exceptionally progressive in the mid-1930s, and had Novalyne been more vocal in her opinion she could have landed herself in a whirlwind of trouble. Completely surprised by Novalyne's perspective, Robert could only stammer, unable to provide a cogent response as to why he disagreed. He did manage to inadequately retort that men have certain needs. Perhaps Robert was shocked by Novalyne's remarks because he was uncomfortable talking about sexual relations with her at this point in their dating. Or he may have been guilty of the kind of behavior she was criticizing.

It is no secret that Robert, on several occasions, visited the Mexican border town of Piedras Negras, across from Eagle Pass, Texas. There is some evidence that on one of these visits Robert had sexual relations with a Latina prostitute. He seems to indicate as much in an undated let-ter to his friend Tevis Clyde Smith.[20] If this did in fact happen, Robert may have been stammering because he certainly would not have wanted to discuss his own sexual experiences with Novalyne. Instead, he simply asked Novalyne where she got these ideas.

In response, Novalyne explained that when she was a young child, she went on a walk with her mother, her grandmother, and her Aunt Georgia (her mother's sister, who was thirteen at the time), and they stopped and visited with the Georges, a locally known African Amer-ican family. While all the adults chatted among themselves, Novalyne played with the Georges' two girls, who were about her age. Oblivious to any racial divide between them, Novalyne and the George girls played together as if they were close friends. When it came time to leave, Nova-lyne told Robert, she waited for her grandmother to tell the Georges to come and visit sometime. When this did not happen, Novalyne turned to the two girls and invited them to come play at her house. She said she remembered the awkwardness that lingered for a few seconds afterward, followed by uncomfortable laughter from all the adults. She simply did not understand the implication of what she was proposing, but the two African American girls did, and they laughed too. As a child, this sur-prised Novalyne, since she saw the Georges not as a black family in a Jim Crow state but as friends.

On the way home, her Aunt Georgia called Novalyne crazy for in-viting the two girls to their house. What happened next left an indel-ible impression on Novalyne for the rest of her life. As she told Rob-ert, her grandmother responded to Georgia by saying, "Mr. George is a good man. He pays his debts, works hard, and keeps his place look-ing clean and nice. I've never heard a word against him. I'd rather be around him and his family than around some white man who doesn't pay his debts, doesn't keep his place up, runs around, gets drunk, and things like that."[21] Taking her grandmother's words to heart, Novalyne believed that people should be judged by their reputations and their be-havior, not by the color of their skin.

Robert listened to Novalyne's story and sarcastically declared that Novalyne and her grandmother made a fairly strong case, but then re-treated to taking the conventional Jim Crow view of the day. He re-minded her that if blacks were found on the streets in Coleman and other small towns in the area after dark, they would be run out of town, or worse. In spite of those Jim Crow laws, Robert told Novalyne, he did not necessarily disagree with her or her grandmother, insofar as the behavior of black or white men was concerned. He used examples he had heard of former slaves who escaped their masters, moved out west, and made honest citizens of themselves. They had certain standards they adhered to, as all men should. But he then revealed to Novalyne his own racial beliefs, which he had incorporated into a few of his stories.

In that day, Robert held to a popular but faulty idea that African Americans came from a different line, with different blood. If races were mixed and mingled, the result was a mongrel race, and indeed this was one of the root causes, he believed, of the collapse of any civilization. Of course Novalyne disagreed with him; she boldly retorted, "If a man's going to fight to keep his race pure, don't let him go down to the flat and leave a half-white, half-black child down there."[22] She reiterated her belief about the rights of a mixed child and then stressed the failure and hypocrisy of those white men who behaved in such a fashion.

One source of Novalyne's great empathy for African Americans and their plight was the fact that she and her family had once experienced a racial attack. When she was younger and her family lived near Santa Anna, Texas, her father was mistakenly identified as a Native American. His life was threatened, and she and her family barely made it out of town alive. No matter what Robert's opinions were, or how hard he tried to convince her otherwise, she held fast to her views, remaining far more progressive and sympathetic to people of different races than Robert was.

By the middle of 1935, after many dates, discussions, movies, and drives on country roads, both Novalyne and Robert had hinted at their love for each other. They had discussions about marriage, and about spending their lives together. Novalyne never grew accustomed to the way Robert talked about his mother, placing her on a pedestal. She also was never comfortable with Robert's incessant need to make certain that his mother was cared for, even if that meant stopping by his house while they were out on a date. She maintained the opinion that Dr. Howard, not Robert, should be responsible for the care of Mrs. Howard.[23] The longer they dated, however, Mrs. Howard's behavior changed. She became friendlier to Novalyne, especially when Novalyne telephoned. Mrs. Howard would greet her politely and ask her to wait while she got Robert on the phone. Still, Novalyne remained ambivalent. And though she continued to date Robert and to assess him as a potential spouse, she was cautious. Then Robert removed all doubt from her mind.

One evening when Robert was discussing cowboys and their freedom (possibly related to a story he was working on), he explained to Novalyne that "cowboys had to be free. They couldn't be tied down to a woman; a woman cramps a man's style. A man's got to be free—free to roam the world." Robert then admitted feeling that "a wife would handicap a man."[24] Novalyne listened and remained silent. She later explained in her book, "I knew that no wife could ever keep his feet so firmly planted in the plot of ground he resided on as his mother kept his. I wondered, as he raved and ranted about a woman's handicapping a man, killing his freedom, if he felt his mother's chains."[25] This was the irony that Novalyne noticed in Robert's claim, at least as she perceived it. In her view, Mrs. Howard had stolen Robert's freedom, and she wasn't entirely wrong. Novalyne assured Robert that she wasn't planning on asking him to marry her and emphasized that she enjoyed her freedom too.

Robert made it clear on that day, and on subsequent dates, that any wife of his would stay at home, cook his meals, keep the house clean, wash his clothes, answer his phone calls, and guard the front door. All the things his mother did for him. Novalyne was unwilling to be that kind of wife, especially since she had plans of her own. It wasn't long after this that she began to date other men. When she dated Truett Vinson, Robert's friend from Brownwood, a few times, she and Robert had a falling-out. A brief but heated altercation ensued, conducted through letters, but after a while they reconciled and began casually dating again.

It was never the same. From that point on, Novalyne considered Robert strictly a friend. She had been good for Robert at a time when he may have needed her most. Between 1934 and 1936, most of Robert's friends were either married or involved in their own careers. She provided a good outlet for his ideas, thoughts, and feelings and was also brave enough to put him in his place when needed.

Robert sometimes expressed his frustration—often in the context of *Weird Tales* not paying him what they owed him—about not being able to help his mother as much as he would have liked. It became apparent to Novalyne that Robert was paying for his mother's medical expenses. Like many other rural areas in the United States, Cross Plains was suffering financially from the Great Depression. This part of the country survived by hunting and canning meat and by farming, both home gardens and large crops. Cash was somewhat scarce during this time, and Dr. Howard compassionately would often receive livestock or produce as payment for his services. This left the Howards cash-deficient, and the onus was on Robert to use what money he made to tie up the financial loose ends. Robert stoically helped, but the strain was tremendous. He rarely discussed personal family matters with anyone, not even with his closest friends. Novalyne had developed a relationship with him like no other he had experienced, however, and he occasionally confided in her about these matters.

On one such occasion, Robert told Novalyne, "My dad has a great talent, more than a place like Cross Plains realizes; Brownwood would have been much better; but if he were to leave here, he'd settle for some place no bigger and no better than Cross Plains." After he confessed this, Novalyne reports that Robert immediately slipped into a comedic and breezy kind of caballero act. It was as if he was using humor to remove himself from the situation—to escape a harsh reality. Robert "started [singing] that old tune of his about a woman tying a man down, keeping him from being free." She bravely asked if that was the way Dr. Howard felt about Mrs. Howard. Robert immediately stopped singing, took a deep breath, and began to defend his father. He explained that when his father was younger, he thought he could save the world through medicine. Robert paused, then turned his attention back to his mother, his responsibility to her and commitment to taking care of her. Novalyne didn't want to hear this. Robert then admitted, "I suppose the truth is that as good a man as my father is, he doesn't always appreciate how helpful and good Mother has been to him. If he'd gone to a larger place like Brownwood, he might have been able to be at home more; then Mother and I wouldn't have been left alone so much at night."[26]

Even though Robert defended his parents, it is likely that he was frustrated with them, especially his father, for placing a financial burden on him. Robert, of course, was never actually obligated to continue living with his parents. He made enough money to support himself. To a certain degree, he may have felt trapped, being his mother's primary caregiver. He may have felt that he owed it to her for the care and support she gave him as a child and in his early years as an aspiring writer. Whatever the case, despite his feelings of frustration toward his parents, Robert stayed devoted to his mother and continued to defend his father. Nevertheless, the burden of helping the one and standing up for the other, verbally and financially, likely took a heavy toll on him.

Robert's revelation about his mother's frustration with Dr. Howard's payment practices causing a serious cash deficiency and his being away most of the time may have led Novalyne to ask Robert why Mrs. Howard did not just leave Dr. Howard if she was that unhappy with him. He was shocked that she could suggest such an idea. In an attempt to justify her suggestion, Novalyne explained the circumstances behind her mother's separation and divorce from both her father and stepfather,

her mother's second husband. With some disapproval, Robert explained that his mother believed that once you marry, you ought to stay married regardless of the circumstances. With this response, Robert essentially admitted that because of his mother's adamant stance about marriage and divorce, she would sacrifice and endure anything in her life with Dr. Howard. Of course, this admission reveals only Mrs. Howard's strong stance about staying married no matter what, not anything about any frustrations she may have had with Dr. Howard. Nor does it reveal a possible desire on her part to divorce him. Both possibilities, however, are strongly implied. In all this, Robert never revealed anything further than the frustration he expressed to Novalyne in this conversation about his parents.

Novalyne ultimately realized that she would never be anything to Robert except his friend. An ambitious young woman, she eventually admitted that she preferred teaching over a writing career. To that end, she applied to the graduate department for speech at Louisiana State University (LSU). After being accepted, she left for Louisiana in the middle of May 1936, intending to keep in touch with Robert through correspondence, but she never saw or heard from him again. On June 15, 1936, Novalyne received a telegram, dated June 11, 1936, from Pat Allen, a friend she dated briefly in Cross Plains. The telegram, which was delivered several days late, conveyed the tragic news about Robert.

CHAPTER ELEVEN

Broken on the Plowshare of Fate

*For life to be worth living, a man—a man or woman—must have
a great love or a great cause. I have neither.*

ROBERT E. HOWARD TO NOVALYNE PRICE ELLIS,
IN *ONE WHO WALKED ALONE* (1986, P. 269)

Robert E. Howard had endured difficult circumstances before,
but none like what he endured the last year of his life. Events
transpired and accumulated that caused him a great deal of
stress, drained his energy, and threatened his creative mind. Taken together, these events were like a sword of Damocles suspended over him,
revealing the perilous nature of his happiness and freedom.

To begin with, Robert's relationship with Novalyne Price had never
been completely stable. By the summer of 1935, the two were slowly
growing apart. Since Robert had indicated more than once that he did
not want to be tied down by a woman, Novalyne began to date other men
and develop her own career plans.

In the meantime, Robert's writing career, while not necessarily
stalled, was shifting directions. He confessed to Novalyne that he was
growing tired of writing Conan stories and wanted to turn his attention
to writing a novel about frontier Texas. He also feared that his creative
well was running dry. To make matters worse, *Weird Tales* was slow in
paying him for some stories it had already published. From 1935 to June
1936, the amount that *Weird Tales* owed Robert kept mounting.

His changing relationship with Novalyne and concerns about his
writing career only compounded the stress he experienced from his
mother's declining health. He spent quite a lot of time taking her to var-

ious hospitals, health specialists, and clinics. And when Dr. Howard was unable to pay for her care, Robert took on the financial burden of covering those costs. The time he devoted to caring for his mother also heavily taxed his writing time, compounding the frustrating sense that his writing career was toppling around him. Ironically, the very thing that had provided him with the freedom to write—the support of his parents, especially his mother—was now demanding that freedom back.

In *One Who Walked Alone*, Novalyne reports that on February 24, 1936, Robert was waiting for her at the Hemphill boardinghouse when she arrived home from work. He wore his nice brown suit that she enjoyed so much. Novalyne sensed that something was wrong. Robert's shoulders drooped, he looked distracted and weary, and his eyes were filled with questions. He wanted to drive around for a while, admitting that he had something to tell her.

During the time Robert and Novalyne dated, each felt love for the other, but never at the same time. There were moments when Novalyne wanted Robert to tell her that he loved her, but he never did. Hurt by this, she had hoped that a day would come when the tables were turned, when Robert would want to hear a declaration of love from her but she would remain silent. She thought that this might be that moment finally, but she hoped against hope that it was not. To offset her fear, all Novalyne could think to do was make jokes to lighten the mood, teasing him, for instance, about his mustache. But Robert was not in the mood for jokes. His mood was quite sullen, and he was reaching out. This was a cry for help.

They drove to nearby Rising Star, talking along the way. Novalyne asked Robert how Mrs. Howard was doing, and he responded that she was not well. He then confessed, "Everything is falling in on me at once. I'm going to do all I can to get her to hang on and get well."[1] Robert explained that the constant care his mother required had made him unable to write and he felt utterly defeated. This upset Novalyne. She wondered what might happen to Robert when his mother died. How would he react to her death? Would he continue to write? He told her that his mother was suffering serious night sweats and that the need to change her wet bedding was keeping him up all night. Novalyne protested and asked why Dr. Howard was not helping. Hurt and defeated, Robert explained that with his father away much of the time, he felt responsible for helping his mother and simply did what needed to be done.

Novalyne continued to protest that the responsibility was not his alone and suggested that he and Dr. Howard hire a nurse to help with the care. She was genuinely concerned about Robert's livelihood, probably because she understood that writing was Robert's passion, his dream. She emphasized the need for him to write. Feeling as if she was missing the point, Robert desperately confessed, "Work is not worth a damn, unless you work for somebody you love. All my life I've loved and needed her. I'm losing her. I know that. Damn it to hell, I know that. I want to live. You hear that?" Then the one thing Novalyne feared most happened. Robert spoke up and said, "I want to live! I want a woman to love, a woman to share my life and believe in me, to want me and love me. Don't you know that? My God, My God. Can't you see that? I want to live and to love."[2] Panicked, Novalyne reverted back to teasing Robert about his mustache, which merely made him feel dismissed and defeated.

Once again, Robert and Novalyne were not on the same page in their relationship. She had moved on because of her previous attempts to express her love for him, and he was realizing what he wanted, but too late. Novalyne was unwilling to replace Mrs. Howard in Robert's life, not because she was incapable or unworthy, but because she was so fiercely independent and unwilling to take on providing the services that Mrs. Howard had provided her son. Not knowing how to respond, she once again made light of the situation and joked about Robert's mustache. Unamused, Robert grabbed her, pulled her close, and said, "If you don't love me, say so, damn it. I know you loved me once. Is it over?"[3] Confused and saddened, Novalyne again emphasized Robert's need to write, to not lose that passion. She complimented his talent, his brilliance as a writer, and warned against putting aside his writing to care for his mother. Then, in tears, she confessed that she did not love him, or anyone else for that matter.

Then Novalyne told Robert that she had been accepted into the master's program for speech at Louisiana State University, and that she intended to leave Cross Plains in May. Defeated, Robert slumped back down into his seat. He assured her that she would make a great teacher. After a long silence, he started the car, turned it around, and drove back to Cross Plains. On the drive home, Novalyne expressed her passion for teaching; however much she loved to write, she said, she felt that teaching was her true calling. "You have a great cause," Robert responded. "For life to be worth living, a man—a man or woman—must have a great love or a great cause. I have neither." Still trying to be whimsical, Novalyne replied, "Shave your mustache and love will come."[4] She laughed at her own joke, but not Robert. He remained silent the rest of the drive back to the boardinghouse as Novalyne continued to assure him about his writing talent and opportunities. Frustrated, Robert asked her to not say another word.

As they pulled up to the boardinghouse, Novalyne told Robert that there was no need for him to walk her to the door. She got out of the car and walked toward the front porch. Robert just stared at her. She turned and said that she hoped Mrs. Howard would feel better soon. He remained silent. Novalyne watched Robert for a minute, hoping he might say something. He kept his empty gaze down the street, no longer acknowledging her presence. It was at this point, Novalyne admits in *One Who Walked Alone*, that she fully realized how ineptly she had handled the situation. A feeling of remorseful anger washed over her. She noticed Robert's shoulders sagging and how terribly defeated he looked. Without saying good-bye, he started the car and slowly drove away.

Decades later, Novalyne realized that this moment in Robert's life had been critical. She came to understand the amount of stress he was enduring and the sacrifice he made to care for his mother, to the point of sacrificing the thing he loved most: his writing. In a speech at the 1988 World Science Fiction Convention in New Orleans, Novalyne declared:

> The spring of 1936 was so full of stress that Bob was overcome. With his pessimistic view of life, his lack of self-confidence, his many problems, his lack of sleep . . . stress did not permit him to look beyond these crises to *hope* they would pass and that life would be worth living. He could not hope. He could not believe.[5]

By late spring of 1936, the Howard house was a flurry of activity. Dr. Howard and Robert had hired several nurses and a maid.[6] Dr. Howard moved his office from Smith's Drugstore to his house, making it much easier for him to attend to Mrs. Howard while still having access to his patients. This change of locale brought people who needed his services to the house at all hours of the day and night. To provide help, colleagues of Dr. Howard's periodically visited the house to perform whatever services were needed for Mrs. Howard. Having spent years being guarded by his mother, who maintained silence in the household so that he could focus and work, Robert now had to try to write in this swirl of noise and interruptions. He was simply unable to do so.

On several occasions between July 1935 and April 1936, Robert traveled to various hospitals and clinics with his mother (or both his parents) for her to undergo certain procedures.[7] The driving involved in several of these trips to closer locales, like Coleman, Texas, ate away at the time

Robert spent researching and writing. In his letters, he had told several people that the care he gave his mother was often overwhelming and always time-consuming.[8] Dr. Howard would report to H. P. Lovecraft on some of Robert's behavior during one of these trips:

> Last March, a year ago, again when his mother was very low, in the Kings Daughters Hospital in Temple, Texas, Dr. McCelvey expressed fear that she would not recover. [Robert] began to talk to me about his business, and I at once understood what it meant. I began to talk to him, trying to dissuade him from such a course, but his mother began to improve.[9]

Thereafter, Dr. Howard kept watch over Robert, as best as he could. This was not the first time Robert had expressed that he might take his own life after his mother passed. On one such occasion, Dr. Daughtery of Brownwood asked Novalyne Price if Robert had ever indicated that he wanted to take his own life after his mother died.[10] The thought (and threat) was always present that Robert might take his own life, possibly before his mother died but more likely afterward. In fact, Dr. Howard wrote E. Hoffmann Price that

> three times [Robert] made complete preparation to do this thing [take his own life] during his mother's illness of something more than a year. Each time that his mother began to get in a bad way and death was expected, Robert would begin to set his house in order and tell me that he did not intend to stay on this earth after his mother was gone. I tried to persuade him from this and talked to him a great deal, but each time complete preparations were made for going, but as his mother would react and show promise of even partial recovery, he would become normal again and spring into his work with renewed energy.[11]

By the late spring of 1936, Dr. Howard was on high alert, keeping his eye on Robert as Mrs. Howard's health worsened.

By 1936, Robert relied more on his agent Otis Adelbert Kline to submit stories to new markets, in hopes of not only expanding his markets but to also garner additional income to help pay for his mother's medical expenses. Kline sold to *Action Stories* several of Robert's humorous westerns that featured Breckinridge Elkins. Kline also managed to sell a few more of Robert's western stories to *Argosy*.[12] As mentioned earlier, between the Great Depression and poor money management, *Weird Tales*

"A BOX OF MONKEY'S"

Hester Jane Ervin (center) with her half-siblings. Photo was probably taken in Exeter, Missouri (date unknown).

Robert E. Howard, age seven or eight, circa 1913–1914.

Cross Plains, Texas, circa 1910s.

Truett Vinson in his front yard in Brownwood, Texas, December 28, 1924.

Dr. Isaac Howard, studio portrait (date unknown).

Tevis Clyde Smith,
circa 1927.

Robert E. Howard and Patches in front of the Howard house, Cross Plains, Texas
(date unknown).

Robert E. Howard (left), Lindsey Tyson (center), and Tevis Clyde Smith (right) (date and place unknown).

Robert E. Howard, teen boxer (date unknown).

H. P. Lovecraft.

HOWARD P. LOVECRAFT
First Vice-President U. A. P. A.

Robert E. Howard (date and place unknown).

Novalyne Price (Ellis), photo taken at the time she and Robert E. Howard dated.

Robert E. Howard, studio photo taken specifically for Novalyne Price.

Robert E. Howard with his parents: Robert, Hester, and Isaac (date unknown).

Robert E. Howard at Fort McKavett in Menard County, Texas, July 9, 1933. "I like this snap; it makes me feel kind of like a Vandal or Goth standing amidst the ruins of a Roman fortress or palace" (Howard to H. P. Lovecraft).

had slowed payments to its authors, but the magazine continued publishing their stories. This put a heavy strain on Robert's finances. Novalyne Price confirmed in *One Who Walked Alone* that Robert was in fact making sales to *Argosy* and *Action Stories*, and she indicated that *Weird Tales* owed him about $1,000.[13] The amount *Weird Tales* owed Robert would only increase. At one point, Robert wrote *Weird Tales* editor Farnsworth Wright, pleading for the money the magazine owed him.[14] Robert probably received an empty promise from Wright that *Weird Tales* would make good on what it owed him. But Robert needed money, not empty promises.

By mid-May of 1936, Robert, for the most part, had given up trying to write. He did, however, have a substantial output of previously written stories that he and Kline continued to submit to various magazines. Some of these stories had been accepted for publication in *Weird Tales* in 1935 and were slated to appear in a summer 1936 issue (or later).[15] Instead of writing, Robert was devoting all of his time and attention to his mother, whose death, he knew, was imminent. In a May 9, 1936, letter to fellow pulp writer August Derleth, he wrote, "When a man dies young he misses much suffering, but the old have only life as a possession and somehow to me the tearing of a pitiful remnant from weak old fingers is more tragic than the looting of a life in its full rich prime." Robert admitted to Derleth, "I don't want to live to be old. I want to die when my time comes, quickly and suddenly, in the full tide of my strength and health."[16] Robert may have been hinting to his fellow pulp writers that he intended to end his own life, but these other writers were distant, thousands of miles away, and had no idea how much stress Robert was enduring.

Though Robert was surrounded by people in his house, he was very much alone. Novalyne had left for Louisiana, and Robert's Brownwood and Cross Plains friends were either married or deeply involved in their own careers. With his mother suffering and her death looming, Robert began putting his house in order. By the second week of June 1936, he was spending his time going back and forth between his mother's bedside and his own room. While in his room, he kept the door closed. Kate Merryman, one of Mrs. Howard's caregivers, said later that when Robert's door was open, she had seen papers scattered everywhere.[17] Dr. Howard continued to do his best to keep an eye on Robert.

Among the people present in the Howard home during this time was Dr. Dill, a colleague of Dr. Howard's and another Cross Plains medical doctor who frequently came to the Howard house to help care for

Mrs. Howard. Kate Merryman reported that another doctor, this one from Brownwood, possibly Dr. Daughtery, would also make trips to Cross Plains to drain fluid from Mrs. Howard's lungs.[18] Mrs. Green, a licensed nurse, was at the Howard house more frequently, to assist Dr. Howard and Dr. Dill. Finally, Leah King, a maid hired by Dr. Howard, helped clean dishes, cook, and clean the house during the shifts when Merryman and her sister Alice Younglove were off.

Between shifts, Kate Merryman would sometimes cook for the men in the house. She reported that Robert loved it when she made pancakes. Just days before his mother's death, Robert began drinking large amounts of coffee to keep himself awake. This was unusual since he had never enjoyed coffee. When he was not in his room working or at his mother's side trying to comfort her, he paced. According to Merryman, he "walked a lot. Just walked the floors. He'd go in there and stay with [Mrs. Howard], and she pretended to be better than she was."[19] This would raise Robert's spirits a little, but he soon went back to worrying and pacing.

In interviews from the 1970s, Merryman revealed that Mrs. Howard confided to her that Robert wanted to take his own life once she died, but also said that Mrs. Howard was certain she had talked Robert out of that idea.[20] Other than Dr. Howard and Kate Merryman, there is no indication in any of the extant interviews or letters that anyone else in the house knew about Robert's intention to take his own life. Dr. Howard would later regret not telling the other doctors and nurses about Robert's potential plan.[21]

On the morning of June 10, 1936, Mrs. Howard slipped into a coma.[22] For the better part of that day, Robert stayed by his mother's side. On the evening of that same day, Dr. Howard was relaxing on the front porch swing, most likely trying to rest and get a bit of fresh air.[23] Robert went outside with him and began pacing up and down the concrete walkway. Alice Younglove reported that Robert "walked out to the end of [the concrete walkway], and he'd come back and face the porch, and he'd stop and look at Doctor Howard. Then he'd go back and walk some more; and every time he'd come up to the porch, though, he'd just stop and look at his daddy." Dr. Howard watched Robert as he paced, probably wondering if Robert was about to follow through on his threat to take his own life. "Doctor Howard said he believed that [Robert] was going to kill him [Dr. Howard]," she said, "because he [Dr. Howard] went down there [to Greenleaf Cemetery in Brownwood] and prepared for three funerals."[24] It is possible that Dr. Howard thought Robert might kill him at the same time he intended to kill himself. However, Dr. Howard did not purchase cemetery plots from Greenleaf Cemetery in Brownwood until June 14, 1936.[25]

It is more likely that when Robert was pacing up and down the walkway, stopping at the porch and staring at his father, he was deciding his own final fate and wondering how his father would be affected. As he paced back and forth on the front walkway, he may also have wondered whether the death of Mrs. Howard followed by his own would cause Dr. Howard to have a fatal stress-related heart attack. The idea of killing his father probably never entered Robert's mind. It seems extraordinarily dubious that Robert was even capable of murder, much less the murder of his own father.

All that night, as during the two previous nights, Robert remained awake and drank cup after cup of coffee. Dr. Howard and others in the house reported that Robert was oddly cheerful. Dr. Howard even said that sometime in the small hours of the morning Robert approached him and said, "Buck up, you are equal to it; you will go through it all right."[26] Given how he had reacted the previous times Mrs. Howard was on the verge of death, Robert's behavior completely disarmed Dr. Howard, and he let his guard slip ever so slightly.

The next morning, on June 11, 1936, Robert asked one of the attending nurses if she thought Mrs. Howard would ever recognize him again.[27] She feared not, the nurse told Robert. He did not respond, but simply walked away, knowing this was his opportunity. Dr. Howard did not realize that Robert had spoken to the nurse. Afterward he admitted in a letter, "I did not think [Robert] would kill himself before [Mrs. Howard] died, but I knew it would be difficult to prevent it afterward."[28] After speaking with the nurse, Robert quietly slipped out the back door, walked to his car, and rolled up the windows. He paused a moment, then put a gun to his head and pulled the trigger. The bullet entered "just above the temple, just above and behind the left ear. It came out the other side."[29] He survived the gunshot wound for approximately eight hours and never regained consciousness. Robert E. Howard died at 4:00 p.m. on June 11, 1936. His mother, Mrs. Hester Jane Ervin Howard, died thirty-one hours later, at approximately 11:00 p.m. on June 12, 1936.

CHAPTER TWELVE

The Aftermath

He was a man—take him for all in all, I shall not look upon his like again.

H. P. LOVECRAFT ON ROBERT E. HOWARD (QUOTING *HAMLET*), IN DERLETH AND TURNER, EDS., *H. P. LOVECRAFT: SELECTED LETTERS: 1934–1937*, VOL. 5

A loud scream jolted Dr. Howard when he was drinking coffee and conversing with another doctor who was at the Howard house the morning of June 11, 1936.[1] The cook cried out that Robert had just shot himself.[2] Both men jumped up and darted out the back door toward Robert's car. Dr. Howard recalled the event in a letter to H. P. Lovecraft:

> The cook standing at the window at the back part of the house, saw him go get in his car. She thought he was fixing to drive to town as he usually did, when she heard the muffled sound of the gun, she saw him fall over the steering wheel. She ran in the house and called the physician who was in the house. The doctor was taking a cup of coffee in the dining room and I was talking with him. We rushed to the car and found him. We at first thought that it was a death shot, but the bullet had passed through the brain.[3]

Dr. Howard and his colleague carried Robert to the back porch of the house and helped him as best they could, but both quickly realized that nothing could be done. The next eight hours may have been the longest eight hours of Dr. Howard's life. He reported later that Robert never regained consciousness. Alice Younglove, who was at the house as Robert lay dying, thought that he might have been suffering. Years later, she reported, "I just felt badly when he [Robert] was dying. He was suffering so. . . . Oh he was suffering. I looked at him . . . every breath was a moan."[4] Younglove's account is interesting, but even if Robert was moaning, he was probably not conscious, as Dr. Howard indicated in his letters.

Word about Robert's death spread through the small community of Cross Plains. A few people hurried to the Howard house to offer help. By 12:00 p.m., Jack Scott from the *Cross Plains Review* had arrived to get the facts about Robert's situation.[5] That afternoon, the *Brownwood Bulletin* carried a story on the lower front page of its afternoon paper: "Robt. Howard, Cross Plains, Tries Suicide."[6] The *Abilene Daily Reporter* also ran a story on the front page of its afternoon newspaper, headlined "Young Author Shoots Self."[7] When these stories went to print, Robert was still alive. The next morning, after Robert's death but before Mrs. Howard's death, the headline for the June 12 *Cross Plains Review* read: "Tragedy Shocks City Thursday."[8] This report, probably written by Jack Scott, provides details about Robert's suicide and briefly describes some of his publishing accomplishments. All of these stories featured similar accounts of the event, likely stemming from Jack Scott's initial report on June 11.

Between Robert's and Hester's deaths, the other doctors present at the Howard house attempted to convince Dr. Howard to check into a hospital. They feared that the stress of Robert's suicide and Hester's imminent death might be too much for him to bear and he might suffer a heart attack.[9] Witnesses at the house said that Dr. Howard was terribly upset, and they feared he might collapse. Despite these warnings, Dr. Howard refused to go to a hospital. When Robert finally succumbed to his gunshot wound, his body was taken and prepared for burial. Still exhausted from his son's suicide, Dr. Howard turned all his attention to Mrs. Howard, who died the following evening.

It is uncertain what caused Mrs. Howard's death. If there was ever a formal written diagnosis, it has not surfaced. On her death certificate, Dr. Howard indicated three causes of death: chronic ulcerative tuberculosis, uremia, and senility. In a letter to Farnsworth Wright, pleading for money owed him for stories already published, Robert had revealed that Mrs. Howard had her gall bladder removed sometime around April 1935, a dangerous surgery at the time for a woman her age (she was sixty-four). Complications arose after the surgery and an abscess developed. She was then taken to a hospital in Coleman, Texas.[10] Seven months later, in November 1935, Mrs. Howard was checked into the Torbett Sanatorium in Marlin, Texas, where, according to Robert, more than a gallon of fluid was extracted from her pleura.[11] Pleural effusion can be caused by tuberculosis, as well as by kidney disease. This would certainly explain Dr. Howard's diagnosis of uremia on Mrs. Howard's death certificate.

By the time his wife died, Dr. Howard was probably experiencing extreme stress and fatigue. But somehow, undoubtedly with the help of close friends and colleagues, Dr. Howard managed to organize a double funeral for his wife and son. On June 14, 1936, the day of the double funeral, Dr. Howard purchased five burial plots at Greenleaf Cemetery in Brownwood.[12] Earlier in the week, he had selected identical caskets. The funeral services, held at 10:00 a.m. at Baptist Tabernacle in Cross Plains, were quite an affair, with multiple ministers and a large attendance. To allow people plenty of time to arrange transportation to the interment, it was not held until the afternoon, at 1:00 p.m. at the cemetery. The June 19 issue of the *Cross Plains Review* reported that members of Mrs. Howard's family from Ponca City, Oklahoma, and Exeter, Missouri, attended the funeral. Dr. Howard's brother David and his wife, who were living in Mart, Texas, also arrived to help support and care for Dr. Howard.

The Baptist Tabernacle sanctuary filled quickly that morning, and some had to stand in the back or wait outside. Those who were present later declared that one thousand or more people attended. The officiant was Reverend B. G. Richburg, a Baptist minister in Big Spring, Texas, and former pastor in Cross Plains, and a friend of Dr. Howard's. He was assisted by Reverend Mann, a local Methodist minister, and the Reverend S. P. Collins, a local Presbyterian minister. Reverend Mann was probably there on behalf of Mrs. Howard, who had been an active member of the Methodist church in Cross Plains and Burkett. It is uncertain why Collins was present. The Baptist Tabernacle pastor, V. W. Tatum, also assisted. To the surprise of many who attended, considering everything he had endured in the previous few days, Dr. Howard spoke during the service. Publicly, Dr. Howard expressed joy at how well the service and burial were performed. Privately, he confided to a few friends about being frustrated with one of the preachers and his sermon. Years later, in a 1977 interview, Norris Chambers, a close family friend of the Howards', admitted, "Dr. Howard wasn't satisfied with the sermon. For weeks he talked about the preacher sending his boy to Hell. And he was tore up about that: he wasn't satisfied at all."[13] The offending preacher was never mentioned by name. It has been suggested that it was the Reverend Richburg, and that he preached a hellfire-and-brimstone sermon from I Samuel 31:4.[14] That passage is about the suicide of Saul, the first king of Israel, and the implication of the sermon was condemnation for those who kill themselves.

After the service and interment, when everyone had returned to their daily lives, Dr. Howard focused on organizing his house and, more specifically, Robert's room, papers, and estate. This would have been a daunting task for anyone, let alone a man of Dr. Howard's age. Seeing the immense undertaking that confronted him, Kate Merryman and Norris Chambers offered their help. Chambers not only helped organize but also typed letters and official documents for Dr. Howard.

Initially, the work was simply sorting through the pages of Robert's stories, which were scattered about the room. As they sorted pages, Kate Merryman found a single-page document in Robert's handwriting. As far as she could determine, it was a will indicating that Lindsey Tyson was to be the recipient of all of Robert's property. Merryman handed the piece of paper to Dr. Howard. He read it, jumped to his feet, and told her not to mention what she had found to anyone else. He then left the room with it, and the document was never seen again.[15] Whatever attempts Dr. Howard made to hide the handwritten will, Lindsey Tyson admitted years later that he was aware of its existence. In a 1978 interview, Tyson declared, "A few days after the suicide, on the street in Cross Plains, a lawyer said to me that Bob had made a will leaving everything to me; but Dr. Howard had destroyed the will. I didn't feel like trying to do anything about it."[16] Tyson probably could have done little at the time without possession of the actual document. And why Dr. Howard did what he did was never explained, by him or by anyone else.

Days after the funeral, the pulp writer Catherine L. Moore received a letter about Robert's death from Thurston Torbett of Marlin, Texas, who was a close friend of the Howards. Moore then sent H. P. Lovecraft a postcard, on June 16, informing him of Robert's death. From that postcard, the news spread rapidly throughout the pulp writing community. On June 24, Dr. Howard wrote Moore about Robert's death (though she knew about it by then), and Moore replied the following day. Within twenty-four to forty-eight hours after he wrote to Moore, Dr. Howard sent letters to E. Hoffmann Price and Lovecraft. Soon these authors were writing return letters of condolence, igniting a regular correspondence. The *Weird Tales* community (mainly Lovecraft's core group of writer correspondents, later called the Lovecraft Circle) rallied together to write memorials for some of the various magazines, informing readers of Robert E. Howard's death. Dr. Howard also contacted Kline and Wright in an attempt to collect money owed to Robert and to decide what needed to be done about those stories that had been accepted but were not yet published.

The July 1936 issue of *Weird Tales* was already at the press and being printed when Robert died. Wright, still struggling to keep the magazine afloat (and still late in paying his writers for their stories), combined August and September 1936 into a single issue to curb costs. It was in that August/September 1936 issue of *Weird Tales* that Robert's death was announced in "The Eyrie." Wright declared: "Mr. Howard for years has been one of the most popular magazine authors in the country. He was master of a vivid literary style and possessed an inexhaustible imagination."[17] After praising and briefly describing Robert's characters, Wright then claimed credit for discovering the budding author. But his tribute mistakenly included several inaccurate details about Robert's life. For instance, Wright said that Robert had his first story published in *Weird Tales* while he was a student at the University of Texas.[18] This was one of several inaccuracies about Robert's life and suicide that circulated for several decades (a few of which will be examined later in this chapter).

Wright's memorial tribute would trigger an outpouring of letters to *Weird Tales*. Readers, stunned by the news of Robert's death, sent letters of condolence, praising his stories. These responses continued for months after the initial announcement. Wright noted in the January 1937 issue of *Weird Tales* that letters about "Robert E. Howard's untimely death continue to come in to the editor's desk. They are letters of appreciation of his genius, and of sympathy and condolence."[19] *Weird Tales* published several more of Robert's stories: "The Black Hounds of Death" (November 1936), "The Fire of Asshurbanipal" (December 1936), and "Dig Me No Grave" (February 1937). The month following Robert's death, in July 1936, *Weird Tales* published the first part of the three-part series "Red Nails," the last published Conan story. The second and third parts appeared in the August/September and October 1936 issues. The first part was the cover story for the July issue and would be the last *Weird Tales* cover story for Robert E. Howard's character Conan the Cimmerian.[20]

Even though *Weird Tales* continued to publish its backlog of Robert E. Howard stories, fans knew that this would not last forever. In the February 1937 issue, one fan expressed his dismay: "It fills one with an almost nameless dread to contemplate future issues of WEIRD TALES without the name Robert E. Howard gracing its pages."[21] Other fans wrote in requesting reprints of Robert's stories. Julius Hopkins of Washington, DC, wrote to *Weird Tales* and declared, "Robert E. Howard's death is truly a great loss to our magazine, for he was one of the real masters of weird fiction. . . . I suggest that you print a collection of his best works, selections made by the readers of WT."[22] This idea was discussed in "The Eyrie" in several subsequent issues, but without results. However, the idea was not completely lost. After establishing Arkham House Publishers in 1939, August Derleth and Donald Wandrei were the first in the United States to publish a collection of Robert's work, *Skull Face and Others*, published in 1946.

On other fronts, Julius Schwartz's *Fantasy Magazine* published H. P. Lovecraft's "In Memoriam: Robert Ervin Howard" in September 1936. In his October 1936 "Eyrie" column, Farnsworth Wright printed a portion of a July 1, 1936, letter from Lovecraft about Robert's death, as well as a portion of E. Hoffmann Price's memorial.[23] Wright concluded with a small bit of information that had been circulating about a couplet that Robert typed shortly before his death:

> All fled—all done, so lift me on the pyre;
> The feast is over and the lamps expire.

At the time, these lines were believed to have been a paraphrase from a line in Ernest Dowson's poem "Nom Sum Qualis Eram Bonae sub Regno Cynarae" (shortened to "Cynara"): "But when the feast is finished and the lamps expire."[24] Years later, however, it was discovered that Dowson's poem was not the source of Robert's couplet.[25] It was more likely that Robert combined several lines from "The House of Caesar" by Viola Garvin. Her poem has five stanzas, each ending with a couplet and the exact same phrase:

> . . .
> All done, all fled, and now we faint and tire—
> The Feast is over and the lamps expire!
>
> . . .
> All well, all good—so hale from sun and mire—
> The Feast is over and the lamps expire!
>
> . . .
> All fled, all done—a Caesar's brief desire—
> The Feast is over and the lamps expire!
>
> . . .
> Lo—we who moved the lofty gods to ire—
> The Feast is over and the lamps expire!

. . .

All dim, all pale—so lift me on the pyre—
The Feast is over and the lamps expire![26]

It is easy to see what Robert did with Garvin's poem to make it his own epitaph. Dr. Howard first mentioned Robert's couplet in the postscript of a June 27, 1936, letter to E. Hoffmann Price. He informed Price that the couplet was found typed on a white slip of paper in a billfold in Robert's hip pocket. Dr. Howard found the slip of paper the same day he wrote to Price. Two days later, in a letter dated June 29, Dr. Howard told Lovecraft the same thing, adding that he thought the lines were typed shortly before Robert's death.

Once Lovecraft received Dr. Howard's letter, he began writing letters to other *Weird Tales* writers. Lovecraft also wrote a letter to Farnsworth Wright, detailing what Dr. Howard relayed to him about the couplet Robert typed prior to his death. This is how the couplet and details about it ended up in "The Eyrie" of the October 1936 issue. Wright assumed that the lines were a paraphrase of Dowson's "Cynara," though his piece did not name Dowson's poem. Several decades after Robert's death, an idea developed that these lines were typed by Robert, then left in his typewriter and discovered later.[27] Dr. Howard's letters and his account of the event certainly correct that false idea.

Dr. Howard spent years attempting to collect the outstanding payments owed by *Weird Tales*. He also worked closely with Otis Adelbert Kline to settle Robert's estate. The two continued to submit manuscripts that had been either rejected before or never submitted. Early on, shortly after Robert's death, Dr. Howard donated his son's personal library and pulp magazine collection to Howard Payne College. The collection included almost three hundred volumes of fiction and nonfiction and approximately fifty volumes of poetry and drama. He asked a few of Robert's colleagues from *Weird Tales* to contribute to the collection in honor of Robert. In a few of his letters, Dr. Howard said that the collection was set apart from the general circulation, but this was probably not the case. The school's library called the collection the Robert E. Howard Memorial Collection, but distinguished these volumes from those in its general circulation only with a bookplate on the inside cover of Robert's books.

Over time many of the books were stolen, lost, or damaged by regular use. On several occasions, Dr. Howard visited the school's library and discovered that the magazines had been so heavily used that the back covers were wearing down or coming completely off.[28] He eventually removed the magazines from the library to preserve them, hoping that they could be used to publish a volume of collected Conan stories.[29] Years later, what books were left from the Robert E. Howard Memorial Collection were gathered and donated to Project Pride of Cross Plains. The few remaining books from the original collection are currently on display in a single lawyer's bookcase at the Howard House and Museum in Cross Plains, Texas.

By 1942, Dr. Howard had moved to Ranger, Texas. He had retired from practicing medicine but answered the high demand for doctors when the United States entered World War II by resuming his practice. In 1943, he sold the house in Cross Plains. Dr. Howard remained in Ranger the rest of his days and died on November 12, 1944. Toward the end of his life, he wrote in a letter that he loved his son's poems. "They are a mirror of himself. He wrote his life into them and behind him stands his quiet, unassuming poetic mother. She was a poet, although she never wrote poetry for publication."[30] It was through Robert's poetry that he saw his son's genius, but recognized the influence of Hester Howard as well. Dr. Howard also understood the quality and value of Robert's Conan stories. For three or four months, from late 1936 to the spring of 1937, he tried very hard to get Farnsworth Wright to release the rights to the Conan stories. On several occasions, Dr. Howard and Otis Adelbert Kline discussed the idea of publishing a single volume of Conan stories, but nothing came of it.

Nevertheless, Conan the Cimmerian and Robert E. Howard's other characters survived the test of time. They continue to be published today. And Conan the Cimmerian eventually became an iconic figure in popular culture.

CHAPTER THIRTEEN

Writing a Legacy
SELECTED STORIES

I am convinced that if stories such as these have any lasting value, it is in revealing the kind of work young pulp-writers were doing in those days when rates were low and one had to make a typewriter smoke in order to keep eating.

HUGH B. CAVE (PULP WRITER AND CONTEMPORARY OF ROBERT E. HOWARD), FROM *MURGUNSTRUMM AND OTHERS* (CHAPEL HILL, NC: CARCOSA PUBLISHERS, 1977), X

Robert E. Howard's professional publishing career lasted a brief twelve years, from 1924 to 1936. In those few years, Robert wrote more words than many other authors write during careers lasting two to three times longer. These twelve years can be somewhat easily divided into three periods: the early fiction (1924–1928), the historical fiction (1928–1932), and the adventure fantasy fiction (1932–1936). Each period lasted approximately four years, and they overlap, as one period transitioned into the next. It should be noted that in many ways Robert's stories respond to events in his own life, including the markets he attempted to breach, his experiences of Texas and the Cross Plains oil booms, the writers who influenced him, and his correspondence. In this sense, he is no different than any other writer. Story was everything for Robert. He was raised on stories and often viewed life in terms of story. Robert was always telling stories, whether telling tall tales to his friends and correspondents or writing stories for various magazines. Everything was a story.

Prior to his first professionally published work, Robert produced a smattering of both humorous and serious history, mystery, and adventure tales as an amateur (juvenile) writer from 1919 to 1923 (interestingly, also a four-year period). This amateur period, while experimental, was a necessary stepping-stone leading him into a professional writing career. As an amateur, Robert submitted works with unabashed courage to professional publishers, mainly the magazines he frequently read. This amateur period was critical in that Robert sharpened his writing skills to a level where he discovered his own voice and developed his trademark narrative style and pace. Both would ebb and flow throughout his early twenties, changing in reaction to circumstances. For instance, his correspondence with Preece and Lovecraft significantly changed both the style and content of his stories. Though he eventually made these his own, his stories would retain the influence of these two writers to the end of his life.

Robert's formative years and his father's nomadic nature and practice were integral to the development of many of his characters, especially his adventure fantasy characters. Even after he moved away from writing Conan stories to focus instead on western fiction, the influence of these early life experiences on his creative mind never waned, not even toward the end of his life. The themes from those frontier experiences of his youth—the ideal freedom and independent ability to survive on one's wits and skill—always resurfaced. In fact, that motif emerges prominently in the bulk of Robert's tales. As we will see, even a few Conan tales failed to escape Robert's passion for frontier and western expansion.

Before examining selected stories, I first present an overview of Robert's three professional publishing periods. The period between 1924 (when "Spear and Fang" was published) and 1928 is what I call Robert's experimental or early fiction period. He experimented with several genres, such as horror, history, and fantasy. It was during this period that Robert began to incorporate adventure elements into his stories. He also nailed down his prose pace, which is arguably the strongest aspect of his fiction. In this early fiction period of discovery, Robert used historical characters and elements to create some nice historical fiction, if somewhat juvenile in style and prose. These early writing experiences led into his second period of publication, what I call his historical fiction period, from 1928 to 1932. This period clearly shows Robert using aspects of the history he was researching at this time, as well as the history he had read earlier.

Between the first period (early fiction) and the second period (historical fiction), Robert published stories that included two key characters: Solomon Kane and Kull of Atlantis. These characters eventually helped to generate the stories of his third period of publication, the adventure fantasy period. The fantasy fiction works from the third period (the Conan the Cimmerian stories), along with the Kull of Atlantis stories, ultimately spawned the sword-and-sorcery subgenre in the modern fantasy fiction publishing industry. From 1932 (with the first publication of Conan) to 1936, Howard's primary attention was on adventure fantasy, set in the Hyborian Age he created. Toward the end of this period, shortly before his death in 1936, Robert turned his attention to writing more westerns. Had he lived and continued writing, it could be argued, he would probably have embarked on a fourth period—western fiction.

Toward the latter part of the first period and up to the early part of the third period, Robert published boxing stories that did not neatly fall into any of the three categories that characterized his three writing periods. The boxing stories, written throughout the three periods, stand alone as their own genre. Robert also wrote a smattering of horror fiction throughout his writing career and utilized horror elements within just about every genre in which he wrote.

A simple chart of Robert E. Howard's writing career looks something like this:

1919–1923	*1924–1928*	*1928–1932*	*1932–1936*
Juvenile, Amateur	*Early Fiction*	*Historical Fiction*	*Adventure Fantasy*
All early stories published in school or local newspapers	Smattering of genres, some historical	Primarily historical, some fantasy	Primarily fantasy, some western

Tracking these periods according to Robert's influences, correspondences, publishing markets, and life events is fairly easy. This chapter examines a selected number of stories and their cultural underpinnings, and what might have inspired Robert to write them. It is important to know that publishing markets had an especially large influence on what Robert wrote and where he published.

Between Robert's historical and fantasy adventure periods (1928–1936), he wrote a number of fantasy fiction tales in which he experimented with an assortment of weird and horrific elements. *Weird Tales* was the perfect platform for this kind of literary ingenuity. The end result was a new species of fantasy fiction. These stories were so influential in the fantasy fiction genre that a decade or so after their first publication a handful of professional authors who wrote stories in a similar vein named this new subgenre of fantasy fiction: sword-and-sorcery.

It is important to note that Robert did not set out to create and develop a new species of fantasy fiction. To a large extent it came about because of Robert's eagerness to expand his publishing market and publish in new pulp magazines. He tried new ideas and subverted several genres in the process. Decades after Robert's death, dozens of new writers cut their writing teeth on Robert's stories and wrote similar fantasy fiction. One group of them gathered to discuss and sometimes quarrel about what genre to call their own works. Some of these writers would become members of a Robert E. Howard fan group known as the Hyborian Legion:

> Beginning in 1950 Gnome Press, one of the small science-fiction specialty houses which sprang up shortly after World War II, brought out a complete edition of the then known Conan stories under John D. Clark's editorship. This was the foundation of the present-day Howard fandom, the Hyborian Legion, and, of course, *Amra*.[1]

How this group found a name for this new species of fantasy fiction is quite intriguing. On November 12, 1955, twelve fans of Robert E. Howard gathered for a group meeting in Philadelphia to establish the Hyborean Legion.[2] (*Hyborian* Legion from here on). The officers for this club were nominated and voted in: Martin "Marty" Greenberg (King of Aquilonia), George Heap (Royal Chancellor), John D. Clark (Count of Poitain), Oswald Train (Royal Sorcerer), L. Sprague de Camp (Royal Chronicler), and Manny Staub (Commander of the Black Dragons). Poul Anderson, Fritz Leiber, and George Scithers were also present. To keep their thoughts and ideas circulating, a few short months after this November meeting the Hyborian Legion developed its own journal, *Amra*, which was published and edited by George Scithers and others.[3]

From this first meeting in 1955 until 1961, various members of the Hyborian Legion discussed and debated what to call this subgenre of fantasy fiction. With the publication of Gnome Press's seven-book Conan series, J. R. R. Tolkien's *Lord of the Rings* (1954–1955), and other fantasy stories and the advent of the mass market paperback book, fantasy fiction, like science fiction, was beginning to experience its golden age of development and publication. Fans of fantasy fiction began to create magazines and fanzines about their favorite authors and their works. One such fanzine, *Ancalagon*, was founded in March 1961 to discuss the works of J. R. R. Tolkien. It was edited by none other than the Hyborian Legion's own Royal Chancellor, George R. Heap. Keeping in step with the ongoing debate about what to call Robert E. Howard's brand of fantasy and similar kinds of fantasy fiction that had been published up to 1961, Heap wrote an article for the first issue of *Ancalagon* titled "On Fantasy-Adventure."

In his essay, George R. Heap explained that the term "fantasy-adventure" was "not actually generally accepted" as the name for the new subgenre. He added that a "better description was discussed at the last Hyborian Legion muster, but of several suggestions, none seemed to be completely satisfactory."[4] To address this dissatisfaction with the terms suggested by that point, Heap offered what he called a "three point definition" to determine three criteria for being able to call a story "fantasy-adventure."[5] Heap's three criteria were (1) a strong element of the supernatural, such as spells, wizardry, and so on; (2) a single strong hero; and (3) the world-background of the story.[6] Interestingly, these have been the primary criteria for several subgenres that fall under the fantasy fiction genre, such as epic fantasy and heroic fantasy. However, Heap's three-point definition served the purposes of the Hyborian Legion's discussion and they used it to move forward in their discussions. Through the ensuing decades the definition would be expanded upon by other writers and by the dictionaries and encyclopedias of fantasy fiction.

Two Hyborian Legion members, L. Sprague de Camp and Fritz Leiber, supported Heap's three-point definition and, in the next issue (April 1961) of *Ancalagon*, offered their own term for the new subgenre. De Camp declared, "I must give my vote to 'fantasy-adventure' as a name for this new literary division; I can't imagine what possible better name the Hyborian Legion could have thought they would find."[7] In addition to proclaiming his support for Heap's term, however, de Camp also provided a two-page caveat correcting (or as de Camp called it, "bone-picking") Heap's three-point definition. In the same issue, Fritz Leiber ignored Heap's suggested term and offered up his own: "sword-and-sorcery." Leiber's term was only one step away from George Scithers's initial ad-hoc term, "sword-play-and-magic type of adventure story."[8] Apparently, Leiber did not necessarily intend to suggest "sword-and-sorcery" as the formal term for the subgenre. He explained:

> At any rate I'll use sword-and-sorcery as a good popular catchphrase for the field. It won't interfere with the use of a more formal designation of the field (such as the "non-historical fantasy adventure" which

Sprague once suggested in a review of Smith's *Abominations of Yondro* [*sic*] in AMRA) when one comes along or is finally settled on.[9]

Leiber used the term "sword-and-sorcery" for the rest of his career. Just one month after Leiber's suggestion was published in the April 1961 *Ancalagon*, a brief article by Michael Moorcock was published in the May 1961 *Amra*. Similar to Heap's "On Fantasy-Adventure," Moorcock's "Putting a Tag on It" suggested a basic general formula for determining which stories belonged to the new subgenre:

A) Hero[10] must get or do something,
B) Villains disapprove,
C) [Protagonist][11] sets out to get what he wants anyway,
D) Villains thwart him one or more times (according to the length of story), and finally,
E) [Protagonist], in face of all odds, does what the reader expects of him.[12]

After delineating his formula—which is akin to Joseph Campbell's "monomyth" in *The Hero with a Thousand Faces*—Moorcock listed stories that he thinks follow it: E. R. Eddison's novel *The Worm Ouroboros* (1922), James Branch Cabell's novel *Jurgen* (1919), J. R. R. Tolkien's *The Lord of the Rings* series (1954–1955), T. H. White's book *The Once and Future King* (1958), Fritz Leiber's Gray Mouser/Fafhrd series, and Robert E. Howard's Conan series. "The roots of most of these stories are legendary, classic romance, and dubious ancient works of 'History.'"[13] All of the stories Moorcock listed are quite different in style, type, and content within the overarching genre of fantasy fiction. The first four are more appropriate for Moorcock's formula than the last two, which are short story series. With that in mind, Moorcock explained how these shorter works fit into his formula:

Conan and the Grey [*sic*] Mouser generally have to start at point A, pass wicked points B and D, and eventually win through to goal— point E. Anything else, in the meantime, is extra—in fact, the extra is that which puts these stories above many others. The Ringbearers in Tolkien's magnificent saga do this also.[14]

Moorcock further explained that "every one of these tales, almost without exception, follows the pattern of the Old Heroic Sagas and Epic Romances."[15] In other words, he considered these stories to be quest stories, with roots that were "legendary, classic romance, mythology, folklore, and dubious ancient works of 'History.'"[16] As such, Moorcock suggested, these were stories in a newly developed subgenre that could be called "epic fantasy."[17]

Both "epic fantasy" and "sword-and-sorcery" would eventually be used, but would designate two distinct fantasy subgenres. The first four stories Moorcock listed—*The Worms of Ouroboros, Jurgen, The Lord of the Rings*, and *The Once and Future King*—would be classified as epic fantasy, along with dozens like them. "Sword-and-sorcery" remained the term used for stories more akin to Robert E. Howard's adventure fantasy stories, such as his Kull and Conan stories. These latter stories met Heap's criteria. Finally, responding to Moorcock's suggestion, Fritz Leiber reiterated in a July *Amra* issue his opinion published in *Ancalagon*:

> I feel more certain than ever [that this field] should be called the sword-and-sorcery story. This accurately describes the points of culture-level and supernatural element and also immediately distinguishes it from the cloak-and-sword (historical adventure story)—and (quite incidentally) from the cloak-and-dagger (international espionage) story too![18]

Both "sword-and-sorcery" and "epic fantasy" are still in use today, and both subgenres remain officially recognized as distinctive. Even so, debate continues about which stories fit into which subgenre.

It is important to understand that the Hyborian Legion included several published and popular science fiction and fantasy authors. These authors were attempting to create a name for a subgenre that included not only Robert E. Howard's work (and other previous authors who wrote in a similar vein) but also their own works in the fantasy fiction field. These writers were particularly influenced by Robert's stories and had written their own popular works for a similar category. The criteria they suggested outlined a "rule of writing," so to speak, for their own work to follow so that it would fit into this new subgenre. It is here that Robert's work, especially his Kull and Conan stories, played an important role: their criteria (especially Heap's three-point definition) were primarily based on Robert's stories. Robert's fantasy adventure stories can be described as "sword-and-sorcery" because these authors considered him the "father" of this subgenre.

As influential as Robert's fantasy fiction was to the development of the fantasy genre, these stories constitute merely a small portion of Robert's entire fictional output. Selecting only a certain number of stories from Robert's twelve-year publishing career to consider in this chapter was not an easy task. There are multiple key stories from each of the three periods of his career—far too many to cover in a single chapter. I would encourage any Robert E. Howard fan to read all of his stories from each period, since each played an important role in his publishing career. That being said, I selected stories based not on the period in which they were published but on other factors: the main protagonist of the story (Solomon Kane, Kull of Atlantis, and so on), the elements in the story (such as the mixing of genres or tropes), and the influence on the story from either Robert's correspondence or outside political or cultural events. Robert wrote his stories for a plethora of reasons, and some are easier to discern within the stories than others. To this end, let us now delve deeply into these selected stories in order to gain a much better understanding of Robert E. Howard, both the person and the writer.

In his brief writing career, Robert professionally published about 138 stories (a few were published posthumously). Among those stories, Robert created several characters who have stood the test of time and have thrived in various other media, including film, comic books, subsequent publications, board games, video games, and graphic novels. To different extents and in different media, four of Howard's characters were more popular than all others: Solomon Kane, Kull of Atlantis, Bran Mak Morn, and Conan the Cimmerian. These four characters inhabit the stories that together constitute the genre Robert is most widely known for—sword-and-sorcery. They also encapsulate the storytelling style that Robert gravitated toward, at least during these twelve years of his life. All of Robert's other stories either point to or reflect the prose style of these stories—action-driven, highly charged narratives that grab hold of readers and keep them absorbed from start to finish.

Most of Robert's literary influences can be seen in one way or another in the stories about these characters. These stories also encapsulate much of his thirty years of living—his experiences of Texas; the sordid people of the two major oil booms in Cross Plains; his travels to other regions of the Southwest, to Louisiana, Oklahoma, Arkansas, and Missouri; and what can be gathered about his thoughts concerning politics and other current events. That is not to say that Robert's life and influences are not reflected in his other stories—of course they are. In fact, a few isolated stories reflect all of these influences better than the stories with his four most popular protagonists. And some of his other stories stand on their own in terms of popularity and content. For instance, the horror story "Pigeons from Hell," with its powerful southern gothic tone and style, is like no other story that Robert wrote. Another distinctive story is "The Black Stone," one of the more popular and influential stories, based on the Cthulhu Mythos. Although heavily influenced by H. P. Lovecraft, it stands on its own merits and demonstrates Robert's keen ability to take Lovecraft's cosmic horror motif and blend it brilliantly with his own captivating narrative and writing style. I could go on about other such stories, and I do discuss a few of his stories that are not written about one of his four main protagonists, but that is not my point here. These stories that do not belong to the subgenres in which Robert excelled demonstrate that he certainly had the ability to broaden the range of his content and bring his signature style to any genre. That style is often shown to best effect, however, in the stories of those four characters.

Robert's discovery of *Adventure* magazine in 1921, at age fifteen, opened a new door to a world of writers who left a lasting impression on his creative mind. By that age, Robert was probably already reading the works of Rudyard Kipling and Jack London. Along with Edgar Rice Burroughs and his Tarzan works, these writers' stories reflect Jean-Jacques Rousseau's idea that it is civilization that inflicts evils on mankind. For Robert, these authors sowed the seed for the idea of the feral protagonist—the notion that when they are away from civilization, people can genuinely thrive in unrestrained freedom and become stronger. We could say that it was these ideas from Robert's early influences combined with the writers Robert read in *Adventure* (Harold Lamb, Rafael Sabatini, Talbot Mundy, and Arthur O. Friel) that produced Solomon Kane, Kull of Atlantis, Bran Mak Morn, and especially Conan the Cimmerian.

The July 3, 1921, issue of *Adventure* carried a story titled "The Prize" by Rafael Sabatini. In that same year, Sabatini's novel *Scaramouche* was published. By the 1920s, Sabatini's stories—pirate tales highly charged with swashbuckling action and adventure—were growing in popularity across the United States. Robert gravitated toward these stories, even as a young child. It is uncertain whether he discovered Sabatini through one of his novels or in *Adventure* magazine. What is certain is that shortly after the summer of 1921, when he discovered *Adventure*, Robert created Solomon Kane.

Solomon Kane inhabits a rich world that combines the swashbuckling pirates of Sabatini's stories with the African jungle settings of stories by Rudyard Kipling and Arthur O. Friel. For Christmas of 1925, when

Robert was nineteen, Tevis Clyde Smith gave his friend a copy of Sabatini's book *The Snare*. In it, Smith wrote a message indicating that the
story's language would shock the sensibilities of the Puritan. Smith went
on to indicate that he and Robert had little love for Puritans. This is not
surprising given that in central west Texas where the two were raised
the normative form of fundamentalist Christianity maintained puritani-
cal ideals and restrictions. Both young men would have rejected such re-
strictive beliefs and behaviors.

It is hardly coincidental that the Solomon Kane stories strongly reflect Sabatini's adventurous swashbuckling style, even though Kane is
a Puritan of the late sixteenth to early seventeenth centuries. Robert's
character roams mainly between Europe and Africa, exacting what he
believes to be God's justice, which, in his estimation, is swift retribu-
tion against those who murder or commit other malicious sins. Like the
pirates of Sabatini's stories, Solomon Kane fights with a rapier. He also
brings a flintlock pistol and dagger to conflicts and confrontations.

Solomon Kane was introduced to the reading public in "Red Shadows," the cover story for the August 1928 *Weird Tales*. Curtis Charles Senf
(C. C. Senf) did the artwork for the cover. Senf was notorious for skim-
ming over the stories he illustrated, if he even read them at all. For "Red
Shadows," he probably read just enough to recognize Sabatini's swashbuckling influence on Robert's story, so his cover art depicts Solomon
Kane as something like a pirate. Kane is wearing a pirate's hat and a red
cape. Solomon Kane looks nothing like Senf's illustration in Robert's description of him in the stories. This would not be the only time Senf mis-
represented this protagonist in his art for the Solomon Kane stories. He
did it again with the interior art accompanying the story "The Footfalls
Within," published in the September 1931 issue of *Weird Tales*. Apparently, not remembering how he depicted Kane for "Red Shadows," Senf
showed him in the art for "The Footfalls Within" as a late nineteenth-
century tropical explorer dressed in the standard cotton canvas safari
garb, with knee-high dark boots and a kind of pith helmet. And instead
of a flintlock musket pistol, Kane is sporting a late nineteenth-century
long-barrel revolver.[19]

Regardless of the artist's blunders, Solomon Kane was well received
by *Weird Tales* readers. Robert's first published Solomon Kane story,
"Red Shadows," is an unequivocally swashbuckling story full of wonderful sword-play and adventure, presented at a quick and captivating narrative pace. After "Red Shadows," one of the ways in which Robert developed his Kane stories was by incorporating elements of horror. He had

previously published two works of horror in *Weird Tales*, "In the Forest of Villefère" and "Wolfshead." Given Robert's pleasure in subverting genres, it is no surprise that for his fourth Kane story published in *Weird Tales*, "The Moon of Skulls," he created a vampire character.

"The Moon of Skulls" was divided into two parts, to be published in two *Weird Tales* issues, and the first part was selected as the June 1930 cover story. The story begins with Solomon Kane struggling to climb the side of a mountainous cliff. Robert slowly develops the setting of the story through the details of its environment and the other characters whom Kane encounters at the beginning of the story. This clever device maintains readers' attention by keeping them guessing about Kane's location. Upon reaching the top of the cliff, Kane encounters a large black tribesman—a hint that the story might be set in Africa. For readers in 1930, this detail also would have given the story line a mysterious tension and sense of awe. After the two awkwardly introduce themselves, Kane tells the tribesman that he is in search of the vampire queen of Negari. Baiting his reader, Robert does not reveal why Kane is looking for the vampiress—whose name, the tribesman reveals, is Nakari. He agrees to lead Kane to her. As they venture forth, more and more tribesmen emerge from hidden places along the path and follow behind Kane and the first tribesman. Sensing an ambush, Kane prepares for the worst. His keen instincts serve him well when an ambush does indeed occur.

From this point in the story, the action increases. Eventually, the story reveals that Kane is actually searching for a captive of Nakari's, a girl named Marylin. Some years before, Marylin was sold to a Barbary rover by Sir John Tafaral, who confessed the deed after Kane fatally pierced him with his rapier in a duel. Now, after escaping the tribesmen's ambush, Kane inadvertently discovers the entrance to a cave where the Negari are hidden underground. He finds the vampire queen Nakari and discovers that she has been abusing Marylin. Lesbianism and sadism are hinted at in the story. Kane is tempted by the beauty of Nakari, described as a mysterious ancient creature who is already old at the height of the Egyptian empire; Nakari is even older than the Babylonian empire. She is a character who lives in a day when the world is young, before recorded time.

"The Moon of Skulls" is somewhat racially charged, as were many of the stories Robert read in *Adventure* magazine. There was widespread stereotyping of minorities in the literature and entertainment of the 1920s and '30s, and Robert engaged in the practice as well. Even so, though the antagonist in "The Moon of Skulls" is typically stereotyped, she is portrayed in a unique fashion. Solomon Kane is clearly infatuated with the ancient black female vampire Nakari and captivated by her beauty and litheness. She tempts the Puritan with the promise of a kingdom if he will join her in ruling the people of Negari by marrying her. This proposal puts Kane in a position similar to that of Jesus being tempted by Satan in the wilderness after his forty days of fasting, or of Samson being seduced by Delilah into telling her the source of his strength, thereby enabling her to ensnare him. The biblical allusions are subtle, but they serve the story well, especially given that the protagonist is a Puritan.

One striking scene in "The Moon of Skulls"—which is sometimes overlooked in light of other elements in this story—is a brief story within the story. As Kane escapes capture in Nakari's palace, he stumbles upon a captive, a dying man who describes his ancient home and how it fell. This man tells Kane of the city of Atlantis and its being engulfed by the sea. He goes on to describe how his own ancient people, the sons of Atlantis (those who escaped Atlantis's demise), eventually enslaved all other races until those races rose up, especially the Negari, to rebel against his ancient people. This brief account is important for several reasons. It nicely supports Robert's character Kull, who is from Atlantis, and neatly weaves a connection between Solomon Kane's world (though Kane admits to the man that he has never heard of Atlantis) and Kull's history. It also presents a motif that Robert uses in many subsequent stories: the detrimental effects of slavery on those nations that incorporate it into their way of life. Robert believed that slavery was especially pernicious when masters practiced miscegenation with their slaves and blended their peoples (as described in "The Moon of Skulls"). We take a closer look at this idea when we discuss "Black Canaan."

Readers liked "The Moon of Skulls" well enough, but were not overly enthusiastic about the story. But the character Solomon Kane soon became one of their favorites as subsequent Solomon Kane stories appeared in *Weird Tales*. From August 1928 to July 1932, Solomon Kane appeared in seven stories published in *Weird Tales*. Since then, the character has been seen in comic books (from Marvel and Dark Horse) and in paperback books (from Centaur Press, Bantam Books, Baen, and others). The latest print iteration is a single Del Rey trade paperback collection of the original Solomon Kane stories titled *The Savage Tales of Solomon Kane*. In addition, the film *Solomon Kane* from director Michael J. Bassett was released in 2009. Though the film lacks any semblance of Robert's original story lines, it is a nice sword-and-sorcery genre film. The Solomon Kane stories are excellent examples of how Robert began incorporating weird elements into his action adventure stories to ultimately develop the sword-and-sorcery subgenre of fantasy fiction. Of course, Robert's first sword-and-sorcery story was not a Solomon Kane story. That honor belongs to another one of his popular characters, Kull of Atlantis.

"The Shadow Kingdom," published in the August 1929 issue of *Weird Tales*, introduced readers to Kull, the exile from Atlantis. "The Shadow Kingdom" was preceded by three Solomon Kane stories: "Red Shadows," "Skulls in the Stars," and "Rattle of Bones." While each of these Kane stories, in its own way, contained hints of weird elements, it was in "The Shadow Kingdom" that Robert began using more such elements. It is quite possible that the success of "The Shadow Kingdom" was one of the reasons why Robert incorporated more weird elements into his Solomon Kane stories. Up to that time, "The Shadow Kingdom" was Robert's weirdest story. It was also his first published fantasy fiction story, and some have argued that it is the progenitor of the modern sword-and-sorcery genre.

It took Robert a year to write "The Shadow Kingdom." He began working on it in the fall of 1926 and finally completed it, after several starts and stops, in the summer of 1927. Accepted by *Weird Tales* in October 1927, it would not see print until two years later. Robert probably imagined the character from his study of history, specifically his study of biblical history, the early history of the British Isles, Celtic folklore, and mythology. Robert also had a healthy interest in the mysteries of Atlantis, which he discussed in his early letters and in a few of his letters to H. P. Lovecraft. In all, Robert wrote ten complete Kull stories (although some are very brief), along with several fragmented pieces, untitled drafts, and several poems. Even though only two complete Kull stories were published in Robert's lifetime, Kull remains one of Robert's more popular characters to this day.

Kull was Robert's first published barbarian protagonist. "The Shadow Kingdom" introduces Kull with great pomp and pageantry. Right away readers are informed that Kull is the king of Valusia (though he is Atlantean). Having seized a decaying throne, Kull maintains it with a heavy hand. But trouble is brewing in Valusia, right in Kull's own living quarters, though he is completely unaware of the impending danger. The story begins with a visit to Kull by Ka-nu, a Pict and the ambassador of the western isles. Aware of the danger afoot in Kull's court, Ka-nu is a bit cryptic with Kull about what is going on, but he assigns Brule the spearslayer to help Kull. Ka-nu brazenly tells Kull to implicitly trust Brule as much as he trusts himself. This is not an easy task for a king of Kull's stature. As "The Shadow Kingdom" unfolds, readers experience the events as Kull does, blindly walking into them while not knowing what to expect. This helps build the tension and pace of the story as events unfold and the danger is revealed. It also establishes a nice anticipatory tone for the entire story.

In "The Shadow Kingdom," Robert juxtaposes two extraordinary barbarians, one a Pict (Brule), the other an Atlantean (Kull). Of the two, Brule is clearly the more savage and less civilized. In many ways, Brule's skills are sharper than Kull's, and he manages to save Kull in this and other stories. To a certain degree, the trappings of civilization have softened Kull's rough edges and his barbarian instincts. Aware of these changes, Kull tends to worry and brood, and he is often hard on himself. In one scene, Robert deftly uses the Valusian architecture—its ancient walls and buildings—to undermine Kull's confidence. As he rides among its ancient structures, reflecting on what the city has seen of previous kings, Kull hears himself mocked in the clattering cadence of his horse's hooves: "Kull—the—king! Kull—the—fool!"[20] This wonderful onomatopoeia conveys a sense of Kull's private insecurity through the sound of the hooves.

Kull's brooding behavior makes him an interesting character. He is a deeper thinker than Conan, and a vastly different barbarian. Conan is a barbarian's barbarian, and Kull is not. In many ways, Kull is a civilized barbarian: still possessed of strong barbaric instincts, he is too often stymied by politics and philosophy and often compelled to reflect and think before he acts. Even so, there are times when his instincts take over and he does what all of Robert's barbarians do: encounter, react, and conquer. In many ways, the contrast between his barbarian instincts and his engagement with a civilized world makes him one of Robert's more interesting characters.

In "The Shadow Kingdom," Kull eventually discovers, with the help of Brule, that his court is overrun by ancient Serpent-Men. Serpent-Men have the ability to shape-shift into the form of anyone they choose, thus killing their victims and stealing their identity. Kull's house is filled with these creatures, and their aim is to kill him and conquer Valusia. With the intelligence that Ka-nu has gleaned, Brule and Kull confront the impending danger from the Serpent-Men and put a stop to it. Along the way, Kull discovers aspects of his kingdom and court of which he had been unaware.

Robert incorporated ghosts and other weird and fantastical elements into "The Shadow Kingdom." He also created a new world from an actual historical setting, as he would continue to do on a larger scale in his Conan stories. "The Shadow Kingdom" was a new kind of fantasy fiction, unlike any other fantasy story that preceded it, and Robert kept writing fantasy fiction in this vein. Up to this point in his publishing career, "The Shadow Kingdom" was Robert's most mature work, especially considering that he began the story at age twenty.

Picts play a prominent role in the Kull stories. As we have seen in a previous chapter, Robert discovered the Picts at age twelve in a public library while briefly living in New Orleans with his parents. He first incorporated the Picts into a story with "The Lost Race" (*Weird Tales*, January 1927). "The Shadow Kingdom" is the second story in which Robert uses Picts, and Picts would be a mainstay in many of his subsequent stories. Robert had an affinity for Picts, and he used them in various roles: to help set the tone for a story, to highlight other characters' abilities (as in several of his Conan stories), and to depict the power of a barbarian, like Brule the spear-slayer. He also created Bran Mak Morn, the last of the Pictish kings, as the protagonist in several of his popular tales.

Robert intended for Bran Mak Morn to be a serial character, as H. P. Lovecraft, early on in their correspondence, had encouraged him to do. Lovecraft's advice apparently was based on an early reading of either "The Children of the Night" or "The Dark Man," stories that Robert seems to have shown to Lovecraft in 1930.[21] Both of those stories mention Bran Mak Morn but do not feature the character as the protagonist. "Kings of the Night" would be his first published appearance as a protagonist. In that story, Bran Mak Morn shares the page with Kull—an interesting idea since historically their own stories are set thousands of years apart. Unfortunately, Bran Mak Morn would never become a serial character.

Shortly before "Kings of the Night" and "The Children of the Night" were published in late 1930, several other pulp magazine markets opened for Robert, including *Fight Stories* and *Action Stories*. Both of these magazines were ripe for Robert's boxing stories. *Weird Tales'* editor Farnsworth Wright, before his publications were suffering the ill effects of the deepening Great Depression, began *Oriental Stories* for readers who enjoyed a more straightforward action adventure story.

The opening up of these new magazine markets divided Robert's attention, and to take advantage of them he was working nearly around the clock to finish stories. Bran Mak Morn was introduced to the reading public in 1930, in the middle of his second writing period (his historical period from 1928 to 1932). That same year Howard created a new character for *Oriental Stories*, Cormac FitzGeoffrey. Bran was certainly not shelved, but earlier in 1926 Wright had rejected "Men of the Shadows," which, in Robert's mind, was the foundational story for Bran Mak Morn. In the meantime, from 1926 to 1930, possibly owing to the success of the Kull stories, Robert wrote "Kings of the Night," a Bran Mak Morn story that incorporated Kull. "Kings of the Night" would not only use an already established character but also introduce the reading public to his new character. While Robert busied himself creating characters and tales for *Oriental Stories*, he incorporated Bran Mak Morn into "The Children of the Night" and "The Dark Man," both submitted to *Weird Tales* in 1930 and both finally published in 1931. After these two stories, Bran would not show up again until 1932, in "Worms of the Earth."

Considered by some fans and scholars to be one of the best stories Robert ever wrote—and possibly the best—"Worms of the Earth" is also one of his weirdest. The story begins with a clandestine Bran Mak Morn witnessing one of his subjects being crucified by Titus Sulla, the Roman military governor of Eboracum. Bran vows to exact retributive justice upon Titus Sulla and the whole Roman civilization. To do so Bran visits a witch-woman of Dagon-moor to inquire about a door that leads to the ancient ones known as the Worms of the Earth. Bran follows her directions, steals the Black Stone, hides it, and uses the theft to threaten the ancient ones, who were once humans before they were driven beneath the earth by Bran's own Pictish ancestors. Fearing Bran and his threats, these creatures agree to kill Titus but only if Bran will return the Black Stone to them. Bran agrees and brings the ancient ones the Black Stone. When he does, he finds Titus alive, but driven mad by the mere sight of the Worms of the Earth. Realizing the insanity of what he has done, Bran kills Titus himself, casts the Black Stone at the creatures, and drives them back into the earth, almost losing his own sanity in the process.

The influence of Lovecraft can clearly be seen throughout "Worms of the Earth," especially in the creation of Nameless Ones, Dagon-Barrow, and Dagon-Mere and in the Lovecraftian horrific gloom-and-doom tone. Blended weird elements with the action adventure that Robert is famous for, this wonderful story is a unique work of dark fantasy-horror. It was also the last Bran Mak Morn story published in *Weird Tales*. By the time "Worms of the Earth" was written and published, Robert had moved on to create his staple *Weird Tales* serial character, Conan the Cimmerian.

Between 1928, when "Red Shadows" was published, and 1932, when "Worms of the Earth" was published, Robert began creating an interconnected world based on actual history, especially in the Solomon Kane and Bran Mak Morn stories. Both characters are written inside a recognizable historical setting and time frame. Between his creation of these two characters, Robert also created Kull and placed him in a precataclysmic and prerecorded historical setting, though it was not a setting removed from real history. Kull's time and place are either used or mentioned in "The Moon of Skulls" (Solomon Kane) and "Kings of the Night" (where Bran Mak Morn and Kull appear together). This use of history and historical settings served Robert well, especially when he began writing his Conan stories. An autodidactic and prolific reader of history, Robert was getting his historical inspiration from H. G. Wells's *The Outline of History* (1920), Edward P. Cheyney's *A Short History of England* (1927), E. A. Allen's *The Prehistoric World, or Vanishing Races* (1885), G. F. Scott Elliot's *The Romance of Early British Life* (1906), and similar works.

Robert's attention turned to historical fiction in late 1930, when Farnsworth Wright started *Oriental Stories* in order to publish action adventure stories set in the Orient (Asia and Asia Minor). In the first issue of *Oriental Stories*, Wright tells his readers what to expect from the new magazine:

> *Oriental Stories* will publish not only tales of Asia and Asia Minor, but will include also fascinating tales of the East Indies, of Egypt, and of the littoral of North and East Africa, which is Oriental in language and character though not in geography. We shall present for your delectation not only vivid tales of romance, intrigue, and red war in present-day Asia, but will offer you also vivid historical tales—of Genghis Khan the Red Scourge, of Tamerlane the Magnificent, of Saladin the Intrepid, of the wars between the Cross and the Crescent, of the spread of Mogul conquerors into India, of the British conquest, of the awakening of China and Japan, and of Russian intrigue to set Islam against the British Empire.[22]

It is often declared that Conan the Cimmerian stems from Kull of Atlantis and those stories. To a certain degree this is true. However, it was Robert's work for *Oriental Stories* that actually laid the foundation for Conan.

Robert's historical fiction, which was largely influenced by one of his favorite authors, Harold Lamb, is too often ignored for the more popular Solomon Kane, Kull, Conan, and even Bran Mak Morn stories. But it was a protagonist in several of Robert's historical stories, Cormac Fitz-

Geoffrey, who could be considered the precursor of Robert's most famous literary character, Conan the Cimmerian. Moreover, the motif of the rise and fall of civilization used in these stories, though Robert had used it before, would become a pillar of the Conan stories.

Robert's historical fiction includes some of his emotionally darkest stories. In these stories imbued with Robert's own gloomy, brooding, and melancholic nature, he peers at the underbelly of the human condition, mankind's constant struggle against self and against others, and the unrelenting need to rule, battle, and conquer. Robert told his friend Tevis Clyde Smith that he thought readers would not like his story "The Lame Man" (the title was eventually changed to "Lord of Samarcand"), which was slated to be published in the spring 1932 issue of *Oriental Stories*. "There isn't a gleam of hope in it," Robert admitted. "It's the fiercest and [most] somber thing I've ever tried to write."[23] As it turned out, readers were not put off by the lack of hope in the tale, or its somber nature, but some readers did quibble over a historical detail by pointing out that Timur, as a Muslim, would not have indulged in wine after his defeat of Bayazid, the Turkish sultan.[24] Other fans, however, simply praised Robert for his stories in the magazine.[25]

"Hawks of Outremer," one of Robert's more remarkable tales for *Oriental Stories*, was voted a fan favorite from the spring 1931 issue. That story reveals what is most likely the single largest inspiration for the eventual creation of Conan the Cimmerian. The protagonist of the story, Cormac FitzGeoffrey, is described as having "square-cut, black hair that topped his low broad forehead [and] contrasted strongly with his cold blue eyes."[26] Like Conan later, FitzGeoffrey is a ruthless fighter and the son of a savage race, born to the game of war. At age twelve, he had already killed three men, wore wolfskin, and weighed nearly fourteen stones.[27] In "The Blood of Belshazzar," the ex-Crusader FitzGeoffrey is also a pariah, and therefore a loner. The violence and bloodshed in the FitzGeoffrey stories provide an easy segue into any Conan story. FitzGeoffrey is Celtic and often swears by the pre-Christian pagan god named none other than Crom.[28] Sound familiar? It is easy to see how FitzGeoffrey is merely a stone's throw away from Conan.

Considering the developmental time line of Robert's writing career, it is not necessarily a bold claim to declare that Cormac FitzGeoffrey is a stronger candidate than Kull as the inspiration of Conan. Even though Robert took a rejected Kull story ("By This Axe I Rule") and rewrote it for his character Conan, there is little similarity between Kull and Conan other than Robert's use of that story, and both characters being introduced to readers as kings. All things considered in Robert's stories and his life, there is probably no single character, story, or life event that inspired him to create his most popular character, but rather a combination of ideas and influences. Be that as it may, between his Conan-like characteristics and the overshadowing of the characters and stories from this period of Robert's writing career by his more popular characters and stories, FitzGeoffrey is too often overlooked as one of the more prominent stepping-stones to Conan.

The year 1932 was pivotal for Robert. In February, while spending time in Mission, Texas, he penned one of his most famous poems, "Cimmeria." The poem was inspired by his memory of the hill country just north of Fredericksburg, Texas, experienced through a misty winter rain. Writing "Cimmeria" was unquestionably one of the pivotal segues to Robert's creation of Conan. Meanwhile, in the summer of that year, as the Great Depression worsened, Farnsworth Wright stopped publishing *Oriental Stories*. Not wanting to surrender so easily, Wright regrouped six months later and revived *Oriental Stories* by revamping its policies, reducing its price, and giving it a new title, *The Magic Carpet*.[29]

It was also in 1932 that Robert began reworking the Kull story "By This Axe I Rule!," which had been rejected by both *Argosy* and *Adventure*. The end result, "The Phoenix on the Sword," introduced the reading public to Conan the Cimmerian. Robert used some passages from the original Kull story in "The Phoenix on the Sword," but he modified the plot a bit and added different supernatural and horror elements. Besides this first Conan story, Robert submitted to *Weird Tales* two other Conan stories, "The Frost-Giant's Daughter" and "God in the Bowl." They were rejected by Wright, who also sent "The Phoenix on the Sword" back for revision. Robert quickly revised the story and resubmitted it, and Wright published it in the December 1932 issue of *Weird Tales*.

After several attempts to establish a serial character in the pulp magazines, Robert had finally succeeded. Conan would become a staple character in *Weird Tales*, which would eventually publish seventeen Conan stories. Several of them stand out as some of the greatest stories Robert ever wrote. In the summer of 1932, Robert and Lovecraft began debating in their letters about the differences (positive and negative) between civilization and barbarism, and some of the insights and themes of this debate would make their way into several Conan stories. "Beyond the Black River" is one of the best examples of the influence of this ongoing debate (it lasted several years) on Robert's storytelling.

Besides the appearance of horror elements (ghosts, vampires, and

so on) in several genres of Robert's published works, including his boxing and western stories, his horror fiction would periodically be picked
up by various pulp magazine markets throughout his twelve-year career.
By 1932, Robert was writing and publishing stories in the western genre.
"The Horror from the Mound" was his first professionally published
western story—although it is technically a horror story with a western
setting. Somewhat slowly in the beginning, Robert would periodically
write and publish western fiction after "The Horror from the Mound."
By 1934, when "Beyond the Black River" was published in *Weird Tales*, he
had published ten westerns, and he continued to write and publish many
more before his death in 1936.

Written and published in the latter part of Robert's publishing career, "Beyond the Black River" is in many ways a frontier/western story
with a barbarian protagonist. It is essentially a frontier expansion story
in the same vein as James Fenimore Cooper's stories (*Last of the Mohi-
cans, The Deerslayer: or The First Warpath*). Once again, the Picts play a
prominent role in his story. In fact, it is easy to see that they are analo-
gous to the Native Americans during the historic expansion of the western frontier. In "Beyond the Black River," the Picts are fighting to save
their territory, which is being encroached upon by the border settlers.
The story is a kind of literary anachronism. Although it is set during the
prehistoric Hyborian Age, it effectively incorporates historic western
frontier language, using words like "fort," "settler," "cabin," "buckskin,"
"pack mule," and "otter pelts" and place names like Thunder River and
Scalp Creek. Robert also portrays the Picts not as a united people but
as divided into small clans (or tribes). This was certainly the case with
Native Americans during the western expansion of the North American
frontier in the eighteenth and nineteenth centuries.

By the time "Beyond the Black River" was published in May 1935,
Robert had argued his case for barbarism to Lovecraft, using the frontier
and its settlers and claiming that they were hardly inferior to educated
civilized people, but rather stronger and more adventurous. Though
neither writer ever completely defined what he meant by "barbarian"
or "barbarism" in their debate, both used examples of various peoples
from history to support their arguments. "Beyond the Black River" was
Robert's exemplum for his argument favoring barbarism. Being a voracious reader of history, he was well aware of the rise of groups from a
base or barbarian state to a more sophisticated and civilized state, and
he knew about their subsequent decline through either their own behavior or their defeat by other greater barbarous groups. Robert cleverly uti-

lized this history not only in his debate with Lovecraft but especially in his stories.

In "Beyond the Black River," Robert juxtaposes and contrasts two characters: Conan, who is a consummate barbarian, and Balthus, a more civilized warrior. This contrast highlights not only Robert's thinking from his ongoing debate with Lovecraft but also the barbarian potency of his protagonist Conan. To underscore the differences that, Robert believed, existed between barbarian warriors and civilized warriors, he has another character in the story, a borderer, witness this contrast. This character utters one of Robert's more popular lines: "Barbarism is the natural state of mankind. . . . Civilization is unnatural. It is a whim of circumstance. And barbarism must always ultimately triumph."[30]

"Beyond the Black River" is a seminal piece in Robert's literary oeuvre, as well as unique among all the Conan stories. Though he continues to use supernatural and weird elements (such as the incantations and sorcery that summon Jhebbal Sag), Robert brings no lost cities or abandoned exotic settings to this story. Instead, he writes in an efficient and powerful new style, with a new setting. Robert told Novalyne Price that "Beyond the Black River" focused on the significance of civilization and how committed to it some men were, enough to die defending it.[31] Robert talked about this story with such high regard because it essentially encapsulates what he had learned from the old-timers who told him stories about Native Americans, frontier life, and the frontier expansion in his own home state of Texas. The success of "Beyond the Black River" probably spurred his desire to write a novel about the western frontier that he had in mind. That idea would never come to fruition.

Robert was a product of his place and time as a writer, and also in his personal views about the political and social issues of his day. He lived in central west Texas during the time of Jim Crow laws, when African Americans were not allowed to remain in some smaller communities after sunset. The Ku Klux Klan was active there, and social divides were clearly drawn. Everyday discussions were permeated by rhetoric about African Americans and their roles in the segregated society of the 1920s and 1930s. African American, Chinese, Japanese, and Mexican racial stereotypes were also replete in the social life and entertainment culture of the entire country—especially in films, advertisements, newspapers, magazines, and cartoons. During this period, newspaper articles appeared almost daily in Cross Plains and the surrounding areas about KKK activities. Larger towns like Brownwood and Abilene had segregated areas where African Americans lived and socialized. Even before the emancipation of the slaves in the South, there had been several slave revolts and uprisings in the region, and to fearful southern whites they remained an underlying threat.

Having grown up in a place pervaded by the notion that African Americans should be suppressed and segregated, Robert could hardly have been immune to racial tensions. In addition, his family heritage could be traced back to the antebellum South. He had heard stories about plantation life, about slavery, and certainly about the slave revolts and uprisings in several southern states, including Arkansas, home to several of his relatives in the 1800s. It cannot be denied that Robert was susceptible to such thinking and acquiesced to it. His opinions about social issues, especially racial issues, made their way into several of his stories. In fact, his thinking on racial issues figures prominently in his story "Black Canaan."

Robert believed that slavery was wrong, not because the practice was morally repugnant, but because it led, he argued, to the cataclysmic downfall of civilizations. He embraced the idea that civilizations that practiced slavery were doomed to be overrun and controlled eventually by those who had been enslaved. He also believed that those civilizations that took the practice of slavery to the point of miscegenation, creating what Robert referred to as a mongrel race, were especially susceptible to such a downfall. He thought that allowing such behavior was detrimental to civilizations. From the end of the Civil War through the 1950s, this kind of thinking was common in the South, and it is still embraced by some today.

Robert's ideas about miscegenation appeared in his early stories, including the one we have already examined in this chapter, "The Moon of Skulls." The ancient stranger imprisoned for many years by Nakari tells Solomon Kane the history behind the people of Negari, who were held as slaves by his own ancient race. Eventually his people practiced miscegenation with their slaves, and ultimately the slaves became the masters themselves and destroyed their old masters. Nakari and her people, who are presented as the antagonists in the story, were the end result. Robert dwells on this idea only briefly in "The Moon of Skulls," but it is the main theme of his story "Black Canaan."

Set in southern Louisiana and Arkansas, "Black Canaan" is the best example of Robert's thinking about slavery, miscegenation, and black uprisings in the South. While stories such as "Kelly the Conjure Man," "The Horror from the Mound," and "Pigeons from Hell" contain racially charged language and some of the racial stereotypes common for the day, "Black Canaan" is a blatantly racist story. Written in late 1932 or early 1933, Robert gave his agent Otis Adelbert Kline the story in September 1933. *Weird Tales* accepted the story a month later and published it in the June 1936 issue.

The protagonist of "Black Canaan" is Kirby Buckner, born and raised in the area known as Canaan, a swampy area between Tularoosa Creek and Black River where early white frontiersmen settled with their families and slaves. Buckner is a prominent landowner and leader in Canaan. While visiting New Orleans, Buckner learns of trouble back home. Worried, he travels back to Canaan and is met along the way by a mysterious female quadroon.[32] Buckner is struck by her untamed and lawless beauty, seemingly intended to madden and make a man dizzy—in other words, to sexually arouse and tempt him.

Kirby Buckner is not the first of Robert's protagonists to be tempted by a black or foreign woman. In fact, his protagonists are tempted this way often enough to make one wonder if Robert himself was infatuated with women of color. This idea has been suggested elsewhere.[33] At one point Robert published a poem in the *Junto*, a magazine privately circulated between Robert and several of his friends, "Etched in Ebony." This poem details an aggressive, if not violent, sexual encounter between a white man and a black woman. There is also some evidence that Robert may have had relations with a Mexican prostitute in the border town of Piedras Negras.[34] And as we saw in chapter 10, Robert made a weak attempt to explain to Novalyne Price that white men visited a certain African American district in Brownwood to fulfill their "needs." All these seem to support Robert's alleged infatuation. To be fair, it is uncertain whether Robert detailed sexual temptations between white men and black women in his stories (and in "Etched in Ebony") to comment on the shamefulness of such temptations or to signal the shame he felt over his own tendency to feel so tempted. Whatever the case, Robert almost always used this scenario to emphasize his idea that the kind of black (or slave) uprisings that had occurred in the past could still occur in his own day. Robert believed that this kind of temptation was one of the root causes.

The reader of "Black Canaan" eventually finds out that this quadroon temptress was sent by the black conjurer Saul Stark to tempt Buckner into a sexual act and thus lure him away from Canaan, where Stark could then incite the local blacks to rise up and conquer Canaan's white people. The racial slurs and language throughout the story ought to make the average twenty-first-century reader cringe, but back in the

1930s when "Black Canaan" was first published, there were probably few people who found it offensive. In fact, it was voted by readers as the best story for the June 1936 issue of *Weird Tales*.

To make the story "weird," Robert used the folklore and mythos of black magic that was well known in southern states among both whites and blacks. Saul Stark is a conjurer, a worker of magic, and he uses magic to manipulate the blacks of Canaan to revolt. Benjamin Garstad, in his excellent article "'Death to the Masters!' The Role of Slave Revolt in the Fiction of Robert E. Howard," rightly points out that "Howard's slave revolts are most often led by wizards or priests."[35] Of course, the magazines in which Robert published, especially *Weird Tales*, would require a weird element, and "Black Canaan" certainly meets that expectation. Aside from the repugnant racism in "Black Canaan," the story is a good example of an early twentieth-century American southern gothic tale, written with a nicely controlled narrative pace and in Robert's signature style.

We need to know the historical context in which Robert E. Howard wrote in order to understand the racial slurs and stereotyping in "Black Canaan" and several other stories, and why authors like him wrote such stories, especially when we find ourselves offended by them. Today we are much more concerned about racial issues and their negative effects than were previous generations, and rightly so. As I have stated elsewhere, "For twenty-first-century readers, historical accuracy can be more highly valued than political correctness when reading previous generations' history and fiction."[36] Our political correctness can sometimes benefit us as we deal with our own moral, political, social, and racial issues in the twenty-first century. "But to take what we think now and force it on a previous generation that had no such ideas is not only anachronistic but wrong-headed."[37] No matter how offensive we might find previous generations' thoughts, ideas, and fiction, our generation can certainly learn something from what they wrote. As Garstad perceptively points out, "After a fashion, Robert E. Howard's accounts of slave revolts are rare and valuable documents giving us insight into the popular thought of the South on the conflict between the races."[38] Let me be clear that I am not attempting to justify Robert's racism, but simply to point out that despite the archaic and negative nature of his ideas for us today, dismissing his work on that basis would perhaps be a disservice to American literature. There is much to be learned from Robert E. Howard stories.

All of Robert's stories have something to tell us as readers. Some read them purely to be entertained, while others read them to become informed about early twentieth-century social norms and their effects on the writers of that time. Robert's fantasy works demonstrate that he was the progenitor of a subgenre of modern fantasy fiction and also one of the earliest twentieth-century authors who built worlds in his fiction. He did so not only within the framework of his Conan stories (and its Hyborian Age) but also in the stories that were precursors to this mythos. In a short span of twelve years, Robert E. Howard established himself as an important and prominent writer in the popular fiction industry of the 1920s and '30s, a time when the Great Depression made it almost impossible to maintain a living as a writer. Nearly one hundred years later, his work has withstood the test of time and is still widely read.

CHAPTER FOURTEEN

Full Circle

THE PUBLISHING JOURNEY OF A BARBARIAN

The only man who could write a Robert E. Howard story was Robert E. Howard. Read Howard pastiches as you will—but don't let anyone kid you that you're reading Robert E. Howard.

KARL EDWARD WAGNER, "FOREWORD," ROBERT E. HOWARD, *THE HOUR OF THE DRAGON* (NEW YORK: G. P. PUTNAM'S SONS, 1977), 7

R obert E. Howard created a number of remarkable characters in his brief writing career, each one seasoned with some aspect of his creator's personality. There is Solomon Kane, the swashbuckling Puritan swordsman and adventurer, bent on exercising his retributive justice upon those who commit evil acts against innocent victims. Another is the mighty warrior Bran Mak Morn, who rules as the last king of a moribund race of Picts. The warrior Kull of Atlantis is a brooding and philosophical barbarian who was once a slave, a pirate, and a gladiator, and eventually the conquering king of Valusia. Then there is El Borak, the Texas gunman from El Paso who wanders the deserts of Afghanistan looking for raw adventure and action. Some of Howard's western stories relate the hilarious mishaps and comedic catastrophes of the humorous characters Breckinridge Elkins, Pike Bearfield, and Buckner J. Grimes. But all these characters pale in popularity next to Howard's broadsword-wielding Conan the Cimmerian—or as he is more commonly known today, Conan the Barbarian.

In December 1932, *Weird Tales* published "The Phoenix on the Sword," a Howard story that introduced a new adventure fantasy protagonist. Initially, Conan the Cimmerian received moderate acclaim. "The

Phoenix on the Sword" placed second in a vote by the readers for the December '32 issue, tied with Seabury Quinn's "The Door to Yesterday." More positive feedback from readers appeared in "The Eyrie" of subsequent issues. As a result, Farnsworth Wright continued publishing Robert's Conan stories. Little did Robert and his readers know that Conan the Cimmerian would unwittingly shape the history of adventure fantasy and eventually become an iconic character in popular culture. By June 1933, Conan was gracing the cover of *Weird Tales* as the protagonist of Robert's story "Black Colossus." The illustrator for this cover was Margaret Brundage, an up-and-coming artist for *Weird Tales*. "A young fashion illustrator," Brundage "had done two popular covers in 1932, both featuring her trademark: beautiful, near-nude women."[1] Brundage illustrated nine subsequent Conan covers for *Weird Tales* from 1932 to 1936. Along with the action, intense pace, and swordplay of the Conan stories, each of the Brundage covers helped bolster the popularity of the barbarian.

From Conan's first appearance in 1932 to Robert's untimely death in 1936, the character amassed a large following of readers. Several other *Weird Tales* writers eventually published stories that were influenced by Robert and Conan. The first was C. L. Moore's story "Black God's Kiss," featuring the first female protagonist—Jirel of Joiry—in the "sword-and-sorcery" fantasy subgenre. When Moore's story was featured on the cover of the October 1934 *Weird Tales*, Jirel was called by one reader "a sort of feminine version of Conan the Cimmerian."[2] Another reader suggested how wonderful it would be for Conan and Jirel to meet in a collaborative story.[3] Of course this never happened, but it was nonetheless an interesting idea. *Weird Tales* continued to publish Moore's Jirel stories until April 1939.[4]

Around the time of Robert's death in 1936, *Weird Tales* serialized two Conan stories. The first was "The Hour of the Dragon," a story Robert attempted to publish as a novel in England through the British publisher Denis Archer and Pawling & Ness Limited. After almost two years of correspondence and submissions, Archer ultimately rejected Robert's work.[5] *Weird Tales* edited "The Hour of the Dragon" into five parts and began publishing it as a series in December 1935, six months prior to Robert's death. Robert submitted the second story, "Red Nails," to *Weird Tales* in 1935 but would not see it published. *Weird Tales* ran it posthumously as a three-part series, beginning with the cover story of the July 1936 issue.

Several other *Weird Tales* writers (and one reader) attempted to fill the void left by Robert's death by creating their own Conan-like characters and adventure fantasy stories. In a brief letter he wrote to *Weird Tales*, Clifford Ball, a longtime reader of the magazine, stated:

> I feel moved to offer my condolences upon the death of Mr. Howard. A hundred international Tarzans could never erase the memory of Conan the Cimmerian. Neither Northwest Smith nor Jirel of Jory [*sic*]—and in Moore you have an excellent author—can quite supplant his glory. When I read that *Red Nails* would be the last of Conan's exploits I felt as though some sort of income, or expected resource, had been suddenly severed.[6]

Prompted by Robert's death, and possibly as a homage to him, Ball wrote his own fantasy adventure stories, four of which were published by *Weird Tales*, from May 1937 to March 1939. Ball's attempt to keep Robert's adventure fantasy tradition alive was met with moderate success.

Thus, had it not been for Henry Kuttner, the adventure fantasy subgenre could have died with its creator. Kuttner created a Conan-like character called Elak of Atlantis and published four Elak stories in *Weird Tales* from May 1938 to January 1941. One of those stories, "Dragon Moon," was the last of its kind to be published in *Weird Tales*. The magazine was beginning to direct its attention to other genres, so Kuttner submitted his Elak stories in different markets and succeeded in having them accepted for publication. Another Howardian character he created was Prince Raynor; after he submitted two Prince Raynor tales to *Strange Stories*, that magazine published both, in its April and August 1939 issues. Clifford Ball would achieve only moderate success with his stories, but Kuttner thrived in this endeavor and rightly deserves the credit for advancing the fantasy subgenre initiated by Robert E. Howard.

By 1940 or 1941, *Weird Tales* changed direction and stopped publishing adventure fantasy in order to turn its attention to other genres, mainly weird horror. Kuttner's "Dragon Moon" was the last Howardian adventure fantasy published in *Weird Tales*, in the January 1941 issue. In 1936, Farnsworth Wright rejected the first of Fritz Leiber's Fafhrd and the Gray Mouser stories, "Adept's Gambit."[7] This was a poor decision. The story would have introduced to the reading public Fafhrd, a seven-foot-tall barbarian protagonist, and his adventuring friend, the small but adroit Gray Mouser, whose weapon of choice was a rapier. When *Weird Tales* rejected the Fafhrd and the Gray Mouser stories, Leiber submitted them to *Unknown* magazine. *Unknown*, which ran from 1939 to 1943, was the brainchild of John W. Campbell Jr., who reveled in the opportunity to publish Leiber's work.[8] Leiber's stories took Robert's adventure fantasy genre to a whole new level with a broader and eager audience.

In the meantime, Robert's agent Otis Adelbert Kline was now working on behalf of Robert's father. Kline's efforts at posthumously publishing Robert's extant manuscripts resulted in a successful run of publications from 1936 to 1939. Based on his connections in the fantasy and science fiction publishing industry, Kline succeeded where Robert had failed and managed to publish Robert's comedic westerns in *Argosy*. During this same period, Kline published around two dozen other Howard stories in *Action Stories, Complete Stories, Star Western, Spicy Adventure Stories* (using the nom de plume Sam Walser), *Thrilling Adventures, Smashing Novels, Cowboy Stories,* and *Fight Stories*. Kline had exponentially expanded Robert's publication arm. Even so, the publication of stories written by Robert E. Howard stopped in 1939 after the appearance of "Almuric" in the May issue of *Weird Tales*. Other than the writers creating Conan-esque characters and writing Howardian-style stories, there was nothing new in the publishing market that would keep Robert's name alive. Then two *Weird Tales* writers, August Derleth and Donald Wandrei, created Arkham House.

Soon after H. P. Lovecraft died in March 1937, Derleth and Wandrei were motivated to team up to preserve Lovecraft's works in a single volume, which they submitted to several of the larger publishing houses in New York. In 1938, Charles Scribner's Sons seriously considered publishing the collection, but ultimately decided against it.[9] Frustrated, Derleth and Wandrei took matters into their own hands and in 1939 established an independent publishing house in Sauk City, Wisconsin. Using George Banta Company, a Wisconsin printer, they printed 1,268 copies of their 550-page manuscript of Lovecraft's collected works, titled *The Outsider and Others*. This launched a long publishing run that has lasted from 1939 to the present day.[10]

By 1946, Derleth and Wandrei turned their publishing attention to Robert E. Howard. Arkham House brought Robert's work, which had been out of the public eye for seven years, back into circulation with a collection titled *Skull-Face and Others*.[11] Approximately 3,000 copies of the 475-page book were printed. It included several poems, about twenty stories, and an introduction by August Derleth. It also contained two memoriams previously published in *Weird Tales* shortly after Robert's death—one by H. P. Lovecraft, the other by E. Hoffmann Price. If only on a small scale, Robert's work was back in circulation, at least among ardent fans. One such fan was Donald Allen Wollheim.

During the 1930s—the golden era of *Weird Tales* and pulp magazines—several pulp fans established their own magazines, known as "fanzines." Donald A. Wollheim stood out among those fans. His influence in fandom and the science fiction and fantasy publishing industry was paramount. He published several semiprofessional zines and fanzines in the early to mid-1930s: *Fanciful Tales of Space and Time* (a semiprofessional zine, one issue only) and *The Phantagraph*. Aside from being the founder of science fiction conventions, Wollheim eventually began writing, editing, and publishing science fiction and fantasy works. In 1947, he was hired by Avon Publishers to be the editor of the *Avon Fantasy Reader*, "one of the most notable weird reprint magazines."[12] Being the first reprint publication, Wollheim republished some of his favorite *Weird Tales* writers, bringing them to a much larger audience than Arkham House had at the time. His reprints of "Queen of the Black Coast" (1948) and "A Witch Shall Be Born" (1949) helped put Robert E. Howard back into the spotlight.

Another pulp fiction fan who played a pivotal role in the 1950s and 1960s revival of Robert's character Conan the Cimmerian was Dr. John D. Clark. Clark collaborated with fellow pulp fan and science fiction writer P. Schuyler Miller in what could be considered the first academic essay on Robert's work, "A Probable Outline of Conan's Career." Donald Wollheim included the final edited copy of Clark and Miller's essay in a chapbook he created in 1938, *The Hyborian Age*, published by LANY Cooperative Publications.[13] Prior to the essay's publication, "Miller wrote Howard in early 1936 and enclosed a rough draft of the chronology of Conan's career he and Clark had devised based on the information in the stories that had been published up to that point." Miller also enclosed a map that he and Clark had created of Conan's world. On March 10, 1936, Robert responded to Miller's letter and confirmed the accuracy of their outlined essay, pointing out only a few minor errors and discrepancies. In that letter, Robert added further details about Conan's history, explained why he wrote the stories out of chronological sequence, discussed political aspects of the various tribes and peoples in the Hyborian Age, and included his own map. "Miller and Clark used the information supplied by Howard to revise their outline before its publication in the LANY *The Hyborian Age* chapbook."[14] Wollheim's chapbook, Robert's *The Hyborian Age* essay, and Miller and Clark's es-

say, along with Clark's connections in the publishing world, were critical to the revival of Robert's Conan stories in the 1950s by Gnome Press,
a small upstart publishing company.

In the late 1940s, Dr. Clark moved to New York City from Schenec-
tady, where he had worked for General Electric. In New York City, Clark
met several fantasy and science fiction writers and eventually joined
their social organization, the Hydra Club. Through his association with
the Hydra Club, Clark met and befriended Martin Greenberg. In 1948,
Greenberg, along with David Kyle—another member of the Hydra
Club—established the small independent publishing company Gnome
Press. Their first publication was a collaborative work by two other Hydra Club members, Fletcher Pratt and L. Sprague de Camp, titled *The
Carnelian Cube*. Gnome Press focused on science fiction, but as an avid
fan of Robert E. Howard, especially his character Conan, Clark convinced Greenberg of the merits of publishing a series of books devoted
to Conan stories. Moreover, "when Gnome Press reprinted Howard's
Conan stories from *Weird Tales*, Clark served as the editor."[15] The first of
these Conan books, *Conan the Conqueror*, appeared in 1950. Clark wrote
the introduction and edited the book, which was merely a retitled edition of Robert's story "The Hour of the Dragon." The six other volumes
that followed would amount to "more than 10% of Gnome's entire output
over the next seven years."[16]

While working on finalizing *Conan the Conqueror*, Greenberg sent
out review copies to his writer friends to get promotional review blurbs
from them. One of these writers, Fletcher Pratt, did not care for Robert or his Conan tales. He handed his copy over to his friend and previous collaborator, L. Sprague de Camp. According to various written
accounts, de Camp, a latecomer to Robert's works, was fascinated with
Conan the Conqueror, which sparked his creative imagination.[17] De
Camp was already involved with Gnome Press via *The Carnelian Cube*,
and John D. Clark was his former college roommate at California In-
stitute of Technology. Because of this, de Camp attempted to interpose
himself in the Gnome Press Conan saga.

Since Robert's agent Otis Adelbert Kline had died in October 1946
and Dr. Howard had died even earlier, on November 12, 1944, the agent
duties were passed to Oscar Friend, another pulp era writer and a close
friend of Kline's. The Howard estate had been left to Dr. Pere M. Kuy-
kendall of Ranger, Texas, a close friend of Dr. Howard's. Prior to his involvement with the Gnome Press Conan saga de Camp had read the last
issue of *Avon Fantasy Reader*, which contained a story by Robert, "The

House of Arabu," retitled "The Witch from Hell's Kitchen" by Donald A. Wollheim for that issue.[18] Robert's story compelled de Camp to telephone Wollheim to inquire "where he obtained this story and whether any more like it existed." Wollheim told de Camp that Robert's agent, Oscar J. Friend, had "a whole pile of unpublished manuscripts."[19] When Wollheim asked de Camp whether he knew Oscar Friend, de Camp said that he did and then abruptly ended the phone call. At once de Camp called Friend and inquired about the pile of manuscripts. Friend confirmed that he had a box of Robert's manuscripts that Kline had left him, along with the duty of serving as Robert's literary agent. Friend informed de Camp that there might be a few unpublished Conan manuscripts in the box.

Excited about the prospect of undiscovered Robert E. Howard manuscripts, de Camp arranged a meeting at Friend's place. "On November 30, 1951, I went to Friend's apartment and dug through the pile, finding three apparently unpublished Conan stories; 'The Frost Giant's Daughter,' 'The God in the Bowl' and 'The Black Stranger.'"[20] De Camp reported that Friend lent him these three stories to edit and/or rewrite and "to see if he could fit them into the Conan Saga that Greenberg was publishing and make it possible to sell them for magazine publication."[21] De Camp had been attempting to get involved with the Gnome Press Conan saga since reading Fletcher Pratt's review copy of *Conan the Conqueror*, without success. Being the brainchild of John D. Clark, who was also the acting editor of the two volumes in circulation in 1951, Greenberg felt that the Conan saga was in capable hands. It is likely that when de Camp initially tried to wedge his way into the project, Greenberg asked de Camp what he could offer that Clark was not already doing. When de Camp took possession of the three unpublished Conan manuscripts from Oscar Friend, he probably used those stories to entice Greenberg and Clark to let him into the project. And as it turned out, these stories were the key to de Camp's participation in the third Conan volume, *King Conan*.

King Conan contained one of the unpublished Conan stories, "The Black Stranger," heavily edited and rewritten in parts by de Camp. He also retitled it "The Treasure of Tranicos." While Clark maintained his status as general editor of the series, de Camp became the editor of this volume. He also wrote the book's introduction, wherein he explained how he discovered the unpublished Conan stories. This clever move by de Camp allowed him to boast about newly discovered unpublished Conan manuscripts and gave him leverage to continue his involvement in the series. De Camp added the two other unpublished stories, "The

Frost-Giant's Daughter" and "The God in the Bowl," to the fourth volume, *The Coming of Conan*. De Camp also began to commandeer some of Robert's Kull stories: he edited and rewrote portions of "The Mirrors of Tuzan Thume" and "The Shadow Kingdom," as well as the poem "The King and the Oak," to turn them into Conan stories. By the sixth volume, *Tales of Conan*, the series was entirely divested of Robert E. Howard's Conan, and de Camp would have made a staple practice of taking Robert's other non-Conan stories and rewriting them as Conan stories. Examples include "The Blood-Stained God" (originally titled "The Curse of the Crimson God"), an unpublished historical adventure story featuring Kirby O'Donnell, and "The Flame Knife" (originally titled "Three-Bladed Doom"), another unpublished historical adventure story featuring Francis X. Gordon. De Camp revised these two stories, set them in the Hyborian Age, and changed their protagonist to Conan. In addition, de Camp was writing his own Conan pastiches (for example, "The Road of the Eagles") and now had his name on the cover, billed equally with Robert E. Howard as coauthor.

The seventh volume—and what ended up being the last—was entirely devoid of Robert E. Howard works. *The Return of Conan* was a pastiche written by Björn Nyberg, a Swedish fan of Robert's stories. When Martin Greenberg received Nyberg's manuscript, he was relatively impressed and asked de Camp to edit and/or rewrite it where necessary to improve and prepare it for publication.

The Gnome Press Conan saga was successful during the period when the books were published. Each of the seven books had a press run of five thousand copies, and each sold relatively fast. The Arkham House books had fewer press runs and sold more slowly, but reached more influential fans, such as Glenn Lord.[22] Gnome Press reached a wider audience than any other independent book publisher during that time. Seeing Gnome Press's success as a smaller independent publishing company, de Camp realized the potential marketing scale that Conan could achieve if the stories were published through a much larger and more established publishing house.

The publishing industry was struggling in the late 1940s and throughout the 1950s. Paper rationing during World War II had forced most magazines to go from an already low grade of paper quality to an even lower grade. Some magazines went bankrupt as a consequence and ceased publication. To stay viable the publishing industry was forced to think outside the box, and many publishers decided to shift from magazines to low-grade hardback or mass market paperback books.

While Gnome Press was successful in selling its books, the company struggled financially, owing in part to its debt load. As Greenberg became slow to pay his writers, they began to take their work to larger publishing houses. In the early 1960s, Gnome Press slipped into a serious financial free fall. Desperate to survive, Greenberg had to consider other publishing options. The "paperback reprint market was beginning to develop, though slowly, and Greenberg saw possible daylight ahead through the sale of reprint rights in the proceeds of which Gnome Press as original publisher would share."[23] Greenberg approached Bantam Books and offered them Gnome's collection of Conan books for a paperback series. During the negotiations with Bantam Books, without Greenberg's knowledge or consent, de Camp struck a deal with Lancer Books for the same series in a mass market paperback edition. This spawned a lawsuit between Greenberg and de Camp.

In the end, Greenberg and Gnome Press lost the lawsuit, which put the final nail in their coffin. Lloyd Arthur Eshbach, in his book *Over My Shoulder: Reflections on a Science Fiction Era*, quotes Greenberg on the situation. "I made arrangements to sell the rights to the Conan series to Bantam," Greenberg said,

> But L. Sprague de Camp, without my knowledge, sold the rights to Lancer Books. I got an injunction to stop publication, and the cost of the suit—which we lost—just about broke us. I believe the sale of the Conan series would have brought in sufficient capital to allow us to recoup and get back into full production. My printer at this time took possession of our inventory to cover bills, and that put the finishing touch to Gnome Press.[24]

In the late 1950s, Gnome Press had lost many of its best authors because Greenberg simply failed to pay them royalties. But even with the departure of these authors, Greenberg was correct that if Bantam Books had acquired the rights to publish the Conan series, the sales from the series probably would have kept Gnome Press alive, at least for a few more years. In the final analysis, "the fact that de Camp won the court battle would indicate that he acted within his legal rights."[25] Conan the Cimmerian was now about to be published as a paperback series that would not only change the publishing landscape of fantasy fiction but also elevate Robert E. Howard—or at least Conan—to a staggeringly iconic level.

Regarding the whole Gnome Press Conan saga, de Camp declared later in his life, somewhat piously, "My brief adventures in the Hyborian Age had been fun, but the profits were only pennies and I had a living to make."[26] Although de Camp never admitted as much, his remark seems to carry a double meaning: Greenberg never paid his writers, and de Camp saw the potential in the Conan saga and therefore legally commandeered the series. Lin Carter, who also played a pivotal role in the Lancer Conan series, explains de Camp's actions in *Imaginary Worlds*:

> Early in the 1960s, de Camp's unquenchable enthusiasm for the Howardian *oeuvres* led him into a new venture. Science fiction had become immensely popular in the burgeoning field of paperback publishing, and Sprague was convinced that Sword & Sorcery could rival its audience. Obtaining permission from Howard's estate, he took the series around to the various paperback firms, eventually interesting Lancer Books in the idea.[27]

Established in 1961, Lancer Books capitalized on the growing paperback market by making paperbacks its sole focus. The founders of Lancer Books, Irwin Stein (the former owner of Royal Publications, a magazine company) and Walter Zacharius (previously employed by the magazine company Macfadden Publications), published stories from a variety of genres, including science fiction and fantasy. "Persuaded by L. Sprague de Camp, Lancer Books, Inc. launched in 1966 an 11-volume mass market paperback series based on the Conan stories."[28] Keeping to the chronological time frame that John D. Clark had established for the Gnome Press Conan saga, de Camp added his own pastiches to the series, along with various unfinished fragments of Conan stories found after Robert's death. According to de Camp, he did so to fill the time gaps in Conan's linear chronology.

Artwork for the new Lancer Conan series was critical. Since 1951, when Gnome Press released its Conan saga, the artistic landscape had changed. In the 1950s, Gnome Press's cover art made Conan look like a Roman centurion, reflecting the popular cultural film and media trend of the day. But science fiction and fantasy had evolved since the '50s. Donald A. Wollheim and the early 1960s Ace pocket paperback books for the Edgar Rice Burroughs reprints were largely responsible for this change. Wollheim employed Roy G. Krenkel as his primary cover artist because he "wanted to bring back the St. John look for their Burroughs line."[29] J. Allen St. John was a well-known artist who illustrated many of Burroughs's stories published in books and the pulp magazines. St. John's illustrations have stood the test of time and are about as popular today as they were then. Though assigned a fairly daunting task, Krenkel got the job done. Wollheim kept Krenkel so busy that he had a difficult time staying ahead of the workload. Krenkel suggested his friend Frank Frazetta as someone who could lighten the load. "The two had been friends going way back to the fifties when they worked for E.C. Publications together."[30]

In the book *Icon: A Retrospective by the Grand Master of Fantastic Art*, Frazetta recounts his initial experience with illustrating a Burroughs cover for Ace. "They reluctantly gave me one cover to do in 1962—and their sales took off. It happened again and again and again."[31] The success of Frazetta's covers for Ace's Burroughs series turned heads at Lancer Books. "Aware of the phenomenal success Ace was experiencing with the [Burroughs] novels featuring Frazetta's paintings, Lancer approached the artist in 1965 with the commission for the Conan covers."[32] In 1964, Frazetta had already worked for Lancer on the cover art for *The Secret People*. It was just a small step from doing that cover for Lancer's editor Larry T. Shaw to doing the cover art for the up-and-coming Conan series. This may have been the best decision that Lancer made regarding its eleven-volume Conan series.

Robert E. Howard's stories, coupled with Frank Frazetta's cover art, created the perfect publishing storm. If there was ever a moment in publishing history when the popular axiom "never judge a book by its cover" did *not* apply, this would have been that moment. Charged with a great deal of energy, Frazetta's cover art depicted the action so well that fantasy fiction readers were compelled to grab a Lancer Conan book off the shelf and thumb through its pages. And of course, Robert's larger-than-life stories were an easy sell for those seeking high adventure. Well over three million copies of the Lancer editions sold prior to the demise of Lancer Books in 1973, when the company filed for bankruptcy.[33]

When the dust settled, the Lancer Conan books turned out to have been both a blessing and a curse. Although the books were "commercially successful and brought a universal revival and broader appreciation for Robert E. Howard's work, the downside was that many of the stories were textually compromised because of the editing, rewriting, or expansions done by L. Sprague de Camp and his collaborator at the time, Lin Carter."[34] After Lancer Books folded, Ace Books contracted for the series in 1977 and simply picked up where Lancer left off, adding a twelfth volume—*Conan of Aquilonia*, written entirely by de Camp and Carter. Ace Books published the series from 1977 to the mid-1980s.

The 1960s was a busy decade for Robert E. Howard's work. In September 1960, NBC launched the popular television series *Thriller*. The show "was the creation of Hubbell Robinson, a 54-year-old producer who had been programme director, then executive vice president, at CBS."[35] Robinson had produced other popular shows, such as *Studio One* and *Playhouse 90*, which featured Boris Karloff, so it made sense that Robinson would get Karloff to host *Thriller*. The pilot aired on September 13, 1960. Titled "Twisted Image," the episode starred Leslie Nielson. Toward the end of the first season, the television series adapted Robert's story "Pigeons from Hell" for episode 36, which aired on June 6, 1961.

On other media fronts, Donald A. Wollheim, the editor during the early 1960s at Ace Books, published Robert's short novel *Almuric* in 1964. Unfinished by Robert, *Almuric* is a sword-and-planet story in the same vein as Edgar Rice Burroughs's *John Carter of Mars*, so it was apropos for Wollheim to republish it during the publication of Ace's Burroughs series in the early '60s. Later, in 1969, Ace Books would reissue *Almuric* with a new cover.

While he worked alongside de Camp contributing to the Lancer Conan series, Lin Carter edited the exceptionally popular "Adult Fantasy" series from Ballantine Books. Recognizing his prowess, Lancer commissioned Carter to assemble a new Robert E. Howard collection. The result would be the 1967 Lancer book *King Kull*, which contained original Kull stories by Robert (though edited and rewritten in various places) and several Kull stories that had been left incomplete by Robert and were finished by Carter.[36] And though Carter created neither Kull nor Conan, by the third printing of *King Kull* Lancer was headlining Carter as one of the creators of both.

The late 1960s and early 1970s was a lucrative time for the Lancer Conan series. By then, the Conan market had a vast readership. When the Lancer Conan books reached their pinnacle in 1970, associate editor Roy Thomas at Marvel Comics convinced Stan Lee to take Robert's barbarian and immortalize him in the pages of a comic book series. Thomas was largely responding to pressure from the many readers who had written to the Marvel editors requesting a Conan comic book series. In several brief essays, Thomas detailed the creation of Marvel's popular *Conan the Barbarian* comic book. "By 1969 Marvel . . . was receiving mail begging us to adapt certain literary creations into our pages—particularly Edgar Rice Burroughs's Tarzan and John Carter of Mars, J. R. R. Tolkien's Lord of the Rings, Doc Savage—and Robert E. Howard's Conan the Cimmerian."[37] Thus, at the behest of readers, Stan Lee and Roy Thomas went to work on a new comic book.

Thomas started with the idea of Conan, since he had already "purchased a few mid-'60s Conan paperbacks, mostly for their Frank Frazetta covers, but hadn't bothered to read a single story all the way through." So, Conan was already in the forefront of his mind based on the Lancer Conan books. With Stan Lee's encouragement, Thomas wrote a memo to Martin Goodman, Marvel's publisher, detailing the idea for a new comic book line. Trying to avoid mentioning the sorcery aspect too soon, the memo focused on the protagonist being quite powerful but possessing no real superpowers or even donning a costume. To bolster readers' interest, the new line would include a host of monsters and "plenty of beautiful women in attendance."[38] Goodman was sold on the idea, but allowed only a minuscule amount of money per issue for the rights of any paperback character Lee and Thomas chose to use. Right away Thomas assumed that this condition left Conan the Cimmerian off the negotiation table.

With a meager $150 per issue to offer, and assuming Conan was out of their price range, Lee and Thomas turned their attention to Lin Carter's Thongor of Lemuria, who was obviously a derivative character. Since Thongor was a combination of Robert E. Howard's Conan and Edgar Rice Burroughs's John Carter of Mars, Lee and Thomas thought that they were getting the best of both in one character. Lee placed a strong importance on character names, and he liked the name Thongor better than Conan. According to Thomas, "*Thongor in the City of Magicians* had been the very first S&S [sword & sorcery] book I had actually read all the way through." So negotiations began. But with such a small amount being offered, Lin Carter's agent dragged his feet on the negotiations. Meanwhile, Thomas purchased the latest Lancer Conan book and spent an evening perusing its pages. Thomas "noticed in L. Sprague de Camp's introduction the name and address of one Glenn Lord, listed as 'literary agent for the estate of Robert E. Howard.'"[39] On a whim, Thomas decided to write Lord and make him an offer for Conan. Thomas would later recall Lord's response:

> To my happy surprise, despite the meager payment we offered, Glenn saw virtue in my contention that such a comic would give Conan (and Robert E. Howard) exposure to many new readers. Indeed, I learned there'd been a few recent attempts to get a Conan comic off the ground—one by artist Gil Kane for his own company; and Glenn had once tried to interest Creepy, a horror black-and-white comic of the period. Neither effort had gotten far.

Thomas's hunch paid off. Lord agreed to Marvel's offer. Consequently, Carter, dubbed as one of the creators of Conan and Kull in the third edition of Lancer's *King Kull*, was set aside in favor of the real author and the "Real McConan."[40]

Marvel knew that the artist they selected would be critical for this project, especially since Frank Frazetta had so firmly placed his artistic stamp on the barbarian's image. Despite this pressure, Thomas said, "Stan and I agreed at once on the perfect artist to illustrate young Conan's exploits." Thomas approached John Buscema, Marvel's first choice, about the project and gave him copies of the available Lancer Conan editions. After reading the works, Buscema became an instant fan of both Robert E. Howard and Conan. In the meantime, publisher Martin Goodman was putting pressure on Lee and Thomas to keep expenses low, and Thomas had already exceeded his allotted budget. This left Buscema, one of Marvel's premier artists, out of the picture. Buscema's rate was simply too high to justify using him. So Thomas shopped around for another artist. What Marvel needed was an excellent artist who had yet to be given a large project but could handle the job. After considering various artists, Thomas offered the project to a twenty-one-year-old British artist named Barry Smith. Two years prior to Thomas's idea for a Conan comic book, Smith (who later went by the name Barry Windsor-Smith) mailed some of his Jack Kirby–inspired work to Marvel. Stan Lee was impressed enough to use Smith as a filler artist on several stories, including an *X-Men* issue. "Barry (with his friend Steve Parkhouse) must've hopped the next boat west, for he was soon knocking on our door."[41]

While Smith was working on fill-in stories for Marvel, he worked with both Lee and Thomas on *Daredevil*, where his work showed commendable improvement. Around this same time, the US government discovered that Smith was in the country illegally and gave him twenty-four hours to leave. "Back to Britain he went, to begin anew the long, laborious process of returning to the US."[42] All seemed potentially lost, but Marvel and Smith agreed to move forward even though he was back in Britain—Smith could mail his work to Marvel from there. Sometime later, in collaboration with Thomas on a sword and sorcery character named Starr the Slayer, Smith had created a few other sword and sorcery drawings similar to what Thomas had in mind for his Conan project. Impressed, Thomas pitched to Smith the idea of doing Conan. Thus was the Marvel Conan comic book series born. Little did the fellows at Marvel know that "no prior period would match the tremendous cross-cultural success that character would achieve during the 1970s. This decade saw a veritable explosion of all things Conan: new books, new critiques, new fans, and new fanzines—and all because of Conan's association with an as-yet untapped medium, comic books."[43]

Marvel's Conan series ran from October 1970 to December 1993 with a total of 275 books and 12 annuals. Barry Windsor-Smith drew the artwork from 1970 to 1973, when John Buscema picked up where Windsor-Smith left off. Buscema worked on the Conan series regularly until 1987. Marvel's Conan comic book series was so popular during the '70s that it spawned several other comic books based on other Robert E. Howard characters. In 1971, Marvel launched *Kull the Conqueror*, which had a brief run from 1971 to 1973. This was followed by *Kull the Destroyer*, which ran from 1973 to 1978. These series were rebooted in the early to mid-'80s. Marvel's *Chamber of Chills* series, launched in 1972, included two early adaptations of Robert's stories, "The Horror from the Mound" (renamed "The Monster from the Mound") for issue 2 and "The Thing on the Roof" for issue 3. To escape being under the thumb of the Comics Code Authority in the early 1970s, Marvel developed a Conan "magazine" called *The Savage Sword of Conan*. This allowed Marvel to do more with the character than it could in the standard comic book format. The magazine also became a magnet for artists, who were allowed more freedom in their artwork than the Marvel comic books. *The Savage Sword of Conan* became one of the more popular publications in the 1970s and is now considered a cult classic by many collectors.

By the 1980s and beyond, Solomon Kane was a staple character in several comic book series: Marvel's *The Sword of Solomon Kane* and Dark Horse Comics' *Solomon Kane*. In the last four decades, other short comic book series, team-ups, and *What If?* books were published that included several of Howard's characters.

The only market that had not been tapped for Robert's works and characters was film. With that in mind, "as early as 1970, Conan pastiche scribe Lin Carter announced that negotiations were underway to mount the first Cimmerian movie."[44] Even if Carter's claim was correct, the idea would hit a serious speed bump when Lancer entered complex legal proceedings with its distributor, Curtis Circulation Company.[45] Lancer's legal problems initially forced the publisher to suspend its book operations, and ultimately the company was forced to sell its Conan series, placing the character in publishing limbo. "All Conan rights, including movie rights, were soon frozen in a number of lawsuits, the main suit having been brought by L. Sprague de Camp against Lancer for breach of contract."[46] The years of legal entanglements left the idea of a Conan film unrealized in the 1970s. Nevertheless, much was going on in that decade that would finally lead to a movie being released by the early 1980s. Since space does not permit a fully detailed account, the following is a brief summary of how the film became a reality.[47]

Edward Summer, a New York University graduate in television and motion pictures, had been a fan of Robert E. Howard since childhood. Summer was asked by director Brian De Palma to help him redo 20th Century Fox's advertising campaign for the film *Phantom of the Paradise*. Through Summer's involvement in that campaign, he met producer Edward R. Pressman, who sought Summer's advice on film projects that might be commercially successful. Summer suggested a Conan film. Curious about the idea, Pressman encouraged Summer to put together a film studios presentation for such a film. Summer's package included Frazetta's artwork for the Lancer covers, Marvel's current Conan comic book series, and an assortment of Howard's Conan stories. "At roughly the same time, Summer met the actor/bodybuilder Arnold Schwarzenegger."[48] When Pressman invited Summer to an early screening of *Pumping Iron*, Summer realized that Schwarzenegger—who looked like he had just stepped out of a Frazetta Conan book cover—would be a good fit for the Conan character.

By 1977, Summer and Pressman had united with other Conan film participants to form Conan Properties, Inc. Summer invited Marvel's Roy Thomas to collaborate on a screenplay, and the team managed to gain the attention of Paramount Pictures. Paramount representatives, who apparently had heard of neither Summer nor Thomas, expressed interest only if the screenplay was written by someone known in the industry. This mandate brought in Oliver Stone, an Oscar winner for his screenplay *Midnight Express*. Stone presented Pressman with a fresh screenplay "based on two REH Conan stories, 'Black Colossus,' and 'A Witch Shall Be Born.'"[49] But bringing on someone of Stone's caliber would increase the film's budget, and the filmmakers were unable to do that. In searching for a director, Pressman and Summer met with a few, including Ridley Scott (*Alien*), Philip Kaufman (*The Right Stuff*), and John Milius (*The Wind and the Lion*). Of these three, Milius was the best candidate since he had directed as well as contributed to scripts (for example, several of the *Dirty Harry* films). Besides being able to write, Milius was also shortlisted because he had flown under the radar in the film industry in the 1970s, and that made him affordable.

"By 1979, Milius's *Conan* had been given a budget of $19.5 million. This mid-tier figure was based on Milius's re-written script, which he'd begun in late 1978."[50] After years of footwork and effort, the film had garnered a budget, a director, a script, and a main actor—Arnold Schwarzenegger. After they added all the other elements that go into creating a film (actors, set designer, and so on), shooting began in Madrid, Spain, in late 1980. *Conan the Barbarian* was finally released in May 1982. "Following its release, *Conan* went on to gross over $100 million," Paul Sammon wrote in concluding his account of the making of the film. When his book *Conan the Phenomenon* was published in 2007, DVD sales had contributed significantly to grosses on the film, Sammon reported, which at that point exceeded $300 million.[51]

In the years following the release of the Milius film, fans have debated, sometimes to a fever pitch, about how well the movie presents Robert E. Howard's character. The film's story line fails to follow in any noticeable manner the story lines from Robert's short stories. Milius included certain elements of Robert's stories, such as the "tree of woe," where Conan is nailed to a tree, a scene stripped from "A Witch Shall Be Born" but altered from its context. And unlike Robert, Milius created an origin story for Conan. "Interestingly, Milius's origin story would later become the most problematic aspect of [*Conan the Barbarian*] for hardcore Howard fans and scholars."[52] Milius added an antagonist—Thulsa Doom—who never existed in Robert's Conan stories. In fact, Thulsa Doom is an enemy of Kull's, from Robert's story "Delcardes' Cat." All things considered, the film is a poor representation of Robert's character and stories. That being said, it is the first major sword-and-sorcery film, and it "became the standard by which all other sword-and-sorcery films were measured, until writer/director Peter Jackson's *The Fellowship of the Ring* was released in 1999."[53]

In 1984, two years after the release of *Conan the Barbarian*, Universal Pictures released another Conan film, *Conan the Destroyer*. This second film did not fare as well at the box office as the first, grossing just over $100 million worldwide and only $31 million in the United States.[54] Conan would not grace the silver screen again until August 11, 2011, when Lionsgate released its iteration by the same title, *Conan the Barbarian*, starring Jason Momoa as Conan. Though Lionsgate's film managed to renew interest in Robert's character, the film lost money at the box office, earning a worldwide gross of just over $41 million against a budget of $90 million. Once again, the film contained few elements from Robert's original stories.

In between Universal's *Conan the Destroyer* and Lionsgate's *Conan the Barbarian*, two other major motion pictures based on Robert's characters were released, though neither utilized story lines from his original works. The first was *Kull the Conqueror*, released in August 1997 and starring Kevin Sorbo of *Hercules: The Legendary Journeys* fame. The second was *Solomon Kane* (2009), written and directed by British filmmaker Michael J. Bassett.

From the 1960s with the Lancer Conan series to the 1970s with Marvel's Conan comic book series and on into the 1980s and '90s with the various films, Robert's original stories were buried under a morass of pastiche-based stories and media. In these four decades, only a handful of collections contained Robert E. Howard's own stories, but they were not quite as far-reaching as the Lancer series, the Marvel comic books, or the films.

In 1977, Berkley Medallion Books began publishing a series of Robert E. Howard volumes edited by Karl Edward Wagner, with manuscripts and letters provided by Glenn Lord, who was at the time the agent for the Howard estate. The first three volumes in the series—*The Hour of the Dragon*, *Red Nails*, and *The People of the Black Circle*—were devoted to several of Robert's Conan stories. *The People of the Black Circle* also included "The Devil in Iron," "A Witch Shall Be Born," and "Jewels of Gwahlur." The Conan volumes were published in both hardcover and mass market paperback. The paperback editions contained small perforated foldout posters with Ken Kelly's artwork. These foldout posters were a delightful addition to the volumes and would raise their collectible value over the years. In many ways, the Berkley series was launched in reaction to the de Camp–Carter Conan series published by Lancer and Ace. Those books were textually edited to varying degrees and included Conan pastiches, which the purist Robert E. Howard fan often scorned.

In the 1970s, Robert E. Howard aficionados became more vocal about their preference for pure Howard stories. Arguments in fandom regarding the validity and quality of Conan fragment completions ("posthumous collaborations"), pastiches, and pastiches based on other Robert E. Howard characters (such as Bran Mak Morn) sometimes became heated, splitting fandom into factions: those purists who felt that Robert's stories should remain unaltered, and those who enjoyed not only the edited versions but also the pastiches. Most of those taking sides in this debate were involved in Howard fanzines, collecting, and scholarship. The average reader and fan was unaware that these issues were being debated.

This debate was partly responsible for the publication of the Berkley volumes. On its Conan book covers, Berkley announced that its books were the "Authorized Editions." Karl Edward Wagner, in Berkley's *The Hour of the Dragon*, took great care to explain that pastiches reflected mere shadows of the real Robert E. Howard stories and characters and too often failed to capture the true spirit of Robert's work.[55] The stories in the Berkley books were presented as they were originally published, with very few edits or alterations and with no pastiches. Aside from the first three Conan books, Berkley would publish seven more Robert E. Howard volumes (though no new Conan books). The Berkley series ended in the late '70s as a direct result of de Camp's opposition to it. The de Camp–Carter Ace editions of Conan would continue to be published until the late 1980s, along with dozens of additional Conan pastiches. So the debate continued.

In the mid-1990s, British film and music video director Marcelo Anciano joined the Robert E. Howard United Press Association (REHupa) "with plans for [a] Solomon Kane book to be illustrated by Gary Gianni, and hopes of a movie."[56] Anciano's plans were extremely fortuitous, not only for Robert E. Howard fans but for Howard purists as well. Longtime Robert E. Howard fan Rusty Burke, also a member of REHupa, and a Howard scholar who eventually became the president of the Robert E. Howard (REH) Foundation, wrote Anciano to "let him know about the textual problems in the Kane stories published up to that time."[57] Burke also "offered to help provide him with good texts." Little did Burke know at the time that his letter would launch him into the project of his life. According to Burke,

> Marcelo had proposed that it [a Solomon Kane book] be the first of a "Robert E. Howard Library of Classics," modeled on the old Scribner's Classics that had been illustrated by Wyeth, et al. He pitched the idea to his partners in Wandering Star, the Berrow brothers, and to Jack and Barbara Baum [owners of the Howard estate at the time], and they agreed.[58]

This idea morphed into the limited and leather-bound illustrated editions of the *Robert E. Howard Library of Classics* published by Wandering Star Media. The project was spearheaded by Anciano with the help of the best Robert E. Howard scholars of the day, who were all textual purists. Limited editions of five volumes were published, and the price tag on each was steep. Anciano got the Frank Frazetta family involved in one of the Conan volumes, *The Ultimate Triumph*, which is lushly illustrated by

Frazetta's artwork. Anciano "recruited and worked with the artists," and he also took charge of "all the art direction" for the book collection.[59] The project was enormously beneficial because it led to a contract with Del Rey, a major science fiction and fantasy publishing house, for a series of eleven Robert E. Howard volumes.

Initially, Del Rey published the first five Wandering Star titles in hardcover and then later in trade paperback editions. More importantly, to allow readers to better understand the stories as they were originally published in *Weird Tales* and other pulp magazines in the 1920s and 1930s, the texts were very lightly edited. According to Burke, the subsequent six volumes in the series were "produced for Del Rey by the Wandering Star team." Burke further explains, "Marcelo Anciano, the originator and mastermind, left us after the Best Of books (*Crimson Shadows* and *Grim Lands*), but the rest of us carried on and I think we all felt that Marcelo was still with us, in the fact that we were still inspired by him and guided by the format he'd established for the Library."[60] Both the Wandering Star and Del Rey editions contain scholarly introductions, essays, chronologies, and textual notes to help the reader gain a better understanding of Robert E. Howard's work. The Del Rey editions, which remain in print, are without a doubt the most significant collection of Robert E. Howard's work ever to be produced, aside from the original works in the pulp magazines.

Ever since Robert's stories, especially his Conan stories, were published in the pulp magazines, they have endured textual revisions, additions, character changes to suit particular stories, and other major and minor edits. Likewise, several of Robert's fragmentary works have been completed and used for stories in the Gnome, Lancer, and Marvel Conan series. Since the 1950s, Conan has been slowly altered to a degree that an entire generation of fans might not recognize the character in the stories as originally published in *Weird Tales*. And many fans who came to know Robert E. Howard through Hollywood, even those who also read the Marvel or Ace Conan books of the '70s and '80s, may not have had an opportunity to see or read Conan as he was originally created by Robert E. Howard. The Del Rey series brought Robert's publishing history full circle, giving back to the reader his original work.

Through the publishing history of Robert E. Howard's works, his characters have garnered a greater amount of popularity than he has himself. As it turns out, Conan is more popular than his creator. This is not unusual in the literary world. Sherlock Holmes is far better known than his creator, Sir Arthur Conan Doyle. Like Doyle, Robert E. Howard the person is somewhat obscure, and many of those who recognize his name may be misinformed about him, perhaps having read a poorly written introduction in a volume of his altered works or an early biography that speculated, sometimes wildly, about his family and his life.[61] By whatever means fans were introduced to Robert E. Howard and his works, his family, his childhood and upbringing, his education, and his struggle to break out of a series of dead-end jobs and begin a writing career, the fact remains that the stories of Robert E. Howard have had an impact lasting almost a century, and that is paramount to understanding not only those stories but *his* story as well.

Afterword

Robert E. Howard's stories and characters are still alive and well today, especially in the video gaming community. *Conan Exiles* is the most recent video game developed around Howard's famous character. Designed by Oscar Lopez Lacalle and published by Funcom, *Conan Exiles* was released on May 8, 2018, and can be played on Microsoft Windows, PlayStation 4, and Xbox One.[1] Set in the world of Conan the Barbarian, *Conan Exiles* is an open-world survival game. At the start, players choose their character, male or female. To a large degree, players can customize their character's race and religion (Stygian, Cimmerian, Hyborian, and so on) and features (looks, body type, and so on).

The custom-created character begins the game being saved from certain death by Conan and then is released into a harsh, wild, and vast exile land with not only deserts but also mountainous regions, plains, and rain forests. After being saved by Conan, players begin the game with a small water-skin and pretty much nothing else. Surviving and thriving in this fictional exile land of the prehistoric Hyborian Age is the basic premise. The character must hunt, find water, plant crops, and build shelter. Players can chooses to play in a PVP (player-versus-player) mode, fending off attacks from other players as well as from the game-established characters and creatures.[2] During an early access period in 2017, *Conan Exiles* sold over 320,000 copies via Steam (a digital distribution platform created by the Valve Corporation). According to Funcom, as of May 2018, over a million copies of *Conan Exiles* had been sold.[3] The game is still growing in popularity and continues to sell. For players who may be having a difficult time with the game, hundreds of YouTube videos have been created by successful players to help "noobs" (new players) survive and thrive.

In the comic book industry, Marvel announced that it had once again acquired the rights to Conan the Barbarian and released the first issue of the new comic book in January 2019. The new Conan series is written by the highly acclaimed Jason Aaron, who is working with the equally acclaimed artist Mahmud Asrar. In several interviews and articles, Aaron said that at age thirteen he discovered Robert E. Howard's character Conan in a used bookstore in his hometown of Jasper, Alabama. Being an ardent fan, Aaron has claimed that he will remain as faithful as possible to Robert E. Howard's original stories in the new Marvel comic book series.[4]

On other media fronts, HBO aired its season finale of the popular *Game of Thrones* series in the spring of 2019. The series is based on George R. R. Martin's epic sword-and-sorcery fantasy book series *A Song of Ice and Fire*. Martin has announced his intention to resume work on the print series, but given his track record, fans are not holding their breath to see the results anytime soon. Martin has repeatedly told readers (and viewers of the HBO shows) that Robert E. Howard's Conan stories were a pivotal influence on *A Song of Ice and Fire*, and on his blog he recommends Howard's works to his readers. Martin claims that were it not for Robert E. Howard, J. R. R. Tolkien, C. L. Moore, and a few others, he could never have written *A Song of Ice and Fire*.[5] Martin's output, both the books and the HBO television series, is an excellent example of the perfected development of sword-and-sorcery, the modern fantasy fiction subgenre that Robert E. Howard created. If you have enjoyed *Game of Thrones*, then take George R. R. Martin's advice and read Robert E. Howard.

In 2006, under the direction of Rusty Burke, the Robert E. Howard Foundation was established to foster an understanding of the life and works of Robert E. Howard.[6] Since its inception, the REH Foundation has acquired, conserved, and managed archives and collections related to Robert E. Howard and his family. The foundation has also published Robert's unreleased manuscripts, fragmented works, and sketches. Some of these items are from Glenn Lord's collection, a large portion of which is housed at the Harry Ransom Center at the University of Texas at Austin.

In 2009, the REH Foundation published a seven-hundred-page collection of Robert's poetry, another game-changer in Howard scholarship. All three print runs sold out fairly quickly. Since its publication, more of Robert's poetry and fragments of his poetry have been discovered, and a revised version of this volume to include this newly discovered material is in the works. The REH Foundation is also working to revise its popular (and currently sold out) three-volume set of all of Robert's letters.

With the wild popularity of *Conan Exiles* and the video gaming industry generally, Marvel comic books, and Martin's *Game of Thrones* TV series, the influence of Robert E. Howard is evident on various media fronts. With several yet to be tapped areas within the vast landscape of his literature and characters, Robert E. Howard's legacy, stories, and characters are likely to thrive and develop further as the second century of his notoriety and influence continues.

Acknowledgments

Ihave been a fan of Robert E. Howard and his stories since 1981, and this book is the result. Eighteen of those years were spent in academic research and writing about Howard, three of them devoted solely to this book. As such, I owe a debt of gratitude to a host of people. I would first like to thank my editor at the University of Texas Press, Jim Burr. From our first conversation at the 2016 PCA/ACA in Seattle, Washington, to the volume you currently hold, he guided me through the entire process, offering suggestions and redirecting me when necessary. Burr has the patience of Job, and I am most grateful to him. A hearty thanks to Howard historian Rob Roehm for enabling my Howard obsession by providing me with documents from his many years of research—newly discovered court documents, Howard family documents, and so on. If Roehm did not have a document, he would tell me where to find it (making sure I made copies for him too). I owe a big thanks to Bobby Derie for his help with the letters of the various pulp writers and for further facilitating my book-buying habit by pointing me to several resources. I would also like to extend thanks to Rusty Burke for answering my emails, providing me with several resources, and answering my questions.

I would like to thank S. T. Joshi and Karen Kohoutek for reading the manuscript. Their suggestions vastly improved the scope and content of the book.

A big thanks to my good friend David Piske. He'll say I dragged him kicking and screaming into Howard fandom, but he loves it. Thanks for those many discussions about Lovecraft and Howard and Conan the Cimmerian while imbibing perhaps too many glasses of wine.

I would like to extend a special thanks to copy editor Cynthia Buck for her care with my manuscript, to Lynne Ferguson for facilitating the editing, and to the staff at the University of Texas Press for their care and attention to the publication of this book.

I would also like to thank the numerous people who, in one way or another, aided and abetted this project: Grace G. Hansen and the staff at the Harry Ransom Center, University of Texas at Austin; William Fliss at the John P. Raynor, S.J. Library, Marquette University; Rob E. King at the Southwest Collection/Special Collections Library, Texas Tech University; and Joshua Seachris, Christopher Oldham, Terry Baker, Scotty Henderson, Patrice Louinet, Mark Finn, Ben Friberg, Jason Ray Carney, Jeffrey Shanks, Michael Scott Myers, Gary Romeo, and Lee Breakiron.

Notes

INTRODUCTION. WHO IS ROBERT E. HOWARD?

1. H. P. Lovecraft, "861: To E. Hoffmann Price," in *H. P. Lovecraft: Selected Letters 1934–1937*, ed. August Derleth and James Turner (Sauk City, WI: Arkham House, 1976), 278.

2. Ibid., 272.

3. Ibid.

4. Michael Merschel, "How Did 'Wonder Boys' Novelist Kill Time in Texas? He Dropped by Conan the Barbarian's Creator's Home," *Dallas Morning News*, October 3, 2017, https://www.dallasnews.com/arts-entertainment/books/2017/10/04/how-did-wonder-boys-novelist-kill-time-in-texas-he-dropped-by-conan-the-barbarian-creator-s-home/.

CHAPTER 1. PIONEERING STORIES

1. I use Howard's first name throughout this book, not to imply a particularly intimate knowledge of or relationship with him but to help in distinguishing between members of his family. When discussing his parents, I usually refer to them as Dr. Howard (but as Isaac when appropriate) and Mrs. Howard (or Hester).

2. George W. Ervin enlisted in the Confederate Army on December 4, 1862, and appeared on General Forest's Tenth Mississippi Cavalry muster roll by March 9, 1863. It is unknown whether Ervin achieved the rank of colonel. It's likely that "Colonel" was an honorific title.

3. Glenn Lord, "The Wandering Years," in *The Last Celt: A Bio-Bibliography of Robert E. Howard* (West Kingston, RI: Donald Grant Publishers, 1976), 24.

4. Howard provides 1866 as the year the Ervins moved to Texas in his essay "The Wandering Years" (ibid., 23–28), but this date is uncertain. In fact, there are several errors in Howard's essay, and recent findings by Howard historians Rob

Roehm and Patrice Louinet have cast suspicion on the chronology in Howard's essay. However, it can be determined where the Ervin family lived prior to moving to Texas from the birth certificates of Hester Ervin Howard's older siblings. Moreover, Hester's older brother, Robert T. Ervin, was born in Texas in 1867. Therefore, it is likely that the Ervins did in fact move to Texas sometime in 1866.

5. Robert E. Howard, "1930," in *The Collected Letters of Robert E. Howard*, ed. Rob Roehm, vol. 1 (1923–1929), vol. 2 (1930–1932), and vol. 3 (1933–1936) (Plano, TX: Robert E. Howard Foundation Press, 2007, 2008), 2:136.

6. *Lampasas Leader*, April 20, 1889, "Local Items" section.

7. *El Paso Times*, July 17, 1888.

8. An obituary from the *Dallas Daily Herald*, June 3, 1874, reports that Mrs. Ervin died from a "lingering illness." Since there is no mention of a child in the news clip, it is possible that Mrs. Ervin was suffering from some illness or condition exacerbated by the birth of Lizzie, causing her death.

9. Howard, "1930," in Roehm, *The Collected Letters of Robert E. Howard*, 2:499.

10. Robin Cole-Jett, "Introduction," in *Lewisville* (Charleston, SC: Arcadia Publishing, 2011), 7.

11. See "Title LXXVIII—Public Education—CH. 3," in *Revised Civil Statutes of the State of Texas*, 532, article 3706. Austin: State of Texas, 1879.

12. There is no evidence that Mrs. Howard completed all the years of her education up to and including graduation from high school, though this is possible. I spent several hours over a three-day period talking with various people in the Lewisville Independent School District. They confirmed that a public school was built in Lewisville around 1877, but the town had no school records dating back to that year. In the late 1800s, girls in Texas were typically educated between ages seven and thirteen and became functionally proficient at essential mathematics, reading, and writing.

13. Isaac M. Howard, "Lonely Business 1937," in *The Collected Letters of Dr. Isaac M. Howard*, ed. Rob Roehm (Plano, TX: Robert E. Howard Foundation Press, 2011), 148–149.

14. Isaac Howard, "Loose Ends: 1939–1944," in ibid., 205.

15. Hester (Ervin) Howard had several stepbrothers and sisters, two of whom were born in Lampasas: George Wynneton Ervin (May 14, 1886) and Lulu Ervin (December 24, 1887).

16. The newspaper had changed hands several times, with a name change each time, until it changed ownership in 1890 to a G. A. Beeman and became *The Rustler*. For additional information, see Patrice Louinet, "The Man from Ferris," in *The Long Road to Dark Valley, Part 4*, *REH: Two-Gun Raconteur*, January 23, 2013, https://web.archive.org/web/20150907095149/http://www.rehtwogunraconteur.com/the-long-road-to-dark-valley-part-4/ (accessed November 27, 2017); and Fran Lomas, "The History of Coke County, Texas," March 4, 2003, http://files.usgwarchives.net/tx/coke/history/county/cokehist.txt.

17. The *Ferris Wheel* was originally called the *Ferris Sentinel*, but William Ervin changed the name shortly after he purchased the newspaper.

18. By this time (1899), Frank Ezzell had purchased the *Ferris Wheel* from Hester's brother William.

19. Louinet, "The Man from Ferris."

20. Annie Newton Davis was the younger sister of Austin Newton, Robert E. Howard's close childhood friend in Cross Cut. Annie, along with all the other Newtons, remained close friends with the Howards, even after the Howards moved to Cross Plains. Of all the Howards, Annie was closest to Dr. Howard. It is unknown whether she obtained this information directly from Mrs. Howard or through Dr. Howard. She never named her source in the interview.

21. L. Sprague de Camp and Catherine C. de Camp, interview with Annie Newton Davis, Brownwood, TX, October 18, 1978, De Camp Collection, Harry Ransom Center, University of Texas at Austin (hereafter "De Camp Collection").

22. Existing copies of the *Ferris Wheel* can be found at the University of North Texas's online Texas historical database; see "Ferris Wheel," https://texashistory .unt.edu/explore/collections/FERWH/. It is safe to say that if Hester had visited Ferris between 1901 and 1904, it would have been reported in the *Ferris Wheel* because of her close relationship with the Ezzells.

23. L. Sprague de Camp and Catherine C. de Camp, interview with Annie Newton Davis, Brownwood, TX, October 18, 1978, De Camp Collection.

24. Samuel R. Ezzell, father of Ida, Lesta, and Frank, retired in Lometa. Lesta McCarson retired up the road in Brownwood, where her husband was born and raised. According to Annie Newton Davis, Hester visited that area. It's likely that Frank Ezzell spent time in the area as well, though he would eventually retire to Big Spring, Texas, where he died.

25. For further details about the situation, see Louinet, "The Man from Ferris."

26. See the de Camp interviews housed at the Harry Ransom Center at the University of Texas at Austin. These interviews reveal a consensus among several of the Howards' closest neighboring friends that Dr. Howard was in fact kicked out of his own home on several occasions when he was not making enough money to support his family.

27. I have used the year 1872 based on information in the introduction by Howard scholar Rusty Burke, who discusses discrepancies in the year of Dr. Howard's birth, in Roehm, *The Collected Letters of Dr. Isaac M. Howard*, ix–x.

28. H. P. Lovecraft and Robert E. Howard, "1930," in *A Means to Freedom: The Letters of H. P. Lovecraft and Robert E. Howard: 1930–1932*, ed. S. T. Joshi, David E. Schultz, and Rusty Burke (New York: Hippocampus Press, 2011), 1:89.

29. It is possible that Robert E. Howard confused the names of his grandfather, James W. Henry, with one of his uncles, William Harrison Henry. Whatever the case, all records indicate that Robert E. Howard's grandfather's name was James W. Henry, not James Harrison Henry.

30. It is unknown whether James W. Henry left the Confederate Army owing to an injury or to illness.

31. Lovecraft and Howard, "1935," in Joshi et al., *A Means to Freedom*, 2:833.

32. William B. Howard's death is documented as 1888 in the Howard family Bible. However, on a pension form she filled out, Louisa Howard indicated that William died near Mount Calm, Texas, in 1889.

33. Rusty Burke, "Introduction: A Grief Indescribable," in Roehm, *The Collected Letters of Dr. Isaac M. Howard*, x.

34. Ibid.

35. Rob Roehm, "Isaac M. Howard in the 1800s," *REH: Two-Gun Raconteur*, October 18, 2012, https://web.archive.org/web/20130121130544/http://rehtwogunra conteur.com/?p=20488 (accessed September 15, 2017).

36. Ibid.

37. Howard historian and scholar Rob Roehm recently discovered that Eliza Howard's sister, Margaret, was also married to a medical doctor, Dr. John K. Hodge. The Hodges lived in Arkansas near the rest of the Henrys. This would have provided Isaac with apprenticeship options if he did move back to Arkansas to study medicine. This information was given to me via correspondence with Rob Roehm on September 9, 2017.

38. Rob Roehm, "Training Doctor Howard," *REH: Two-Gun Raconteur*, May 14, 2015, https://web.archive.org/web/20150705020534/http://www.rehtwogun raconteur.com:80/training-dr-howard/ (accessed September 21, 2017).

39. Burke, "Introduction: A Grief Indescribable," x.

40. Lovecraft and Howard, "1932," in Joshi et al., *A Means to Freedom*, 1:379.

41. Roehm, "Training Doctor Howard."

42. Ibid.

43. Dr. Howard may have figured out the age difference on his own. The fact that he sometimes reported his own and his wife's birthdays on different days may indicate that he was unable to remember dates or that the dates were never that important to him.

44. Burke, "Introduction: A Grief Indescribable," xi.

CHAPTER 2. FROM BIRTH TO BAGWELL

1. Vernon A. Garrison, "Peaster Pencilings," *Weatherford Daily Herald*, January 26, 1906.

2. Rob Roehm, "The Howards Are a Moving People," *Howard History*, December 13, 2019, https://howardhistory.com/2019/12/13/the-howards-are-a-moving -people/ (accessed December 13, 2019).

3. L. Sprague de Camp, interview with Wallace C. Howard, Mart, TX, July 22, 1977, De Camp Collection.

4. Robert E. Howard mentions being named after his great-grandfather in a short work titled "An Autobiography," which can be found in Glenn Lord's *The Last Celt*. It should be noted that, in personal correspondence, Rob Roehm wondered whether it might be possible that Robert E. Howard was named after his maternal uncle, Robert T. Ervin: "Hester appears to have visited Galveston around the time of her brother's death, where he lived, which makes me think they might have been close. She at least knew him. She never even met her grandfather." My assumption is that Robert E. Howard's uncle was probably named after his grandfather, who would have been Robert's great-grandfather, so it seems likely he could have been named after either one.

5. The Texas state historical landmark beside Robert E. Howard's grave cites the same birth date recorded on his birth certificate: January 24, 1906.

6. The Howard family Bible was recently brought to Cross Plains, Texas, for the 2015 Robert E. Howard Days.

7. Alberta Lawrence (Chamberlin), "1933–34–35," in *Who's Who among North American Authors*, vol. 6 (Los Angeles: Golden Syndicate, 1933), as cited in Glenn Lord, "Facts of Biography," *The Howard Collector* 1, no. 1 (1961): 5.

8. *Polk's Medical Register and Directory of North America*, 8th ed., rev. (Chicago: R. L. Polk & Publishers, 1904).

9. "Peaster Items," *Weatherford Weekly Herald*, October 19, 1905.

10. Some of the information about the various Texas towns in this chapter was gleaned from the Handbook of Texas, available at the Texas State Historical Association website, https://tshaonline.org/handbook.

11. "Peaster Pencilings," *Weatherford Weekly Herald*, February 22, 1906.

12. Lovecraft and Howard, "1930," in Joshi et al., *A Means to Freedom*, 1:94–95.

13. Ibid., 1:95.

14. This house later became known as "the Old Kyle House."

15. L. Sprague de Camp and Catherine de Camp, interview with Miss Katherine Merryman and Mrs. Alice Younglove, Cross Plains, TX, March 7, 1978, De Camp Collection; and interview with Kate Merryman, Alice Younglove, and Lois Garrett, Merryman-Younglove home, Cross Plains, TX, October 17, 1978, De Camp Collection.

16. William V. Ervin had owned *The Ferris Wheel* in Ferris, TX (see chapter 1).

17. Rob Roehm, "We Spent the Winter in San Antonio," *Howard History*, December 10, 2018, https://howardhistory.com/2018/12/10/we-spent-the-winter-in-san-antonio/ (accessed December 10, 2018).

18. Ibid.

19. "More State Land," *Brownsville Daily Herald*, June 21, 1907.

20. The *Handbook of Texas* declares that the only farming in Seminole around 1906 to 1908 was probably family gardening and small grain crops used as cattle feed. See https://tshaonline.org/handbook.

21. This date is known because Rob Roehm discovered a medical registry that

Dr. Howard filed in Bexar County on November 20, 1909, which contained a hand-written history of the places where he had registered his medical license from 1907 to 1909.

22. Coke County courthouse, Medical Registry Book: Medical License no. 1, page 57.

23. Ira Carleton Chase, ed., "County Societies: Changes of Address from February 15 to March 18, 1909," *Texas State Journal of Medicine* (May 1908–April 1909), IV:337.

24. The railroad tracks were laid through Bronte in 1907, but, oddly, the first train did not actually arrive in Bronte until 1909.

25. Certificates filed at the county clerk's office are dated December 1908, May 1909, and August 27, 1909.

26. The last recorded date marking the presence of the Howards in Bronte was a birth certificate dated August 27, 1909.

27. Dr. Howard filed his medical license in Bexar County on November 20, 1909, and gave his mailing address as San Antonio, Texas.

28. See Rob Roehm, "Down the Nueces," *Howard History*, December 9, 2018, https://howardhistory.com/2018/12/09/down-the-nueces/.

29. Lovecraft and Howard, "1930," in Joshi et al., *A Means to Freedom*, 1:91.

30. L. Sprague de Camp and Catherine C. de Camp, interview with Fannie "Faye" Adamson, October 16, 1978, De Camp Collection.

31. Robert E. Howard, "The Score Board," *Dime Sports Magazine* (June 1936): 108.

32. *Texas State Journal of Medicine* 5 (May 1909–April 1910). "J. M. Howard" is probably a typo and should have read "I. M. Howard." This was a common error due to Dr. Howard's often illegible handwriting.

33. US Department of Commerce and Labor, Bureau of the Census, "Thirteenth Census of the United States: 1910—Population (May 16, 1910) Texas, Palo Pinto, Justice Precinct 1, District 0182."

34. *Polk's Medical Register and Directory of North America*, 11th rev. ed. Detroit: R. L. Polk & Co., 1910.

35. See Roehm, *The Collected Letters of Robert E. Howard*, 1:357, 2:18, 2:67, 2:100, 2:247.

36. According to the paper trail, they lived there from May 16, 1910, to October 18, 1912.

37. S. C. Gwynne, *Empire of the Summer Moon: Quanah Parker and the Rise and Fall of the Comanches, the Most Powerful Indian Tribe in American History* (New York: Scribner, 2010), 173.

38. At the time, the Howards knew her as Mary (Tarkington) Brown; she would later remarry and become Mary Crawford.

39. Howard, "1931," in Roehm, *Collected Letters of Robert E. Howard: 1930–1932*, 2:257. Note that the date Howard uses, 1872, is incorrect: the events Mary Crawford described occurred in 1860.

40. Ibid., 2:247.

41. Ibid.

42. Rusty Burke, "A Deep Dark Current Runs Forever," *Robert E. Howard United Press Association* (*REHupa*) 200 (August 2006), 1. *REHupa* is a fan and aficionado publication in which a few scholars occasionally share unpublished or soon to be published research.

43. Pat B. Clark, *The History of Clarksville and Old Red River County* (Dallas: Mathis, Van Nort & Co., 1937), 19.

44. Lovecraft and Howard, "1930," in Joshi et al., *A Means to Freedom*, 1:43.

45. There is some discrepancy in Mary Bohannon's place of birth. Her death certificate (which misspells her last name, as taken from the Bohannon family) has her place of birth in Tennessee and states a "near estimate" of her birth date as February 23, 1821. Errors such as these are not uncommon, especially for former slaves, minorities, and the poor.

46. In census data from 1860, Henry C. Bohannon's name is spelled "Bohanan," but the family name is spelled "Bohannon" on various cemetery headstones.

47. Burke, "A Deep Dark Current Runs Forever," 4.

48. Red River County land deeds, Deed Book 30, pp. 113–115.

49. Mary Bohannon's residence is confirmed by the 1910 federal census for Red River County. It declares that Mary Bohannon was living with the Dennis family in Red River County, Precinct 4, district 0124, which includes a section of Bagwell just north of the T&P Railroad.

50. Sharon Stephens Black, "Mary Bohannon of Bagwell, Red River Co., Texas," *Red River County Texas Genealogical Society Quarterly* 19 (Spring 2002): 3–7.

51. To a twenty-first-century audience, this language ought to be offensive—and this helps serve my point when I discuss Howard's use of this same kind of language toward slaves and blacks later on in the book. Lovecraft and Howard, "1930," in Joshi et al., *A Means to Freedom*, 1:43–44.

52. Ibid., 1:44.

53. Ibid.

54. Stephen King, *Danse Macabre* (New York: Gallery, 2010), 240.

55. The cemetery researchers Lawrence and Sue Dale have done extensive research on the people (all African Americans) and location of this abandoned cemetery. For their research, see "Bagwell Cemetery" at http://www.findagrave.com /cgi-bin/fg.cgi?page=cr&GRid=62825115&CRid=2347051&.

56. Burke, "A Deep Dark Current Runs Forever," 4.

57. Black, "Mary Bohannon of Bagwell, Red River Co., Texas," 3–7.

58. Lovecraft and Howard, "1930," in Joshi et al., *A Means to Freedom*, 1:45.

59. Ibid.

60. Burke, "A Deep Dark Current Runs Forever," 6.

61. For a full account of this story, see Joshi et al., *A Means to Freedom*, 1:84–85. It's quite possible that this story is a tall tale that Howard used to showboat in his correspondence to Lovecraft.

CHAPTER 3. CROSS CUT AND BURKETT

1. "Prof. J. H. Surles," *Abilene Daily Reporter*, January 17, 1915.

2. "Cross Cut Items" in the *Cross Plains Review*, on January 29, 1915, announced that "Dr. Howard, of Putnam has moved to Cross Cut." The phrase "of Putnam" implies that the Howards may have been living in Putnam (at least for a short time).

3. Another indicator that the Howards probably spent only a short time in Putnam is that, as far as can be determined from courthouse records, around 1915 Dr. Howard did not register his medical license in Callahan County (Putnam, TX).

4. This is speculation on my part based on the de Camp interviews with Norris Chambers, Dr. Chambers's son. On page 12 of these interviews, Norris Chambers indicates that his father and Dr. Howard knew each other prior to Dr. Howard's marriage to Hester Jane Ervin. See L. Sprague de Camp and Catherine de Camp, interview with Norris Chambers, Fort Worth, TX, July 22, 1977, De Camp Collection.

5. "Dr. Howard and Family have moved in[to] the house recently vacated by Mr. Pentecost and Family." "Cross Cut Items," *Cross Plains Review*, June 11, 1915.

6. Land Deed Book 140, pp. 623-624, Brown County Clerk's office, Brownwood, TX.

7. "Cross Cut Items," *Cross Plains Review*, June 11, 1915.

8. L. Sprague de Camp and Catherine de Camp, interview with Mr. and Mrs. L. L. Morgan, Brownwood, TX, March 6, 1978, De Camp Collection.

9. "Cross Cut Items," *Cross Plains Review*, June 23, 1916.

10. "Cross Cut Items," *Cross Plains Review*, November 9, 1917.

11. Austin Newton described these adventures in detail in a phone interview with L. Sprague de Camp, April 2, 1978.

12. Ibid.

13. This is not a bold claim. It is generally accepted that Robert Howard was an introvert. One of the characteristics of introverts is being cautious about whom they allow into their immediate circle. It should be noted that we cannot be sure that the people around Robert caused this behavior, but it may have contributed. Based on my research in various sources, I do think the local townspeople pushed Robert deeper into himself. Certainly, there were other factors involved as well, and these will be revealed in subsequent chapters.

14. L. Sprague de Camp and Jane Whittington Griffin, phone interview with Austin Newton, April 1, 1978, De Camp Collection.

15. Ibid. It would be a few more years—around 1918 or 1919—before Dr. Howard purchased his first automobile.

16. "Cross Cut Items," *Cross Plains Review*, July 13, 1917.

17. His last trip to New Orleans was reported in the *Cross Plains Review* on January 28, 1921.

18. The Tulane University catalog, *The Register*, lists Dr. Howard in the "Catalogue of Students" in its "Graduate School of Medicine" in both its October 1, 1918, and October 1, 2021, issues. On January 28, 1921, the *Cross Plains Review* mentioned

that Dr. Howard had recently returned from postgraduate studies at both Tulane University and Loyola in New Orleans. Rusty Burke provided me with a copy of a $75 receipt for a six-week course Dr. Howard took at Tulane University and his certificate for coursework at Loyola University dated November 26, 1920.

19. This information was provided to me by Frank Hilton at the Martin & Frances Lehnis Railroad Museum in Brownwood, Texas.

20. Several sources seem to confirm this date, including Robert Howard's autobiographical essay about New Orleans, "In His Own Image" (which refers to the capture of the infamous "ax-man"), and an article in the March 10 *New Orleans Times-Picayune* indicating that the ax-man (aka Frank Guagliardo/Frank Jordano) had been captured. For details regarding this event and the Howards' arrival in New Orleans, see Patrice Louinet, "The Axman Cometh or Robert E. Howard in New Orleans," *REHupa* 203 (February 2007), and Rusty Burke, "Robert E. Howard in New Orleans, Part Three," *REHupa* 244 (December 2013).

21. Those dates were determined through the typescript work of Howard scholar Patrice Louinet.

22. The essay was given an ad hoc title by Glenn Lord, a Robert E. Howard collector and aficionado.

23. Robert E. Howard, "In His Own Image," in *The Last of the Trunk*, ed. Patrice Louinet (Plano, TX: Robert E. Howard Foundation Press, 2007), 479–480.

24. For details about these events, see Helena Katz, *Cold Cases: Famous Unsolved Mysteries, Crimes, and Disappearances in America* (Santa Barbara, CA: Greenwood, 2010).

25. Burke, "Robert E. Howard in New Orleans, Part Three."

26. Ibid., 128.

27. Formally known as the National Prohibition Act, the Volstead Act, passed by the 66th US Congress, went into effect on October 27, 1919. Some states, such as Louisiana and other southern states, used the Volstead Act as a preemptive measure leading up to the enforcement of the Eighteenth Amendment and Prohibition. See Ned Hémard, "Prohibition in New Orleans," New Orleans Bar Association, 2013, https://www.neworleansbar.org/uploads/files/Prohibition%20in%20New%20Orleans_1-8.pdf.

28. Lovecraft and Howard, "1931," in Joshi et al., *A Means to Freedom*, 1:122.

29. Rusty Burke, "Robert E. Howard in New Orleans, Part Two," *REHupa* 243 (October 2013): 122–133, 17.

30. Ibid., 21.

31. Lovecraft and Howard, "1931," in Joshi et al., *A Means to Freedom*, 1:255.

32. Robert E. Howard, "Worms of the Earth," *Weird Tales* (November 1932).

33. Lovecraft and Howard, "1931," in Joshi et al., *A Means to Freedom*, 1:272.

34. Patrice Louinet and Rusty Burke, "Robert E. Howard, Bran Mak Morn, and the Picts," in *Bran Mak Morn: The Last King* by Robert E. Howard (New York: Del Rey, 2005), 343–360.

35. Rusty Burke recounts his discovery of *The Romance of Early British Life*

in "Seanchai 97," *REHupa* 166 (December 2000). Burke details some of the congruences that led him to believe that this was most likely the book Howard read in the Canal Street public library.

36. G. F. Scott Elliot, *The Romance of Early British Life: From the Earliest Times to the Coming of the Danes* (London: Seely, Service & Co. Ltd., 1909), 81.

37. Lovecraft and Howard, "1932," in Joshi et al., *A Means to Freedom*, 1:255.

38. Lovecraft and Howard, "1931," in ibid., 147.

39. This time frame was established by Rob Roehm based on the first known birth record with a Burkett address for Dr. Howard, which Roehm discovered at the Coleman County courthouse.

40. T. A. Burns and Merrill Burkett, "Coleman County Communities, Burkett," in *History of Coleman County and Its People*, ed. Coleman County Historical Commission (San Angelo, TX: Anchor Publishing Co., 1985), 1:126–127.

41. Land deed filed at the Coleman County courthouse, June 1, 1918; book [? missing number], pp. 210–211.

42. L. Sprague De Camp, phone interview with Mrs. Alma (Frank R.) Baker King, August 26, 1978.

43. L. Sprague de Camp and Jane W. Griffin, phone interview with Earl J. Baker, Plano, TX, April 2, 1978, De Camp Collection.

CHAPTER 4. THE BIRTH OF A WRITER

1. This information was provided to me by Rob Roehm.

2. T. A. Burns, "Robert E. Howard as a Boy," *Cross Plains Review*, July 10, 1936.

3. Robert E. Howard, "1935," in Roehm, *The Collected Letters of Robert E. Howard*, 3:287.

4. Ann L. Beeler, *Footsteps of Approaching Thousands* (Cross Plains, TX: Cross Plains Public Library, 2011), 1.

5. Ibid., 5.

6. Ibid., 20.

7. Lovecraft and Howard, "1933," in Joshi et al., *A Means to Freedom*, 2:606.

8. Open classrooms are minimally controlled and openly structured self-learning environments, with no walls or strict schedules, where students are given time and freedom to learn things that interest them in a hands-on environment. Unfortunately, open classrooms did not exist in the United States until the 1960s.

9. Lovecraft and Howard, "1933," in Joshi et al., *A Means to Freedom*, 2:607.

10. Ibid., 2:608.

11. Ibid., 2:608–609.

12. Mark Finn, "Introduction," in *Sentiment: An Olio of Rarer Works* by Robert E. Howard, ed. Rob Roehm (Sugar Land, TX: Robert E. Howard Foundation Press, 2009), xii.

13. Robert also submitted the same story in 1921, at age fifteen, to *Western Story* magazine.

14. Lovecraft and Howard, "1931," in Joshi et al., *A Means to Freedom*, 2:155.

15. Brian Stableford, "Introduction," in *Tarzan of the Apes* by Edgar Rice Burroughs (New York: Barnes & Noble, 2014), v.

16. Steve Eng, "Barbarian Bard: The Poetry of Robert E. Howard," in *The Dark Barbarian: The Writings of Robert E. Howard: A Critical Anthology*, ed. Don Herron (Westport, CT: Greenwood Press, 1984), 25.

17. See Robert E. Howard, *Back to School*, ed. Rob Roehm (Sugar Land, TX: Robert E. Howard Foundation Press, 2012), 2–9.

18. This was reported to Glenn Lord by Lindsey Tyson.

19. Roehm, *The Collected Letters of Dr. Isaac M. Howard*, 189. Dr. Howard's claim may be correct, since Hester's father was so successful in business. However, she was probably more concerned that her son be happy, and she certainly supported Robert's decision to be a writer.

20. Rob Roehm and Bob Roehm, *The Brownwood Connection: A Guide for Robert E. Howard Fans* (Plano, TX: Robert E. Howard Foundation Press, 2010), 4.

CHAPTER 5. *TATTLERS AND YELLOW JACKETS*

1. It should be noted that Robert E. Howard's first submissions to *The Tattler* were also likely to have been in response to a contest to win gold coins. The only source for all this information is Tevis Clyde Smith's written recollections.

2. "Cross Plains Boy Writes Good Stories for High School Paper," *Brownwood Bulletin*, December 22, 1922.

3. Ibid.

4. The *Little Blue Book* was a vast series of staple-bound booklets that could fit in the palm of the reader's hand (pocket size). They sold for a nickel or a dime each and covered a wide range of subjects. The series was started by Emanuel Haldeman-Julius of Girard, Kansas, to provide an education to the masses.

5. Tevis Clyde Smith, "The Magic Name," *Fantasy Crossroads* 10/11 (March 1977): 48.

6. Ibid.

7. Robert submitted "Lal Singh—Adventurer" to *Adventure* in early 1923; the manuscript for this story is lost. He submitted "The Feminine [Female] of the Species" to *Argosy-Allstory* in early 1923; the only extant typescript for this story is reprinted in Howard, *Sentiment*. He submitted "The Mystery of Summerton Castle" to *Weird Tales* in early 1923; the manuscript for this story is also lost.

8. Tevis Clyde Smith, *Pecan Valley Days* (Brownwood, TX: T. C. Smith, 1956), 44.

9. For a delineation of these three markets, see Louis L'Amour's book, *Education of a Wandering Man*, Bantam Books, 1990; pp. 139–141.

10. One such early pulp writer was Thomas Lanier Williams (aka Tennessee Williams), who became a playwright and won two Pulitzer Prizes. One of his early short stories, "The Vengeance of Nitocris," was published in the August 1928 *Weird Tales*. The cover story for that issue was "Red Shadows," written by Robert E. Howard.

11. Roehm and Roehm, *The Brownwood Connection*, 8.

12. This idea is suggested in Rob Roehm, "Hawkshaw and Howard," *Howard History*, February 2, 2018, https://howardhistory.com/2018/02/02/hawkshaw-howard/.

13. *Hawkshaw the Detective* would cease publication in 1922, then reappear from 1931 to 1952.

14. Smith, *Pecan Valley Days*, 44.

15. Tevis Clyde Smith, "So Far the Poet . . . Notes for Howard Biography," in *Report on a Writing Man & Other Reminiscences of Robert E. Howard*, ed. Rusty Burke (Necronomicon Press, 1991), 34.

16. For more details, see Herbert Klatt, *Lone Scout of Letters*, ed. Rob Roehm (Lancaster, CA: Roehm's Room Press, 2011).

17. Roehm and Roehm, *The Brownwood Connection*, 14.

18. Ibid. The *Commerce Journal* for the Baylor College for Women was published on May 25, 1923.

19. Howard, "1923," in Roehm, *The Collected Letters of Robert E. Howard*, 1:21.

20. See Roehm, *The Collected Letters of Robert E. Howard*, 1:309. "The Iron Terror" is reprinted in *The Early Adventures of El Borak* (Plano, TX: Robert E. Howard Foundation Press, 2010).

21. There is no evidence that Howard submitted this story to any publication other than *Cosmopolitan*. If he had done so, he probably would have listed it among his other submissions in his February 1929 letter to Tevis Clyde Smith. For more details about this story, see my article "El Borak the Swift & The Iron Terror," *On an Underwood No. 5*, November 17, 2019, http://onanunderwood5.blogspot.com/2019/11/el-borak-swift-iron-terror-by-todd-b.html.

22. The manuscript for this story is lost. See Howard, "1929," in Roehm, *The Collected Letters of Robert E. Howard*, 1:309.

23. The manuscripts for these two stories have been lost.

24. In his interview with L. Sprague and Catherine de Camp on March 7, 1978, Lindsey Tyson mentioned that Dr. Howard wanted Robert to go to college because he initially had no confidence that Robert could make it as a writer. In Dr. Howard's personal correspondence, he mentioned that Hester wanted Robert to be a businessman, and Dr. Howard admitted that he sent Robert to the Howard Payne Academy commercial department to get a business degree. See Roehm, *The Collected Letters of Dr. Isaac M. Howard*, 189.

25. Lovecraft and Howard, "1933," in Joshi et al., *A Means to Freedom*, 2: 548–549.

26. Rob Roehm, ed., *School Days in the Post Oaks* (Plano, TX: Robert E. Howard Foundation Press, 2011), 273.

27. "Mortuary" section, *Brownwood Bulletin*, October 2, 1923, 7.

28. Smith, "The Magic Name," 49.

29. Roehm, *School Days in the Post Oaks*, 274.

30. Ibid., 131.

31. Howard, "1924," in Roehm, *The Collected Letters of Robert E. Howard*, 1:31.

32. Ibid., 1:33.

33. Roehm and Roehm, *The Brownwood Connection*, 22.

34. Lindsey Tyson, born February 16, 1907, was a little over a year younger than Robert, but two grades behind him in school.

35. Roehm and Roehm, *The Brownwood Connection*, 22.

36. Catherine de Camp and L. Sprague de Camp, interview with Lindsey Tyson, Cross Plains, TX, March 7, 1978, De Camp Collection.

37. Roehm, *School Days in the Post Oaks*, 274.

38. Catherine de Camp and L. Sprague de Camp, interview with Lindsey Tyson, Cross Plains, TX, March 7, 1978, De Camp Collection.

39. Ibid.

40. See Tevis Clyde Smith, "Introduction," in *The Grim Land and Others*, ed. Jonathan Bacon (Lamoni, IA: Stygian Isles Press, 1976).

CHAPTER 6. PULP FICTIONEER

1. J. C. Henneberger, letters to Joel Frieman, reprinted in *WT 50: A Tribute to Weird Tales*, ed. Robert Weinberg (Oak Lawn, IL: Robert Weinberg, 1974), 6.

2. J. C. Henneberger, "Out of Space—Out of Time," *Deeper than You Think . . .* 1, no. 2 (July 1968): 3.

3. Henneberger, letters to Joel Frieman, in Weinberg, *WT 50*, 6.

4. Henneberger, "Out of Space—Out of Time," 3.

5. Ibid.

6. Ibid., 3–4.

7. Henneberger, letters to Joel Frieman, in Weinberg, *WT 50*, 4.

8. See Mike Ashley, *The Time Machines: The Story of Science Fiction Pulp Magazines from the Beginning to 1950* (Liverpool, UK: Liverpool University Press, 2000).

9. See Robert Weinberg, *The Weird Tales Story* (Berkley Heights, NJ: Wildside Press, 1999).

10. Ibid.

11. Ashley, *The Time Machines*, 41.

12. John Locke shows evidence that Henneberger probably never had any such assurances. See Locke, *The Thing's Incredible! The Secret Origins of Weird Tales* (Off-Trail Publications, 2018).

13. S. T. Joshi, "For My Own Amusement (1923–1924)," in *I Am Providence* by S. T. Joshi (New York: Hippocampus Press, 2013), 1:451.

14. At one point, Henneberger recruited Harry Houdini to write stories for the magazine, thinking his name would certainly boost sales. It did not.

15. "Dagon," "Arthur Jermyn," The Cats of Ulthar," "The Hound," and "The Statement of Randolph Carter."

16. For instance, because of his work with amateur magazines like *Home Brew*, Lovecraft was accustomed to submitting all his manuscripts single-spaced. Baird requested that Lovecraft retype the manuscripts to make them double-spaced.

17. See Weinberg, *The Weird Tales Story*, and Joshi, *I Am Providence*, vol. 1.

18. H. P. Lovecraft, *Letters to Family and Friends: 1911–1925*, ed. S. T. Joshi and David E. Schultz (New York: Hippocampus Press, forthcoming), 115–116.

19. Farnsworth Wright, "The Eyrie" (editorial), *Weird Tales* (December 1924): 175.

20. Ibid., 181.

21. The November 1924 issue of *Weird Tales* had several ads intended to entice readers to buy the next issue. These ads announced that the next month's issue would appear on newsstands an entire month prior to the actual issue month.

22. Farnsworth Wright, "The Eyrie" (editorial), *Weird Tales* (December 1924): 176–177.

23. See Patrice Louinet, "'The Wright Hook' (or, The Origin of 'Spear and Fang')," *REH: Two-Gun Raconteur*, October 25, 2016, https://web.archive.org/web /20161130132820/https://rehtwogunraconteur.com/the-wright-hook-or-the-origin -of-spear-and-fang/ (accessed March 2, 2018).

24. Wright, "The Eyrie," 177. This quote was reprinted in Louinet, "'The Wright Hook.'"

25. Wright, "The Eyrie," 177.

26. Louinet, "'The Wright Hook.'"

27. This payment upon publication and not acceptance was likely due to *Weird Tales'* financial troubles at the time. However, the magazine never changed this policy in its entire existence.

28. L. Sprague de Camp and Catherine de Camp, interview with Lindsey Tyson, Cross Plains, TX, March 7, 1978, De Camp Collection.

29. Roehm and Roehm, *The Brownwood Connection*, 26.

30. Ibid.

31. Howard, "1925," in Roehm, *The Collected Letters of Robert E. Howard*, 1:55.

32. Ibid., 1:59.

33. Ibid., 1:60.

34. Robert E. Howard, *Post Oaks and Sand Roughs* (Hampton Falls, NH: Donald M. Grant Publisher, 1990). This novella should be read and interpreted with a grain of salt, since it is loosely based on various events in Robert's life.

35. See Roehm, *Collected Letters of Robert E. Howard: 1923–1929*, vol. 1.

36. The name on the fake summons is blank, but Howard was aware that Clyde

had a girlfriend, Echla Laxson, and he may have known a few personal details about that relationship that Clyde shared.

37. Roehm and Roehm, *The Brownwood Connection*, 26.

38. Ibid.

39. Howard, *Post Oaks and Sand Roughs*, 53.

40. Roehm and Roehm, *The Brownwood Connection*, 26.

41. Howard, *Post Oaks and Sand Roughs*, 52.

42. Ibid., 54.

43. Rusty Burke and Rob Roehm, "Gloria," *The Dark Man: The Journal of Robert E. Howard Studies* 6, nos. 1 and 2 (November 2011): 45.

44. Howard, "1925," in Roehm, *The Collected Letters of Robert E. Howard*, 1:61.

45. This idea was suggested to me by Rusty Burke in an email ("Subject: Little Blue Books"), March 8, 2018.

46. Howard, "1925," in Roehm, *The Collected Letters of Robert E. Howard*, 1:62.

47. Ibid., 1:63.

48. Burke, email to author, March 8, 2018.

49. Howard, *Post Oaks and Sand Roughs*, 34.

50. "The Lost Race" finally appeared in the January 1927 issue of *Weird Tales*, two years after Robert submitted it.

CHAPTER 7. THE OTHER SIDE OF THE COUNTER

1. Steve Tompkins, "Introduction," in *Kull: Exile of Atlantis* by Robert E. Howard (New York: Del Rey, 2006), xxiv.

2. Howard, "1925," in Roehm, *The Collected Letters of Robert E. Howard*, 1:71.

3. Roehm and Roehm, *The Brownwood Connection*, 31.

4. Smith, *Pecan Valley Days*, 46–47.

5. L. Sprague de Camp and Catherine de Camp, interview with Lindsey Tyson, Cross Plains, TX, March 7, 1978, De Camp Collection.

6. Howard, "1925," in Roehm, *The Collected Letters of Robert E. Howard*, 1:71.

7. Robert E. Howard, "In the Forest of Villefère," *Weird Tales* (August 1925): 185–87. In the story, Howard had written: "*If I slew the thing as a man its frightful spirit would haunt me forever.*"

8. Robert E. Howard, *The Horror Stories of Robert E. Howard* (New York: Del Rey, 2008), 19 (emphasis in original).

9. H. P. Lovecraft, "The Eyrie" (letter to the editor), *Weird Tales* (March 1924). Lovecraft later admitted in one of his letters to Robert Bloch that Munn had failed in what Lovecraft had suggested. For more details, see my article "The Coincidental Friendship of H. Warner Munn and H. P. Lovecraft," *On an Underwood No. 5*, May 27, 2018, https://onanunderwood5.blogspot.com/2018/05/the-coinciden tal-friendship-of-h-warner.html.

10. James March Jr., "The Eyrie" (letter to the editor), *Weird Tales* (September 1925): 416.

11. A prime example is Howard's story "The Horror from the Mound," in which he subverts the western genre by including a vampire character. Moreover, certain things Howard does with his vampire in this story had never been done in vampire fiction before "The Horror from the Mound" was published in 1932.

12. Lord, *The Last Celt*, 373.

13. Howard, "1926," in Roehm, *The Collected Letters of Robert E. Howard*, 1:81.

14. The manuscript of the rewritten story, as far as we know, no longer exists.

15. Farnsworth Wright, "The Eyrie" (editorial), *Weird Tales* (June 1926): 859.

16. Lovecraft, "861. To E. Hoffmann Price," in Derleth and Turner, *Selected Letters: 1934–1937*, 5:277.

17. Howard, *Post Oaks and Sand Roughs*, 92.

18. Ibid.

19. Ibid., 95.

20. Howard, "1926," Roehm, *The Collected Letters of Robert E. Howard*, 1:77.

21. Howard, *Post Oaks and Sand Roughs*, 95.

22. Howard, "1935," in Roehm, *Collected Letters of Robert E. Howard: 1933–1936*, 3:367–368.

23. Dr. Isaac Howard to E. Hoffmann Price, November 10, 1943, in Roehm, *The Collected Letters of Dr. Isaac M. Howard*, 189.

24. Novalyne Price Ellis, *One Who Walked Alone* (Hampton Falls, NH: Donald M. Grant Publisher, 1986), 23.

25. Tevis Clyde Smith, *Frontier's Generation* (Brownwood, TX: Tevis Clyde Smith, 1980), 149.

26. L. Sprague de Camp and Catherine de Camp, interview with Lindsey Tyson, Cross Plains, TX, March 7, 1978, De Camp Collection. At first, Dr. Howard was cautious and doubtful about his son wanting a career as a freelance writer. But once Robert became a well-established and regularly paid author, Dr. Howard's attitude changed; in fact, he paraded around Cross Plains bragging about his son.

27. See "Fall 1926" entry at Rusty Burke, "Robert E. Howard Fiction and Verse Timeline," *Howard Works*, http://howardworks.com/timeline.htm#1926 (accessed May 1, 2018).

28. Roehm and Roehm, *The Brownwood Connection*, 37.

29. L. Sprague de Camp and Catherine de Camp, interview with Lindsey Tyson, Cross Plains, TX, March 7, 1978, De Camp Collection.

30. See Roehm and Roehm, *The Brownwood Connection*, 38.

31. Howard, *Bran Mak Morn*, 181.

32. Ibid., 179.

33. Roehm and Roehm, *The Brownwood Connection*, 42.

34. Lindsey Tyson to L. Sprague de Camp, October 10, 1977, De Camp Collection.

35. Roehm and Roehm, *The Brownwood Connection*, 43.

36. See Smith, "So Far the Poet . . . Notes for Howard Biography," in Burke, *Report on a Writing Man*.

37. *The Yellow Jacket* published two other Howard stories in 1927: "Ye College Days" on January 20 and "Cupid vs. Pollux" on February 10.

38. Lindsey Tyson to L. Sprague de Camp, October 10, 1977.

CHAPTER 8. A NEW SPECIES OF FANTASY FICTION

1. Howard, "1927," in Roehm, *The Collected Letters of Robert E. Howard*, 1:151.

2. In chapters 11 and 13 of *Post Oaks and Sand Roughs*, Howard details his mother's financial help with clothes and the trip to San Antonio. While *Post Oaks and Sand Roughs* is a semiautobiographical work of fiction, it is likely true that Mrs. Howard helped her son financially, especially during the period of the deal with Robert.

3. Herbert Klatt, *Lone Scout of Letters*, ed. Rob Roehm, (Lancaster, CA: Roehm's Room Press, 2011), 174.

4. Tompkins, "Introduction," in Howard, *Kull*, xix.

5. Lovecraft and Howard, "1933," in Joshi et al., *A Means to Freedom*, 2:651.

6. Jeffrey Shanks, "History, Horror, and Heroic Fantasy: Robert E. Howard and the Creation of the Sword-and-Sorcery Subgenre," in *Critical Insights: Pulp Fiction of the '20s and '30s*, ed. Greg Hoppenstand (Ipswich, MA: Salem Press, 2013), 6.

7. Farnsworth Wright, "The Eyrie" (editorial), *Weird Tales* (October 1929): 436. Readers' responses to a story typically appeared in "The Eyrie" about two months after the story's publication.

8. E. Hoffmann Price, "The Eyrie" (letter to the editor), *Weird Tales* (October 1929): 436.

9. A. Merritt, "The Eyrie" (letter to the editor), *Weird Tales* (October 1929): 438.

10. Originally titled "The Spirit of Tom Molyneaux."

11. Howard did submit the story to *Fight Stories*, which rejected it. He then sent it to *Argosy*, which also rejected it, before submitting it to *Ghost Stories*. For details about "The Apparition in the Prize Ring" and the *Ghost Stories* editor's possible alterations to the story, see Patrice Louinet, "The Lord of the Ring: Part 1," in *Fists of Iron: Collected Boxing Fiction of Robert E. Howard*, vol. 1 (Plano, TX: Robert E. Howard Foundation Press, 2013.

12. "Crowd-Horror" would be the only Howard story published in *Argosy* in his lifetime. Shortly before his death in 1936, through Robert's agent Otis Adelbert Kline, *Argosy* accepted several of his later stories for publication, and he was aware that *Argosy* had accepted them. They began appearing in the magazine shortly after he died.

13. Howard, "1928," in Roehm, *The Collected Letters of Robert E. Howard*, 1:179.

14. S. A. McWilliams to Robert E. Howard, New York, NY, February 20, 1928. Rob Roehm provided me with a scan of this letter.

15. Robert E. Howard, *The Savage Tales of Solomon Kane* (New York: Del Rey, 2004), 32.

16. There is some discrepancy about how much Howard was paid for the story. In *Post Oaks and Sand Roughs*, Howard declares that he was paid $80, but the Howard scholar and fan Glenn Lord documents the payment as $20.

17. "The Voice of El-Lil," "Red Blades of Black Cathay" (cowritten with Tevis Clyde Smith), "Hawks of Outremer," "The Blood of Belshazzar," "The Sowers of the Thunder," and "Lord of Samarcand" would all be published in *Oriental Stories* between 1929 and 1932.

CHAPTER 9. FRIENDS AND LETTERS

1. Howard, "1930," in Roehm, *The Collected Letters of Robert E. Howard*, 2:116.

2. For information about bootlegging in and around Cross Plains in the 1920s and '30s, see Todd B. Vick, "Bootleggers & Gangsters: A Day in the Life of Robert E. Howard," *On an Underwood No. 5*, November 16, 2017, http://onanunderwood5 .blogspot.com/2017/11/bootleggers-gangsters-day-in-life-of.html.

3. Howard, "1932," in Roehm, *The Collected Letters of Robert E. Howard*, 2:426–427.

4. In the late 1920s and early '30s, the Cross Plains icehouse was still a fully functioning business and had certainly not been abandoned.

5. See Paul Herman, interview with Larry McDonough at McDonough's home, October 23, 2000, "Another Thought #1," June 1, 2001, http://www.robert-e-howard .org/AnotherThought1.html. The McDonough family were close friends with the Howard family and lived down the street from the Howards' house in the late 1920s and early 1930s. Larry McDonough was twelve when Robert E. Howard died, but it is likely that he heard stories about Robert E. Howard. In this interview, he recounts stories about boxing (or some form of fighting) and drinking at the icehouse.

6. The first extant letter we have between Preece and Howard is not dated, but it is believed to have been written and mailed in early 1928. See Howard, "1928," in Roehm, *The Collected Letters of Robert E. Howard*, 1:197.

7. See chapter 13 for more detail on Robert E. Howard's twelve-year publishing career. Before this midpoint in his career, he had written some historical fiction but been unsuccessful in getting much of it published.

8. See Howard, "1930" (letter 115), in Roehm, *The Collected Letters of Robert E. Howard*, 2:45.

9. Howard, "1928," in ibid., 1:233.

10. Howard, "1930," in ibid., 2:47.

11. Howard used Wells's *The Outline of History* in several other historical fiction works, as suggested by pulp magazine aficionado Jeffrey Shanks in his essay "Evolutionary Otherness: Anthropological Anxiety in Robert E. Howard's 'Worms

of the Earth,'" in Justin Everett and Jeffrey H. Shanks, eds., *The Unique Legacy of Weird Tales: The Evolution of Modern Fantasy and Horror* (Lanham, MD: Rowman & Littlefield, 2015).

12. Wallace West, "The Souk" (editorial), *Oriental Stories* (December/January 1930–1931): 150.

13. Henry S. Whitehead, "The Souk" (letter to the editor), *Oriental Stories* (Spring 1931): 572.

14. These works were *Frontier's Generation*, *The Cardboard god*, *From Memories of Men*, *Images Out of the Sky*, *Don't Blame the Python*, and *Pecan Valley Days*.

15. "Hawks of Outremer," "The Blood of Belshazzar," "Lord Samarcand," and "The Sowers of the Thunder."

16. Cormac FitzGeoffrey was featured in "The Hawks of Outremer" and "The Blood of Belshazzar." For details about the character and Howard's desire to make a series of stories centered on him, see Howard, "1930" (letter 125), in Roehm, *The Collected Letters of Robert E. Howard*, 2:86.

17. According to Rusty Burke in his introduction to *Swords of the North* (Plano, TX: Robert E. Howard Foundation Press, 2014), the late Steve Tompkins was the first to detect Howard's world-building during this period. Tompkins believed that, beginning with "Men of the Shadows" and all the way through to Howard's unfinished tales like "Nekht Semerkeht" and similar stories, Howard was building a contiguous and sweeping epic akin to the histories (*The Silmarillion*, *The Book[s] of Lost Tales*, *The Children of Hurin*, and so on) of Tolkien's *Lord of the Rings*.

18. Howard used Conan of the Reavers, an Irish protagonist, in "People of the Dark," *Strange Tales* (June 1932).

19. Howard, "1933," in Roehm, *The Collected Letters of Robert E. Howard*, 3:130.

20. *The New Masses* was a popular Marxist Socialist journal published from 1926 to 1948 (changing names several times during that period). Other writers who published in *The New Masses* included William Carlos Williams, Upton Sinclair, Richard Wright, Ralph Ellison, Dorothy Parker, Langston Hughes, and Ernest Hemingway.

21. In addition to his contributions to historical anthologies (for example, *Bits of Silver: Vignettes of the Old West*), Preece wrote several fiction and nonfiction works pertaining to Texas history and the Old West, such as *Lone Star Man: Ira Aten, Last of the Old Texas Rangers*, *The Dalton Gang*, *Dew on Jordan*, and *Living Pioneers*. Preece also wrote articles for *Real West* magazine between March 1964 and February 1975.

22. H. P. Lovecraft, "The Rats in the Walls," *Weird Tales* (June 1930): 853. The reprint in the June 1930 issue of *Weird Tales* was identical to the story's original publication in the March 1924 issue.

23. H. P. Lovecraft, "149. To Frank Belknap Long," in *H. P. Lovecraft: Selected Letters: 1911–1924*, ed. August Derleth and Donald Wandrei (Sauk City, WI: Arkham House, 1965), 1:258.

24. For a detailed account of this episode, see Lovecraft and Howard scholar Bobby Derie's article "Howard, Lovecraft, & The 'Sin-Eater,'" *On an Underwood No. 5*, August 18, 2016, http://onanunderwood5.blogspot.com/2016/08/howard-love craft-sin-eater-by-bobby.html.

25. Howard, "1930," in Roehm, *The Collected Letters of Robert E. Howard*, 2:43. Fiona MacLeod was the pseudonym of the Scottish writer William Sharp (1855–1905).

26. Lovecraft and Howard, "1930," in Joshi et al., *A Means to Freedom*, 1:17.

27. Ibid., 1:24.

28. Rusty Burke, "Introduction," in *The Horror Stories of Robert E. Howard*, xviii.

29. Two years prior to their correspondence, Howard had praised "The Call of Cthulhu" in "The Eyrie," *Weird Tales* (May 1928).

30. Howard's fictitious *Nameless Cults* is a hat-tip to Lovecraft's famous imaginary book of forbidden lore, the *Necronomicon* of the mad Arab Abdul Alhazred. Eventually, Lovecraft, along with E. Hoffmann Price, August Derleth, and others, created the putative German title of von Junzt's work, *Unaussprechlichen Kulten*. S. T. Joshi informed me that this title is ungrammatical German: it should have been either *Die unaussprechlichen Kulten* or *Unaussprechliche Kulten*.

31. Lovecraft used von Junzt and *Nameless Cults* (as well as Justin Geoffrey, introduced in "The Black Stone") in "Out of the Aeons," "The Shadow Out of Time," "The Horror in the Museum," "Dreams in the Witch House," and "The Haunter of the Dark." Justin Geoffrey is a weird and fantastic poet who wrote the poem *The People of the Monolith*, from which a certain verse refers to the Black Stone located in Hungary.

32. Though the Cthulhu Mythos has changed dramatically over the years, books and stories within or attached to the mythos are still being written today by various authors.

33. See Lovecraft and Howard, "1930," in Joshi et al., *A Means to Freedom*, 1:42. While it is not explicitly indicated, it is possible that Lovecraft sent August Derleth's address to Howard along with these others.

34. Lovecraft and Howard, "1931," in ibid., 1:213.

35. Ibid., 1:314.

36. Ibid., 1:315.

37. For details of this event, see E. Hoffmann Price, *Book of the Dead* (Sauk City, WI: Arkham House, 2001), 70. Shortly before Bonnie and Clyde were killed in May 1934, a picture of Bonnie Parker with a cigar in her mouth was confiscated and widely circulated among law enforcement.

38. See Scott Connors, "*Weird Tales* and the Great Depression," in *The Robert E. Howard Reader*, ed. Darrell Schweitzer (Cabin John, MD: Borgos Press, 2010).

39. Price, *Book of the Dead*, 72.

40. Ibid.

41. Ibid., 80.

42. Ibid., 90. These claims made by Price in the *Book of the Dead* have been hotly contested. Even so, there is some truth to Price's observation, and some of Robert's letters bear it out.

43. Howard may have discovered the AFG through Price, who had been reading the AFG journal, *Author & Journalist*, since mid-1932. If not through Price, then Howard most likely received a personal invitation from AFG to join, since by then he was a professional writer.

44. Howard, "1932," in Roehm, *The Collected Letters of Robert E. Howard*, 2:337.

45. Lovecraft and Howard, "1932," in Joshi et al., *A Means to Freedom*, 1:302.

46. Howard, "1933," in Roehm, *The Collected Letters of Robert E. Howard*, 3:149.

47. There is no definitive proof for how Howard discovered Kline's agency. By 1933, when he hired Kline as his agent, Howard was already a member of the AFG and had been corresponding with Price for several years.

48. For details, see chapter 2 in Price's *Book of the Dead*.

49. Bobby Derie, "Conan and the OAK, Part 1—1933," *On an Underwood No. 5*, June 22, 2017, http://onanunderwood5.blogspot.com/2017/06/conan-and-oak-part-1 -1933-by-bobby-derie.html (accessed August 1, 2018).

50. Kline had published his stories in *Argosy*, *Amazing Stories*, *Thrilling Wonder*, and *Weird Tales*, among others.

51. Derie, "Conan and the OAK, Part 1—1933."

52. Marshall B. Tymn and Mike Ashley, eds., *Science Fiction, Fantasy, and Weird Fiction Magazines* (Westport, CT: Greenwood Press, 1985), 626.

53. Howard, "1932," in Roehm, *The Collected Letters of Robert E. Howard*, 2:339.

54. Reavers, also known as Border Reavers, were raiders who lived and raided along the Anglo-Scottish border between the twelfth and sixteenth centuries.

55. Rusty Burke, "Subject: Two Stories," email to author, August 2, 2018.

56. Robert E. Howard, "Cimmeria," in *The Coming of Conan the Cimmerian* by Robert E. Howard (New York: Del Rey, 2003), 3.

57. David Piske, "Barbarism and Civilization in the Letters of Robert E. Howard and H. P. Lovecraft: A Summary with Commentary (Part 1)," *On an Underwood No. 5*, August 19, 2015, http://onanunderwood5.blogspot.com/2015/08/barba rism-and-civilization-in-letters.html (accessed August 3, 2018).

58. Howard, "1932," in Roehm, *The Collected Letters of Robert E. Howard*, 2:329.

59. Rusty Burke, "Seanchai 61," *REHupa* 61 (May 1991): 19–21.

60. Lovecraft and Howard, "1934," in Joshi et al., *A Means to Freedom*, 2:698.

61. Ibid., 1:501–502.

62. Howard, "1928," in Roehm, *The Collected Letters of Robert E. Howard*, 1:233–235.

63. H. P. Lovecraft, "Letters to Natalie H. Wooley," in *H. P. Lovecraft: Letters to Robert Bloch and Others*, ed. David E. Schultz and S. T. Joshi (New York: Hippocampus Press, 2015), 205.

64. H. P. Lovecraft, "Letters: H. P. Lovecraft and C. L. Moore," in *H. P. Lovecraft: Letters to C. L. Moore and Others*, ed. David E. Schultz and S. T. Joshi (New York: Hippocampus Press, 2017), 32–33.

65. Lovecraft and Howard, "1931," in Joshi et al., *A Means to Freedom*, 1:140.

66. Lovecraft and Howard, "1935," in ibid., 2:855.

67. Howard spoke about this idea to his girlfriend at the time, Novalyne Price (Ellis). See her book, Ellis, *One Who Walked Alone*, 77 and 180.

CHAPTER 10. NOVALYNE PRICE

1. In this chapter, I refer to Novalyne Price Ellis by her first name, intending no disrespect but simply to discuss their relationship in a more personal fashion.

2. Tevis Clyde Smith, "In Regard to This Book and the Author," in Ellis, *One Who Walked Alone*, 10.

3. Ellis, *One Who Walked Alone*, 16.

4. Ibid., 23.

5. *The Whole Wide World* is a 1996 motion picture based on Novalyne Price Ellis' book *One Who Walked Alone*. The screenplay was written and adapted by one of Novalyne's former students, Michael Scott Myers, and starred Vincent D'Onofrio and Renée Zellweger.

6. Ellis, *One Who Walked Alone*, 45.

7. L. Sprague de Camp and Catherine de Camp, interview with Leroy Butler and his wife Floyce Butler, Abilene, TX, July 22, 1977, De Camp Collection. Jack Scott was a reporter for the *Cross Plains Review* newspaper.

8. Ellis, *One Who Walked Alone*, 49.

9. Rusty Burke, "A Conversation with Novalyne Price Ellis by Rusty Burke," in *Day of the Stranger: Further Memories of Robert E. Howard* by Rusty Burke (West Warwick, RI: Necronomicon Press, 1989), 12.

10. See Ellis, *One Who Walked Alone*, 127. Ellis does not specify how much either man earned.

11. It was the suggestion of Michael Scott Myers, the screenwriter for the film *The Whole Wide World*, that Mrs. Howard and Robert were in a kind of business relationship. Michael Scott Myers, correspondence with the author, August 22, 2018.

12. Ellis, *One Who Walked Alone*, 54.

13. Robert had researched Genghis Khan out of his own interest but also to inform his collaborative piece written with Tevis Clyde Smith, "Red Blades of Black Cathay," published in the February/March issue of *Oriental Stories*.

14. See Ellis, *One Who Walked Alone*, 83–84.

15. On several occasions, Robert Howard had been seen around town shadowboxing and talking to himself, most likely creating events in his mind to use later in a story. That he typically kept to himself, selected his friends carefully, and did not really socialize with others in town was also viewed by some as odd behavior.

16. Ellis, *One Who Walked Alone*, 86.

17. The term "mulatto," meaning the offspring of a white person and black person, is now considered derogatory. But in the mid-1930s, it was commonly used as a racial classification.

18. Ellis, *One Who Walked Alone*, 93.

19. See Charles C. Alexander, "Crusade for Conformity: The Ku Klux Klan in Texas, 1920–1930," *Texas Gulf Coast Historical Association* 6, no. 1 (August 1962).

20. See Howard, "1936," in Roehm, *The Collected Letters of Robert E. Howard*, 3:504–5. See also Rob Roehm, "The Missing Mexico Trip," *Howard History*, October 19, 2018, https://howardhistory.com/2018/10/19/the-missing-mexico-trip/.

21. Ellis, *One Who Walked Alone*, 92–96, 95.

22. Ibid., 96.

23. This opinion may have derived in part from Novalyne's experience of her mother's second husband, whom she claimed was tied to his own mother's apron strings. That marriage did not go well and ended in a difficult divorce.

24. Ellis, *One Who Walked Alone*, 145.

25. Ibid., 145–146.

26. Ibid., 196.

CHAPTER 11. BROKEN ON THE PLOWSHARE OF FATE

1. Ibid., 266.

2. Ibid., 267.

3. Ibid.

4. Ibid., 269.

5. Novalyne Price Ellis, "Speech about Robert E. Howard," in Burke, *Day of the Stranger*, 47 (emphasis in original).

6. Katherine "Kate" Merryman and her sister Alice Younglove were hired as "nurses" to care for Mrs. Howard, though it is not certain whether either was in fact a registered nurse. Even so, they performed the duties of home care nurses in 1936. Leah King was hired by the Howards as a maid in the spring of 1936.

7. Robert mentioned some of these trips in letters to his various correspondents. See Howard, "1935" and "1936," in Roehm, *Collected Letters of Robert E. Howard: 1933–1936*, 3:382, 3:421, 3:425, and 3:458.

8. See Howard, "1936," in Roehm, *Collected Letters of Robert E. Howard: 1933–1936*, 3:415, 3:458–59, and 3:463.

9. Isaac Howard to H. P. Lovecraft, June 29, 1936, in Roehm, *The Collected Letters of Dr. Isaac M. Howard*, 64.

10. See Ellis, *One Who Walked Alone*, 190.

11. Isaac Howard to E. Hoffmann Price, June 27, 1936, in Roehm, *The Collected Letters of Dr. Isaac M. Howard*, 59.

12. These stories were "A Gent from Pecos" and "Gents on the Lynch" (both

Pike Bearfield stories), "The Dead Remember," "The Riot at Bucksnort," and "Vultures' Sanctuary."

13. See Ellis, *One Who Walked Alone*, 278.

14. See Howard, "1935," in Roehm, *Collected Letters of Robert E. Howard: 1933–1936*, 3:306–308.

15. These stories were "Black Canaan," "Red Nails," and possibly "The Black Hound of Death." *Weird Tales* would also publish "The Fire of Asshurbanipal" in December 1936 and "Dig Me No Grave" in January 1937.

16. Howard, "1936," in Roehm, *Collected Letters of Robert E. Howard: 1933–1936*, 3:437.

17. See L. Sprague de Camp and Catherine de Camp, interview with Kate Merryman and Alice Younglove, July 18, 1977, De Camp Collection.

18. Ibid. The fluid was probably drawn from the pleura around her lungs and may have been the result of a faulty gall bladder surgery performed some time earlier.

19. Ibid.

20. Ibid.

21. See Roehm, *The Collected Letters of Dr. Isaac M. Howard*, 63–64 and 76–77.

22. Ibid., 76.

23. Kate Merryman and Alice Younglove cite this date as "the night before" Robert killed himself. See L. Sprague de Camp and Catherine de Camp, interview with Kate Merryman and Alice Younglove, July 18, 1977, De Camp Collection.

24. L. Sprague de Camp and Catherine de Camp, interview with Katherine Merryman and Alice Younglove, Cross Plains, TX, March 7, 1978, De Camp Collection.

25. This date is several days after both Robert and Mrs. Howard died. The date is taken from the record of purchase for five burial plots at Greenleaf Cemetery in Brownwood, Texas.

26. Howard to H. P. Lovecraft, June 29, 1936, in Roehm, *The Collected Letters of Dr. Isaac M. Howard*, 64.

27. This nurse was most likely Mrs. Green, since Kate Merryman, as she told the de Camps, had already left the house before 8:00 a.m.

28. Howard to W. J. Proctor, July 11, 1936, in Roehm, *The Collected Letters of Dr. Isaac M. Howard*, 77.

29. Howard to H. P. Lovecraft, June 29, 1936, in Roehm, The Collected Letters 63. There are varying accounts of where the bullet entered Robert E. Howard's head. I intentionally quoted Dr. Howard's account since he was the first one, along with another doctor (probably a Dr. Edwards) present at the house, to go to Robert after the shot was fired. That same day, June 11, 1936, the *Brownwood Bulletin* reported that the bullet entered Robert's right temple and ranged upward, coming out the top of his head on the left side.

CHAPTER 12. THE AFTERMATH

1. In his account, Dr. Howard does not mention the other doctor's name. Among the several doctors who were regularly at the Howard house the last week of Robert's and Mrs. Howard's lives, it could have been Dr. Edwards, since in a "Card of Thanks" published by the *Cross Plains Review* on June 19, 1936, Dr. Howard specifically mentions Dr. Edwards's name as one who "stayed with Robert as he was passing."

2. The cook may have been Leah King, who had been hired to cook and clean.

3. Isaac Howard to H. P. Lovecraft, June 29, 1936, in Roehm, *The Collected Letters of Dr. Isaac M. Howard*, 63.

4. L. Sprague de Camp and Catherine de Camp, interview with Kate Merryman, Alice Younglove, and Lois Garrett, Merryman-Younglove home, Cross Plains, TX, October 18, 1978, De Camp Collection.

5. This report was syndicated (or sent directly) to several area newspapers that ran two daily editions (morning and afternoon).

6. "Robt. Howard, Cross Plains, Tries Suicide," *Brownwood Bulletin*, June 11, 1936.

7. "Young Author Shoots Self," *Abilene Daily Reporter*, June 11, 1936. Rob Roehm provided me with this paper.

8. "Tragedy Shocks City Thursday," *Cross Plains Review*, June 12, 1936.

9. L. Sprague de Camp and Catherine de Camp, interview with Kate Merryman, Alice Younglove, and Lois Garrett, Merryman-Younglove home, Cross Plains, TX, October 18, 1978, De Camp Collection.

10. See Howard, "1935," in Roehm, *Collected Letters of Robert E. Howard: 1933–1936*, 3:306.

11. Ibid., 3:388.

12. This information is based on the records on file at Greenleaf Cemetery. There is no explanation (or historical evidence) as to why Dr. Howard bought five plots instead of three. It is likely that Dr. Howard had arranged the purchase of these five plots prior to the funeral date and simply paid for them on the day of the funeral.

13. L. Sprague de Camp and Catherine de Camp, interview with Norris Chambers, Fort Worth, TX, July 22, 1977, De Camp Collection.

14. L. Sprague de Camp writes in his book *Dark Valley Destiny* that the preacher was the Reverend B. G. Richburg and that Richburg used the passage from I Samuel 31:4. I have found no evidence that de Camp's claim is accurate, and he does not cite a source for it. The de Camp interviews with Norris Chambers do not reveal specific details other than Dr. Howard's complaint that one of the preachers "sent his boy to hell."

15. L. Sprague de Camp and Catherine de Camp, interview with Katherine Merryman and Alice Younglove, Cross Plains, TX, March 7, 1978, De Camp Collec-

tion. There is no indication from anyone in any extant interview that Norris Chambers was at the house when this occurred.

16. L. Sprague de Camp and Catherine de Camp, interview with Lindsey Tyson, Cross Plains, March 7, 1978, De Camp Collection.

17. Farnsworth Wright, "The Eyrie" (editorial), *Weird Tales* (August/September 1936): 250.

18. Howard was actually taking classes at the commercial department housed in the Howard Payne Academy.

19. Farnsworth Wright, "The Eyrie" (editorial), *Weird Tales* (January 1937): 122.

20. The last *Weird Tales* cover story for any Robert E. Howard story was "The Fire of Asshurbanipal," in the December 1936 issue.

21. Fred C. Miles, "The Eyrie" (letter to the editor), *Weird Tales* (February 1937): 249.

22. Julius Hopkins, "The Eyrie" (letter to the editor), *Weird Tales* (November 1936): 506.

23. Price's letter was probably addressed to Wright.

24. Ernest Dowson, "Cynara," first published in *The Second Book of the Rhymer's Club* (1894), available at https://allpoetry.com/Cynara.

25. See Rusty Burke, "All Fled, All Done," *The Dark Man: The Journal of Robert E. Howard Studies* 5 (Winter 2001); and Rusty Burke, "The Note," *The Cimmerian* 3, no. 1 (January 2006).

26. Viola Garvin, "The House of Caesar," reprinted in *Songs of Adventure*, ed. Robert Frothingham (Boston: Houghton Mifflin Co., 1926), available at https://all poetry.com/The-House-Of-Caesar.

27. This idea stems from stories by Jack Scott and the de Camps' interviews with him. For clarification of the facts, see Burke, "All Fled, All Done"; and Burke, "The Note."

28. See Roehm, *The Collected Letters of Dr. Isaac M. Howard*, 143.

29. Ibid., 152.

30. Isaac Howard to Otis A. Kline, February 15, 1937, in Roehm, *The Collected Letters of Doctor Isaac M. Howard*, 149.

CHAPTER 13. WRITING A LEGACY

1. Richard H. Eney, "Swords and Sorcery," in *The Conan Swordbook*, Voyager Series (Baltimore, MD: Mirage Press, 1969), xii. See chapter 14 for more details about Gnome Press.

2. This information was gleaned from *Amra* 2, no. 1 (January 1959), which misspells the group's name as "Hyborean." This seems odd, considering that it is well established that John D. Clark was present at that first meeting. Clark, along with P. Schuyler Miller, wrote the essay "The Hyborian Age by Robert E. Howard and a

Probable Outline of Conan's Career." The club corrected the spelling error in *Amra* 2, no. 2 (1959).

3. According to the club, the journal was named *Amra* because Conan the Cimmerian called himself Amra when he was a pirate.

4. George R. Heap, "On Fantasy-Adventure," *Ancalagon* (March 1961): 2.

5. Ibid., 6.

6. Ibid., 3–4. "Hero" is a confusing term; Heap probably means "protagonist." The use of "hero" rather than "protagonist" is an all too common mistake committed in certain literary circles. It should be noted that not all protagonists are heroes per se. See my article "The Mistaken Identity of a Barbarian: Conan, Hero or Anti-Hero?" in *Dark Man Journal of Robert E. Howard and Pulp Fiction Studies* 8, no. 2 (August 2017).

7. L. Sprague de Camp, "The Reverberatory" (editorial), *Ancalagon* (April 1961).

8. George Scithers, "Whence?," *Amra* 2, no. 1 (January 1959): 5.

9. Fritz Leiber, "The Reverberatory" (editorial), *Ancalagon* (April 1961).

10. Moorcock conflates the terms "hero" and "protagonist"; not all protagonists in these works are heroes per se.

11. I have replaced "hero" with "protagonist" to eliminate any confusion between the two terms.

12. Michael Moorcock, "Putting a Tag on It," *Amra* 2, no. 15 (May 1961): 16.

13. Ibid.

14. Ibid., 17 (punctuation slightly edited).

15. Ibid.

16. Ibid., 16.

17. It should be noted that Moorcock has frequently been cited as the originator of the term "sword-and-sorcery," but as I have demonstrated here, this is quite clearly *not* the case. If anything, Moorcock should be credited with coining the term "epic fantasy." Fritz Leiber is the properly credited creator of the term "sword-and-sorcery."

18. Fritz Leiber, "Swackles," *Amra* 2, no. 16 (July 1961): 21.

19. For more details about Senf's art and what some *Weird Tales* authors thought of it, see my article "The Blunders of One Weird Tales Artist: Curtis Charles Senf," *On an Underwood No. 5*, June 3, 2018, http://onanunderwood5.blogspot.com /2018/06/the-blunders-of-one-weird-tales-artist.html.

20. Robert E. Howard, *Kull: Exile of Atlantis*, (New York: Del Rey, 2006), 24.

21. See Lovecraft and Howard, "1930," in Joshi et al., *A Means to Freedom*, 1:45. The letter seems to be missing.

22. Farnsworth Wright, "The Souk" (editorial), *Oriental Stories* (October/ November 1930).

23. Howard, "1931," in Roehm, *Collected Letters of Robert E. Howard: 1930– 1932*, 2:277.

24. For a thorough discussion of this issue, see Bobby Derie, "Fan Mail: Prohi-

bition in 'The Souk,'" in Derie, *Weird Talers: Essays on Robert E. Howard and Others* (New York: Hippocampus Press, 2019), 229–235.

25. One such fan was Jack Darrow, aka Clifford Kornoelje, who went on to serve as assistant director for the re-formed Chicago Science Fiction League in 1939.

26. Robert E. Howard, "Hawks of Outremer," *Oriental Stories* (April/May/June 1931): 438.

27. Howard, "Hawks of Outremer," 436–454.

28. Crom Cruach, in pre-Christian Ireland, was a pagan god. Human sacrifice was necessary to appease Crom Cruach, and worship of this pagan god is believed to have been stopped by Saint Patrick.

29. Farnsworth Wright actually managed to procure renowned writer H. Bedford-Jones for *The Magic Carpet*, though the magazine faltered and ended after one year. The first issue also included two stories by Robert E. Howard: "The Shadow of the Vultures," and another attributed to Patrick Ervin, one of Howard's noms de plume, "Alleys of Darkness," a Dennis Dorgan story.

30. Robert E. Howard, *The Conquering Sword of Conan* (New York: Del Rey, 2005), 100.

31. See Ellis, *One Who Walked Alone*, 178.

32. Since the 1930s when Howard used the word in "Black Canaan," "quadroon" has become offensive and obsolete.

33. See Benjamin Garstad, "'Death to the Masters!' The Role of Slave Revolt in the Fiction of Robert E. Howard," *Slavery and Abolition* 31, no. 2 (June 2009): 233–256.

34. Roehm, "The Missing Mexico Trip."

35. Garstad, "'Death to the Masters!,'" 237.

36. Todd Vick, "Comments on Finn's 'Less an Archive, More an Agenda,'" *The Dark Man: The Journal of Robert E. Howard Studies* 8, no. 1 (2015): 14–22, 20.

37. Ibid., 20.

38. Garstad, "'Death to the Masters!,'" 240.

CHAPTER 14. FULL CIRCLE

1. Randy Broecker, *Fantasy of the 20th Century: An Illustrated History* (Portland, OR: Collectors Press, 2001), 62.

2. Mary A. Conklin, "The Eyrie" (letter to the editor), *Weird Tales* (December 1934): 782.

3. Alvin Earl Perry, "The Eyrie" (letter to the editor), in *Weird Tales* (February 1935): 271.

4. Moore wrote five Jirel stories and collaborated with Henry Kuttner on one story, "Quest of the Star Stone," using Jirel as the protagonist.

5. For a full account of this effort to get the story published as a novel, see Karl

Edward Wagner, "Afterword," in *The Hour of the Dragon* (New York: G. P. Putnam's Sons, 1977), 198–210.

6. Clifford Ball, "The Eyrie" (letter to the editor), *Weird Tales* (January 1937): 125–126.

7. Fritz Leiber would publish horror and science fiction stories for *Weird Tales* beginning in 1940; "Adept's Gambit" was not published until 1947. Farnsworth Wright stepped down as editor of *Weird Tales* in 1940, and Dorothy McIlwraith took over until the magazine folded in 1954.

8. *Unknown* introduced the reading world to Fafhrd and the Gray Mouser when it published Fritz Leiber's "Two Sought Adventure" in August 1939.

9. Dwayne Olsen posted photocopies of the Charles Scribner's Sons letters to Donald Wandrei on the Facebook page of August Derleth and Arkham House Publishers. The letters are dated September 27, 1938, and November 3, 1938. The first indicates a strong interest in publishing the collection pending a consultation with Scribner's famous editor Max Perkins. The second letter, regrettably, is a rejection.

10. Currently Arkham House, as it has been periodically in the past, is in limbo. The last book it published appeared in 2010.

11. Two other story collections had included stories by Robert E. Howard prior to *Skull-Face and Others*. The first was Arkham House's *Beyond the Wall of Sleep* (1943), in which Robert's coauthored story "The Challenge from Beyond" appeared. "The Challenge from Beyond" was a round-robin story collectively written by C. L. Moore, A. Merritt, H. P. Lovecraft, Robert E. Howard, and Frank Belknap Long. Besides his contribution to this collection, Robert's "The Black Stone" was published in *Sleep No More* (1944), edited by August Derleth and published by Farrar & Rinehart, Inc.

12. See Donald H. Tuck, ed., "Who's Who," in *The Encyclopedia of Science Fiction and Fantasy*, vol. 2, *M–Z* (Chicago: Advent Publishers, 1978), 465.

13. *The Hyborian Age* contained an essay, also titled "The Hyborian Age," written by Robert E. Howard, which had been previously published in Wollheim's fanzine *The Phantagraph* as a three-part series.

14. Jeffrey Shanks, "Introduction to the 2015 Facsimile Edition: Construction of an Age Undreamed Of," in *The Hyborian Age: Facsimile Edition* (Tallahassee, FL: Skelos Press, 2015), x.

15. L. Sprague de Camp, "Obituaries," no. 331, *Locus* 21, no. 8 (August 1988): 64–65.

16. Steve Carper, "Conan the Conqueror," *The Gnome Press Release*, April 29, 2013, http://gnomepress.com/single-staters/conan-the-conqueror/ (no longer accessible).

17. See Lin Carter, *Imaginary Worlds: The Art of Fantasy* (New York: Ballantine Books, 1973), 132–33; L. Sprague de Camp, "Conan's Ghost," in *The Spell of Conan* (New York: Ace Books, 1980), 38–43.

18. Over the years and in various written accounts, L. Sprague de Camp's reports on the details of his Gnome Press years and his involvement in and discovery

of Robert E. Howard's works have changed. This account of his reading the last issue of *Avon Fantasy Reader* and encountering Howard's story, however, has remained consistent in all his accounts.

19. L. Sprague de Camp, *Time and Chance: An Autobiography* (Hampton Falls, NH: Donald M. Grant, Publisher, 1996), 229.

20. Ibid.

21. Ibid., 230. According to Sam Moskowitz, Oscar Friend did not actually lend de Camp the stories so much as de Camp "virtually took possession of them." See Sam Moskowitz, "L. Sprague de Camp," in *Seekers of Tomorrow: Masters of Science Fiction* (New York: Ballantine Books, 1967), 167.

22. Glenn Lord was introduced to Robert E. Howard via Arkham House's edition of *Skull-Face and Others*. Lord would go on to be the most influential fan of Robert E. Howard, publishing anthologies and obtaining the largest collection of Howard memorabilia and ephemera, much of which is housed in the Harry Ransom Center at the University of Texas at Austin.

23. Lloyd Arthur Eschbach, *Over My Shoulder: Reflections on a Science Fiction Era* (Philadelphia: Oswald Train, 1983), 219.

24. Ibid.

25. Ibid.

26. De Camp, *Time and Chance*, 232.

27. Carter, *Imaginary Worlds*, 137.

28. Leon Nielson, *Robert E. Howard: A Collector's Descriptive Bibliography of American and British Hardcover, Paperback, Magazine, Special and Amateur Editions, with a Biography* (Jefferson, NC: McFarland & Co., 2010), 55.

29. Arnie Fenner, "Frank Frazetta: Master of Imagination," in *Icon: A Retrospective by the Grand Master of Fantastic Art*, ed. Cathy and Arnie Fenner (Nevada City, CA: Underwood Books, 2003), 27.

30. James A. Bond, *The Definitive Frazetta Reference* (Lakewood, NJ: Vanguard Productions, 2010), 96.

31. Fenner, *Icon*, 27.

32. Ibid., 31.

33. These numbers are an average estimate between Lin Carter's assertions in *Imaginary Worlds*, in which he places the total at three million in 1973, and the numbers I gleaned from the Excel spreadsheet provided to me by Howard scholar and fan Scotty Henderson, based on his years of researching the L. Sprague de Camp professional papers at the Harry Ransom Center and the Lancer bankruptcy papers.

34. Nielsen, *Robert E. Howard*, 55.

35. Stephen Jacobs, *Boris Karloff, More than a Monster: The Authorised Biography* (Sheffield, UK: Tomahawk, 2011), 433.

36. The incomplete manuscripts that Carter completed were "The Black City" (renamed "Black Abyss" for this collection), "Riders Beyond the Sunrise," and "Wizard and Warrior."

37. Roy Thomas, "Conan the Marvelous," *Conan Classic* 1, no. 1 (June 1994): 29.

38. Ibid.

39. Ibid. After Oscar Friend died, Glenn Lord was contacted, on the advice of L. Sprague de Camp, by Kittie West, Oscar Friend's daughter, to see if he would take over Friend's position as literary agent for the Howard estate.

40. Thomas, "Conan the Marvelous," 29.

41. Ibid., 30.

42. Ibid.

43. Paul Sammon, *Conan the Phenomenon: The Legacy of Robert E. Howard's Fantasy Icon* (Milwaukie, OR: Dark Horse Books, 2007), 61.

44. Sammon, *Conan the Phenomenon*, 97.

45. "Lancer Suspends Operation and Files $7.5 Mil Suit," *Publishers' Weekly* 204 (October 1, 1973): 39–40. See also Peter Dzwonkoski, ed., *American Literary Publishing Houses, 1900–1980* (Detroit: Gale, 1986). Special thanks to Scotty Henderson for providing me with these references.

46. Dzwonkoski, *American Literary Publishing Houses, 1900–1980*, 97–98.

47. This summary is based on Paul Sammon's account in his book *Conan the Phenomenon*. Sammon was on the *Conan the Barbarian* movie set as it was being filmed in Spain.

48. Sammon, *Conan the Phenomenon*, 98.

49. Ibid., 101.

50. Ibid., 103.

51. Ibid., 107.

52. Ibid., 103–104.

53. Ibid., 107.

54. These box office figures are based on the information at "Conan the Destroyer (1984)," IMDb, http://www.imdb.com/title/tt0087078/business (accessed August 18, 2017).

55. Wagner himself had written one of the most popular Howard pastiches, *Conan: The Road of Kings* (New York: Bantam, 1979).

56. Rusty Burke, email to author, July 20, 2017. Marcelo Anciano is known for directing music videos for Pat Benatar, Peter Gabriel, and Berlin. He was also the associate producer for Michael J. Bassett's film *Solomon Kane*.

57. To read the mission statement for the REH Foundation, go to http://www.rehfoundation.org/about/.

58. Burke, email to author, July 20, 2017.

59. Ibid.

60. Ibid.

61. From the time of the late Gnome Press volumes to the publication of the Lancer and Ace Conan editions, most of the information available to the reading public about Howard, his family, and his life came from L. Sprague de Camp's introductions. De Camp was also the first to write a full-length biography of Howard, and that book further skewed public understanding of Howard's family and life.

AFTERWORD

1. Oscar Lopez Lacalle also designed *The Park* (2015), *LEGO Minifigures On-line* (2014), *The Secret World* (2012), and *The Scourge Project: Episodes 1 and 2* (2010).

2. PVE (player-versus-environment) is also another option.

3. See Funcom, "Conan Exiles Out Today, over 1 Million Sold," May 8, 2018, http://pr.funcom.com/pressreleases/conan-exiles-out-today-over-1-million-sold -2501619.

4. See Tucker Chet Markus, "Jason Aaron, Mahmud Asrar, and Esad Ribic Lead New Conan the Barbarian Series," *Marvel*, August 24, 2018, https://www .marvel.com/articles/comics/jason-aaron-mahmud-asrar-and-esad-ribic-lead-new -conan-the-barbarian-series.

5. See George R. R. Martin, "Reading Recommendations," *Not a Blog*, March 13, 2013, http://georgerrmartin.com/notablog/2013/03/13/reading-recommendations/.

6. The foundation's website is at http://www.rehfoundation.org.

Index